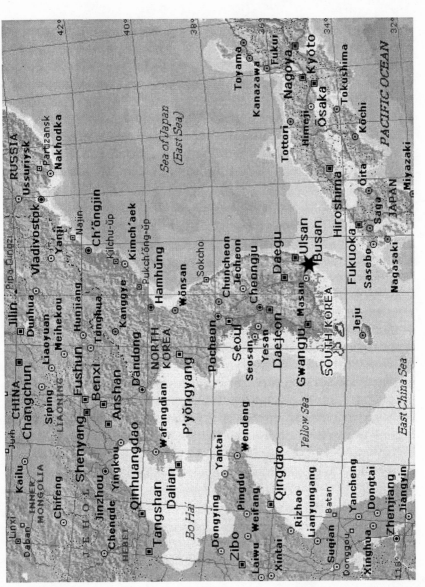

Korean map

BAMBOO
Heart

BAMBOO
Heart

CINDY NESSEN

To order additional copies of this book, contact:
Xlibris Corporation
1-888-795-4274
www.Xlibris.com
Orders@Xlibris.com
54121

Contents

To my beloved son, Edward

Bamboo Heart

Forward

By Ron Nessen

I was introduced to Young-Hee Song—Cindy—in the bar atop the Caravelle Hotel in downtown Saigon in the summer of 1965 as America's involvement in the Vietnam War was accelerating. I was a newly-arrived correspondent for NBC News. She was the leader of a high energy Korean song-and dance troupe—Cindy and the Apples—appearing at a local night club.

For nearly 40 years, we have been lovers, husband and wife, angry adversaries in a vicious divorce, emotional combatants, non-communicating ex-spouses, and, ultimately, admiring, supportive friends.

Over those years, as I have learned the details of Cindy's astounding life—and of the life of her equally intrepid mother—my admiration of their ability to survive and prevail in the face of hardship has grown.

The highs and lows of Cindy's life are almost inconceivable. She writes about them with brutal candor and with hard-won insight.

The depths were low, indeed. Cindy as a child, laboring day after day up to her knees in muck, harvesting rice, plucking leeches from her legs, making crude sandals at night from straw, struggling to keep her impoverished family from starving after her father died. Cindy barely a teenager, trying to keep a half-brother alive by suckling him from her own undeveloped breast after he was virtually abandoned by their mother.

And the heights were high, indeed. Cindy dancing with the President of the Unites States and singing with the Marine Corps Band at a glittering White House state dinner. Cindy as a successful international business consultant bringing together important Korean and American corporate and government officials.

Those are only the bare details of Cindy's truly amazing journey from rice paddies to the White House. In this endlessly fascinating book . . . sometimes horrifying, always engrossing . . . she relates the details of her life and the life of her mother. And from those lives of hardship, perseverance, and eventual triumph, she draws lessons that will inspire all who read this book

Be clear—this is not just another book about an Asian woman coming to America, adapting to an alien culture, and succeeding. It is all that. But it is much more. Mostly this book is about an extraordinary woman telling her own story in her own way.

This book's journey from connection to print was almost as long, twisting, and difficult as the lives it depicts. Frankly, Cindy drove me and many of her friends to distraction at times with her ceaseless efforts to see her life story written and published. But, as with the rest of her life, it was her indefatigable drive and determination to get her story into print that finally enabled her to overcome all obstacles.

I will end on a personal note. I am in the book because I have been in Cindy's life, one way or the other, for almost four decades. Some of what she writes about me is not very flattering. And deservedly so.

We enjoyed a storybook wartime romance in Saigon that ended abruptly when I was wounded by a Viet Cong hand grenade. I'll never forget being driven away from a military hospital, watching Cindy's tearful face growing smaller and smaller in the rear window. But, with her characteristic determination and refusal to accept fate's cruel twists, she besieged the State Department until it finally relented and granted her a visa to come to the Unites States.

We were married in New York City, and I resumed my career as a globe-trotting correspondent. Many times Cindy found herself dropped down in a strange city and a strange culture—Mexico City, London, and eventually Washington—while I took off on yet another reporting assignment. But she survived and prevailed every time.

In those days, and later when I became President Ford's press secretary, I believed my work was more important than my marriage, more important than my daughter from an earlier marriage, more important than anything. Also, I didn't understand the need for commitment and faithfulness in marriage. I wasn't a very nice person in those days.

As a result, my marriage foundered. One day, I packed my bags and walked out the front door, leaving Cindy and our son Edward weeping on the front porch. It's a scene that haunts me still, more than 20 years later.

Eventually, I learned what's important in life. I learned the importance of commitment in a relationship. Cindy and I finally reconciled a few years ago at the funeral of her mother, a gallant and lively woman who suffered through nearly all the tragedies that befell her native Korea in the 20th century as well as in United States . . . and always with a bemused, lop-sided smile on her determined face.

Cindy and I have been friends ever since.

I have strongly encouraged her to tell the story of her life and the lives of her mother even though I am not a very sympathetic character in the books. I encouraged her because hers is an inspiring story that needs to be told, and needs to be read.

The metaphor Cindy has chosen as the title for her life story—Bamboo Heart—is perfect. The strong women she depicts are like the bamboo of their native Asia—they bend in the many storms that sweep through their lives, but they never break.

#####

Bamboo Heart

I sit on the deck overlooking my backyard surrounded by tall bamboo. In the distance, a park, the trees wearing red and gold dresses like the embroidered ones that young Korean girls make for their weddings. I sip my green tea, and hear the soft whisper of the bamboo leaves caressing each other.

Whenever I see bamboo, I am reminded of Master Lee and my calligraphy lessons. When I first went to his apartment, I took off my shoes at the door. Master Lee sat cross-legged in stocking feet in his bare living room. He was thin with graying hair. Seeing him sitting crossed-legged on the floor in his *hanbok*, a white jacket and gray baggy trousers tied at the ankles with baby blue ribbons, I was transported back to my childhood. How long had it been since I had seen a man sitting in this attitude? Years ago my grandfather sat cross-legged like this, his hair silver against the reddish sky.

I bowed. "*An-nyung-hashim-nika?*" How are you?

"*Nae, nae,* please sit down," he said as he pointed to a blue silk cushion on the floor.

I sat with my legs tucked under me, my body bent slightly sideways. A well-mannered Korean woman never sits cross-legged, especially in front of a man. Master Lee's wife entered, carrying a tea tray.

"*An-nyung-hashim-nika?*" she asked as she placed the tray in front of me. How are you?

"*Nae, kam-sa-haminida,*" I answered, inclining my head. Yes , I'm well, thank you. As she left the room, her stocking-clad feet made no sound.

"Have you done calligraphy before?" Master Lee's eyes narrowed.

I'd sat in calligraphy class as a child, trying very hard to sculpt perfect letters on a piece of white rice paper. "When I was very young," I said, "but only letters, not a painting."

From a low shelf, Master Lee brought out a stack of rice paper, placed it in front of him. He put a stone weight on top of the sheets. He held his wide sleeve back as he poured a small amount of water from a porcelain teapot into the ink stone and ground a stick in long strokes until the glistening black liquid turned the proper consistency. He wet the brush from inkstone, rolling this way and that. When the brush was completely wet and perfectly pointed, he pushed the brush down on the corner of the paper and drew upward, ever so gently lifting it up. He did this several times, some short. some long. Then he dotted with tinted reddish brown here and there and transformed the lines into an iris.

Several lessons and many strokes later, I learned how to create beautiful lilies and rocks. Master Lee was pleased. "You need a pen name," he said. Without stopping to consider, he said, "You will be *Jook Shim*, Bamboo Heart."

Not Chrysanthemum, not Plum Flower as is traditionally the case for a woman. In Asia, each kind of flower and tree has symbolic meaning. A chrysanthemum blooms in the fall and lasts well in cold weather which could mean beautiful but yet resilient. Plums bloom early in the cold spring in the snow. Each is a symbolic reference to some aspect of life. But bamboo for a woman?

Master Lee noticed my surprise. "*Bamboo yields to the wind,*" he told me, "*and is thus never broken.*" In his low, husky voice, his words seemed a poem. "*Bamboo has no season. It is strong and straight. Every joint represents growth. And it grows stronger with the passage of time.*"

Images flashed through my mind—of my childhood in Korea, my father's dreams of Japan, the wars and protests that shaped us, the leaders and politicians, both U.S. and Korean, whom I'd met, my dances with a U.S. and a Korean president, my years as a performer, a wife, a mother, a woman alone, a woman guided by her ancestors.

It's so hard to be a single person. As a colonial subject of Japan in Korea, I tried my best to be Korean and Japanese. It didn't work, as it hadn't for my poor grandfather. I've done better as an American, but always I've carried the heritage of my roots, the legacy of Korea. It is a country that has endured civil wars, atrocities, invasions, starvation, and political cleavage—and created untold beauty in art and music and poetry long before its neighbors in Asia were awake. In my soul are the values of humanity, honesty, dignity, and pride that have survived hardship and endured, as they have in the country of my birth.

Every Korean has a story to tell, one that reaches back through the centuries to ancestors unknown, whose tales were passed down from generation to generation.

Master Lee had seen my essence. Somehow he knew that my heart had carried me through storms and troubling winds, and that with each test, I had become stronger.

I had prevailed.

Here is my story.

Young-Hee, the English Princess

Bamboo
This is not a tree
Neither is it a grass
Who made it grow so straight?
And why is it so pure inside?
The seasons come and go
But your green stays forever.

—Yoon Sun Do (1587-1671)

Man is born broken. He lives by mending,
Grace of God is glue.

—Eugene O'Niell
Irish playwright

My name is Song Young Hee. My mother told me that when I was born,
I looked like a boiled egg that had been freshly peeled: "You were
flawless." My mother told me that I was born at six in the morning
in the year of the pig. "I remember the hour because moments after
you were born, my father went out to feed the pigs." Because of the
importance of pigs at my birth, it was prophesied that I would never
starve. "You were such a pretty baby with only a bit of hair on your head,
which I tried to comb down on your forehead, only to have it blown
loose again by the wind."

My father named me Young-Hee, which means "English princess" after the prettiest, most popular princess in Britain at the time, Princess Margaret. The year was 1935, and the Japanese occupied Korea. My family lived in Busan.

"It was a miracle you survived," my mother said to me. "When you were a baby, you had pneumonia, and I pushed you to a corner, thinking you weren't going to make it. But the next day, you moved, and I was certain you would have a long life."

"You left me to die in the corner of a room?" I asked.

"What was I to do? I thought you were dying."

"Didn't you try to save me?" I asked.

"Save you? I didn't need to save you. You saved yourself."

My father was an accountant for a Japanese wholesale fruit company. By the time I was born, he had saved enough money to buy a small plot of land in Cholyang, which was not far from my grandparents' house. While the other residents of Cholyang had houses built low with black clay-tiled roofs, our house had two sections. Facing the main street, a two-story building with a flat roof, stucco walls, and lots of windows. The ground floor was office space, which was empty except for a stack of dried pollack in one corner to be sold. I sometimes invited neighborhood children to inspect the dead fish, poke out the eyes, and eat them. The grown-ups always said that eating fish eyes made our eyes see well.

Then, there was a small garden in between this and the traditional quarters. While everyone else's front gate was made of wood, ours was made of glass. Whenever it was opened, bells jingled. During the winter, we slept downstairs in our *ondol* rooms, which had heated floors. During the summer, we slept on the second floor in a *tatami* room. There we lay on the straw mats beneath a huge mosquito net, which covered the whole room and swayed this way and that in a breeze from a fan.

At a time when the other kids didn't know what vitamins were, my mother made sure I took cod liver oil and Wakamot, a brewer's yeast. Mother rubbed mentholatum on our skin to cure scrapped knees and bugs' bites. She fed us plentiful seasonal fruit brought by the box from my father's work.

My father loved music. I woke in the morning to Leopold Mozart's *Toy Symphony* playing on his radio/phonograph, which was made in Germany and stood three feet tall. Lying in bed listening to the sounds of cuckoos, quails, and nightingales, I imagined myself flying over a fairytale forest, watching the birds busily working. Other times I heard the Russian *Volga* riverboat song sung by an old man. I imagined an old boatman who did backbreaking work of dragging barges and ships laden with everything from wood to salt up and down the slow moving river. Then there was *Peter and the Wolf* with its honking duck and trilling bird.

My father owned a large collection of both classical and popular music. The classical records were ordered through the mail. Every month, two records would arrive. My father handled them carefully, holding them with the tips of his fingers on both sides, telling me never to touch the grooves. He used metal needles for the popular records, but for the classical ones, he only used needles made of soft yellow wood. After they were used a few times, my father cut the needles with a small pair of triangular scissors to sharpen the tips. He would not risk scratching his records. Mother told me that he'd learned to play the harmonica first, then the mandolin, and later the guitar.

During the evenings, my grandparents, granduncles, aunts, and cousins often visited our house full of music and happiness. After dinner, my father played his records. When the American song "*Diana*" played (sung in this case by a Japanese male singer), I would twirl and dance around the room. My family sat around, laughing, clapping, and cheering me on. Sometimes my father held me, and we danced to the Argentine tangos "*La Cumparsita*," or "*Dark Eyes*," sung in Japanese. I was three years old.

My granduncle visited us in the evening. I loved my granduncle. He had jet-black hair, thick black eyebrows, deep-set large eyes, a straight Western nose, and he was always smiling. In summer, he wore a white silk jacket and gray baggy trousers; in fall, a *hanbok* of rust-colored damask with his trousers tied at the ankles with thin silk ribbons; and in winter a blue vest with gold watch chain peeking from his lower pocket. He loved to dress up, and I loved his visits because he always told good stories.

"Ah, Young-Hee yah, Tong-Ho yah, did you eat rice?" he'd ask me and my brother with a big warm smile.

"Granduncle, tell us a story," I would say, pulling on his hand and leading him to the small room where my father kept his books, records, and the big radio/phonograph. My brother would follow, and together we would sit before my granduncle on the warm *ondol* floor.

"What story should I tell you tonight?" he would ask.

"Tell us the story of *Shim Chung*." This was one of my favorites.

"Okay," he would say, and then he would begin.

"*There was once a little girl named Shim Chung. Her mother had died while giving birth to her. In the following years, the blind father supported his daughter by begging until Shim Chung was old enough to take his place. One day, Shim*

Chung was late returning home. Her concerned father started out toward the village to search for her. When he was crossing a bridge, he stumbled and fell into the river. A passing Buddhist monk rescued him and told him that his eyesight would be regained if he donated three hundred sacks of rice to the temple. In his excitement, the father pledged the rice without considering how poor they were. Only later did he regret his decision. When Shim Chung returned, her worried father told her what he had done. She assured him not to worry, but she was deeply concerned herself.

"When the captain of a ship and his sailors came to the village offering money for a maiden to be sacrificed to the sea dragon king during their next voyage, Shim Chung sold herself and gave the money to the monk.

"In the middle of the sea, Shim Chung stood and looked over the water toward her village. After she prayed for her father's long and healthy life, she covered her head with her skirt and jumped into the water.

"When she arrived in the undersea kingdom, she was welcomed by the sea dragon king, who already knew why she was there and praised her for her filial piety. She turned down the prince's offer to become his undersea goddess and asked to return to her father, who, she had learned in a dream, was still blind.

"But you see," my granduncle would say, "because she had a good heart and filial piety for her father, the sea dragon king put her inside of a beautiful lotus flower and floated it in the ponds of a palace belonging to a human king.

"It was time for the prince to marry, and his court had been searching for the right bride for him, but the prince wasn't happy with any of the maidens brought before him. When the prince learned of the mysterious lotus flower in the court pond, he went to see it. And it was then that he saw the beautiful Shim Chung emerge from the floating petals. He knew upon seeing her that she was the one he should marry. But there was a problem. Shim Chung cried all the time. The prince did not know what was wrong with her, and so one day he said, 'My darling Shim Chung, you seem so unhappy. What can I do to make you smile again?' Shim Chung finally said, 'The only thing I wish for is to see my father again.' Upon hearing her story, the king immediately ordered a huge party and invited all the blind men in the country. Shim Chung sat beside the king, examining each man who entered the palace. Many came, but she did not see her beloved father, and she grew despondent again. But then at last an old man arrived. He wore ragged clothes and walked stooped over with a cane. It was her father at last.

"She ran to him.

"'Father, dear Father, it is me, your daughter, Shim Chung,' she cried and hugged him. At that moment, her father opened his eyes, and for the first time in his life, he could see his daughter's face.

"So you see," my grand uncle would say, "if you are good to your parents, God will know this and give you a good life. On the other hand, those without filial piety will always be punished in some way. If your husband or wife dies, you can always get another one. You can have many children, but you have only one set of parents. Always remember that."

While I listened to this story, my little heart was full of sadness, and I promised myself that I would be like Shim Chung, caring for my parents as long as I lived. That promise would become a lifelong commitment, and later, people would nickname me Shim Chung for my devotion to my widowed mother. But I knew none of this then while I sat at the feet of my granduncle and begged him for another story.

My father owned a German-made Leica camera and had a darkroom in the attic. He developed and enlarged his own photographs and would invite me sometimes to watch his miracle work. The room was dark as a tunnel with one small lightbulb hung from the ceiling. "Come and stand here and look in here," he would say. I stood on a low step and leaned close to a large container with water and a big white piece of paper in the bottom. "Watch what happens," he said. He picked up one corner of the paper with a bamboo tong and swished the paper up and down. Soon I saw the shape of a face emerging—mine. He picked it out with bamboo thong and hung it on the line. When I was four and five years old, he took pictures of me every weekend. "Young-Hee yah, come and pose for me." I would put on my red-and-white polka-dot sundress and run into our courtyard smiling and twirling the parasol my father had bought in Seoul. Then I would imitate the poses I had seen the famous Japanese singer Yamaguchi Yoshiko do on stage at the theater downtown.

Sometimes my father told me to sit on the veranda with my brother. "Put your arms around Tong-Ho . . . that's right . . . now, smile . . . that's it." Modeling for my father became second nature to me. My mother told me that Tong-Ho had won third place in a baby contest when he was one hundred days old. "Of course, first and second place were given to Japanese babies," she said. But that was to be expected, living in Korea under Japanese rule.

My dearest memories of my father came from our spring trips, when the cherry blossoms were in full bloom. My mother and father put on their best clothes and dressed me in mine, including a beret that my mother had knitted. Granduncle often came with us as did Chung-Soon, our eleven-year-old maid and babysitter from the countryside, who carried my baby brother on her back. We boarded a streetcar that took us to Tong-Nae Mountain, famous for its cherry blossoms. I had seen my father study portraits in photography magazines, which was how he taught himself. On Tong-Nae Mountain, my father took pictures of my mother. In one, she was strolling up the mountain, wearing her long pink-and-green *hanbok*, her hair tied in a tight bun, her neck wrapped in a chiffon scarf. In another, she was taking a picture of me leaning next to a pine tree. I remember thinking that I heard one of the cuckoos from the *Toy Symphony* floating in the breeze.

As I grew older, I often visited my father's library when he was at work. I was intrigued by his walls of records and world literature translated into Japanese: *War and Peace, Anna Karenina,* and *The Brothers Karamazov.* Since there were no other children of my age in the neighborhood, my playtime was spent exploring my father's library. When I was six or seven, I overheard my father and granduncle feverishly discussing a book called *Crime and Punishment.* I found a copy in my father's study and attempted to read it, but it was written in difficult Chinese characters, and I sadly returned it to the shelf. Next to *Crime and Punishment* were several small books with smooth, shiny covers the color of the sky. They were a collection of Shakespeare's plays. I took one down from the shelf and loved the feel of it in my hands. It was *Hamlet.* I read the lines aloud though they were translated into formal Japanese, which I couldn't understand. Still, I liked it because it was obviously a script for a play. I read it as if I were standing on a stage in front of an audience.

My father had always dreamed of studying at Waseda, a prestigious law school in Japan where most of the well-to-do boys went. But he was too poor to go in his youth. His friend Min-Sang, who later became my aunt's husband, had planted the seed of that dream before my father was married. He told my father, "You can always get married, but it'll be too late once you have your family." But family or no family, he never gave up on his dream. In 1940, when my father was thirty, he prepared for his journey to Japan. He told my mother to stop crying. After all, he said, he wasn't leaving for good. He would send for us as soon as he was settled.

At the time, she did not know that my father was fulfilling his dream of studying law in Japan. He'd studied English and Chinese through mail-order books and records. He'd bought a farm in Yangsan, arranged for a supply of rice and other grains to be provided for his family every year, and bought a second house behind our house, which had ten rooms to rent out. When everything seemed in perfect order, my father quit his job. Even though he was thirty years old, with a wife and two children, he believed a dream should never end as just a dream.

In the early spring, we made the trip to the Busan dock to see my father off to Japan. Mother wore a *hanbok* with a fox fur around her neck. Father had bought it for her from a very famous department store downtown called Minakai. It had beady red eyes, four legs, and a brown bushy tail that wrapped around her neck and ended at a clip underneath its nose. I wore a red dress with a hat to match and white ankle socks with a pair of black patent leather shoes. Holding my father's hand, I skipped and jumped, looking at my shiny shoes. I looked out of the taxi at the streetcar and unfamiliar buildings. In no time we were driving past the docks. There were small boats and big boats. Gulls rose into the sky and dove down into the water to feed on floating debris.

We all got out of the taxi, stepped onto the pier, and saw waves breaking beneath it. Granduncle and Father took the luggage out of the trunk and led the way toward a large wooden gate with a sign that said "**Customs**." We were not allowed to go past the customs landing and departure gates. Everyone said good-bye. Everything smelled like salt, and the sky was blue and bright. Father gave his luggage to a man in a uniform.

"Your father is going to Japan on that boat," my mother said, pointing to the black-and-white steamship ahead. Against the afternoon light, I strained my eyes. To my child's eye, the ship looked like a great monster.

One by one, the passengers disappeared into the steamer, which was draped with red, green, yellow, and blue paper ribbons, fluttering in the wind. I wanted to catch one, hold on to its end, and swing in the breeze. My father touched my hat and said, "Now, you be a good girl. You're big now, so I'm counting on you to take care of your little brother."

As I held on to my mother's leg, I nodded obediently and watched the colorful ribbons dance above my father's shoulder. Mother cried as he walked away, carrying his little bag.

"What are you crying for?" my grandmother scolded my mother. "Why are we standing here like a bunch of fools? We should leave. We can't see him anymore."

With the rest of my family, I left the pier, the ribbons swimming in my memory.

On a sunny morning a few days after his departure, I sat on the veranda and played with my doll, the one my father had bought me.

She had yellow hair and blue eyes the color of my brother's marbles. When I laid her on her back, her eyes closed. When I stood her up, they opened. Her lashes were long, and they curled up to the clouds. I kissed her cheek and patted her hair. My brother was sleeping in the inner room, and my mother was in Father's study, airing out his winter wardrobe. Chung-Soon squatted in the courtyard, scrubbing our dirty clothes on the shiny, flat rocks that were grouted into the ground for that purpose. Her skin was dark, and her face looked as if someone had planted two persimmon pits on her cheeks. I was told that Chun-Soon was a distant cousin of ours, but we looked nothing alike, and I promised myself that my skin would always remain fair. My granduncle once told me that our skin was the perfect color. When I asked him why that was so, he said that when God made white Americans, he didn't bake them in his holy oven long enough. When God made Africans, he cooked them for too long. In his final attempt, he cooked Asians, and their skin came out golden. At first, his story made me laugh because I could not imagine someone like God cooking in a kitchen. Then I thought that God had surely been mistaken in thinking golden skin was perfection because I wanted my skin to be as smooth and fair as that of my yellow-haired doll.

Then someone pounded on our front gate, and my mother yelled at Chun-Soon, "Who is it?"

A man's voice came from the other side. "*Gomen kudasai,*" he said in Japanese. Excuse me.

Chung-Soon opened the sliding door, and policemen entered our courtyard. They wore black hats and black uniforms with shiny golden buttons. My mother came out of the room, slipped on her rubber shoes, and walked out onto the courtyard. I followed, holding on to her skirt.

In Japanese, my mother asked, "What's wrong?"

"We've come to search your house," the leader said. His eyes were hidden underneath the shadow of his hat as he signaled the others to search our rooms. They scattered like mice. My mother rushed me to the inner room, where my baby brother was sleeping, and I crawled underneath the comforter. Had I done something wrong? My parents and granduncle used to tell me to behave myself, or else they would call the police to take me away.

Trembling under the blanket, I listened to the policemen stomping all over our house. They had not even taken off their shoes. When the noise subsided, I crawled out from under the blanket, slid open the door, and peeked through the crack. My mother stood on the veranda and told Chung-Soon to go and get my grandfather. I went to my mother and hid behind her skirt. A policeman in my father's study scattered his books and records on the floor; another was in our privy; another opened our wardrobe, upset a pile of our blankets, and went through our photo album page by page. Then finding books written in English and Chinese, he tore out the pages. I heard footsteps in the attic. A policeman came down, holding my father's camera and strips of negatives. Another policeman found my father's suits laid out on the floor with their pockets turned inside out. He approached my mother and said, "You are a very smart wife, Madame. You cleaned out his pockets before we arrived."

My grandfather rushed in through the front gate. The policeman recognized him and said, "Oh, Sai sang, what are you doing here?" Sai sang was Japanese translation of "Mr. Choi."

"This is my son-in-law's house. What is going on here?"

The policeman told my grandfather that his son-in-law had been detained on suspicion of being a spy for the Korean independence movement, and he was being held at police headquarters.

My father never made it to Japan. When he arrived at the checkpoint of the port, he was stopped, and his bags were inspected. Among other scenes, they found photos of the harbor, which were forbidden, and books translated into Chinese. The Japanese police suspected my father was a spy, and they arrested him. The Sino-Japanese War was intensifying; many Korean freedom fighters were working in China, and the Japanese general Ito Hirobumi was assassinated at the Harbin railroad station in Manchuria by the Korean freedom fighter Ahn Joong-Gun. Japanese authorities were nervous and watchful, suspicious of those with unusual lifestyles. For any Korean, especially one as young as my father, it was unusual to own a big Western-style house. My mother later told me that the Japanese police would not have known of our family's lifestyle if it were not for Mr. Yamamoto, a colleague of my father's from the fruit company. Mr. Yamamoto was in love with a saleslady at a department store that my father frequented. On his way home from work, my father would stop to buy a few items for my mother, brother, and me. The saleslady helped my father regularly. He showed her his camera and photographs and even took pictures of her. They became friends, and Mr. Yamamoto, jealously observing this, reported his suspicions about my father to the authorities.

With the help of his former employer, Mr. Ishihara, my father was released a few weeks later. Mr. Ishihara told the police that not only was my father the most honest person he had ever known, but he had not made so much as a one-penny mistake all the while he was employed at the fruit company. My mother told me that she didn't recognize my father when he was released. "I thought the ghost of some stranger was staggering toward me. When he reached me, he collapsed."

After my father returned home, he did not speak about his days in prison. Mother later learned from his cellmate that my father hadn't touched his food; he only cried. His cellmate had been jailed trying to sell rice that he had grown, but the Japanese forbade this seemingly innocent act also.

With military provocation in Manchuria in 1931, Japanese set up the puppet state of Manchukuo the following year. Continuing clashes with China brought about an all-out war in 1937. Korea was used as a supply base, and the Korean people suffered greatly. Because of the shortage of manpower in Japan, more and more Korean rice went to Japan. Cattle were confiscated for meat. Koreans had to stand in line for rations of the food they had produced. That is, if any was left. We were lucky because Father owned rice paddies, but Mother stood in line for small portions of the meat that my father needed to recover his health, and sometimes she bribed the butcher with rice. My mother nourished my father back to health with chicken ginger soup and eggs, which his mother brought every month from Yangsan, where she lived. My father gained weight, listened to his records, read his books, and one day told us to pack because our family was going to Japan. He was determined; a dream could not remain only a dream.

In the spring of 1940, when I was five, my father, my mother, my brother, and I boarded a boat bound for Tokyo. On the lowest deck, the Koreans were squeezed in like cattle while the Japanese occupied the top of the ship. The hold looked like a huge warehouse with people lying on the bare floor. Many were seasick with their suitcases and bundles under their heads. Lying next to my mother, I was sure the big room was spinning.

But once in Japan, it was as if we'd arrived in heaven. In the evenings, when we walked around Ginza, I was thrilled by the fancy department stores, music in the streets, bright neon signs, and women in colorful kimonos, scurrying with their pigeon-toed walk in wooden slippers, or wearing Western dresses with stylish hats and high heels. They looked as though they had stepped straight out of a movie screen like those in the theaters where people lined up to see American movies.

My mother's long, straight hair was cut and permed. She put away her *hanbok* and instead put on dresses that stopped just below the knee. Her favorite was a short purple dress with puffy sleeves and tiny buttons covered with purple velvet that ran down her chest in two rows. Her boat-shaped rubber shoes were replaced with high heels.

My father told my mother to take a sewing class because dressmakers were in high demand in Tokyo, and her skill would come in handy while he went to school. However, he was not able to immediately enroll in Waseda because our family had arrived after the registration date. While my father desperately sought a way to enroll himself and my mother diligently attended sewing classes, I stayed home.

One evening, I took a black crayon, and on the *shoji* or silk sliding door of my father's room, I drew the hair of a geisha. When he saw what I had done, he punished me. Feeling unwanted and good for nothing, I took off for my uncle's house. My mother had taken me there once, and I was certain that as long as I found the railroad tracks, I could find my way. When I knocked on his door, no one answered. I sat on his step, watching bicycles go by. When I grew tired of waiting, I stood up and began my journey back home. As soon as I crossed the railroad tracks, I saw my mother, running toward me with open arms, calling out my name. She squeezed me tightly and cried, "Where have you been? I've been looking everywhere for you." Holding her hand on the way home, I wondered, "*Why she had been crying? Why did she not know that I would be at my uncle's? Where else in Japan could I go?*"

My father was willing to do anything in order to enroll in Waseda. A man who had heard of my father's trouble visited and told him that special arrangements could be made for a price. Without hesitation, my father gave the man the sum he had named. Then he waited. Spring passed. My father attempted to track the man down, but he was nowhere to be found. Then one day, my grandfather sent a cable from Busan. Our house had been broken into. We should return home immediately. After six months in Japan, our family packed for the journey home, and my father's dream remained just that.

Japanese Colony

When this body of mine dies over and over,
One hundred times over,
My skull becomes dust on the earth,
It makes no difference if there's a soul or mind,
My heart will still go on loving you.

—Jung Mong-Joo (1337-1397)

Give me liberty or give me death.

—Patrick Henry (1736-1799)

My story begins before my birth and is intertwined with the history of my people.

Before the Japanese swallowed up this peaceful country in 1910, and it became a Japanese colony, Korea was called Cho-Sun, the Morning Calm. The Korean people were known as "the white-clad people" because they loved to wear white *hanboks,* the Korean national dress. In the old days, almost all men and women wore these white cotton or linen *hanboks.* Young women washed them in the sparkling water of the creeks that flowed over shiny cobblestones until the clothes again became perfectly white. Perhaps it was a sign of purity.

Why did Korea become a Japanese colony? As an old Korean saying goes, *"The shrimp's back breaks when the whales fight."* In 1903, Russia started to purchase land and put up the buildings near the Yalu River for trade. Since Japan had occupied China ten years prior, the Japanese demanded that Russia move out or fight in Manchuria. When it was clear that Russia was not going to back down, Japan attacked without warning, just as she had struck China. Japan needed a military base from which to wage war with Russia, and that place would be Korea. There Japan made the transparent promise that its military presence would secure the safety of the emperor. On February 8, 1904, Japanese ships opened fire on Port Arthur, bottling up the Russian fleet at anchor there, and war was officially declared. The Korean government declared complete neutrality, but this was a futile gesture. Japanese troops landed at Inchon and marched into Seoul. The government was forced to sign a protocol with the following provisions: Korea accepts Japanese advice on the improvement of facilities; Japan assures the Korean government of independence and territorial integrity; if and when there is danger to the personal safety of the Korean emperor, the Japanese government will take such steps as the occasion demands, and the Korean government will give complete cooperation; the Japanese government may make use of any part of Korean territory for military operations in securing the emperor's safety; and the Korean government is to conclude no treaties with other governments without the consent of Japan.

From then on, in everything but name, Korea became the puppet of the Japanese empire. July of 1905 brought the Taft-Katsura Agreement, in which the United States recognized Japan's interests in Korea in return for a Japanese promise not to interfere over American rule in the Philippines. In August a similar agreement was reached with Britain, with Japan promising to support British rule in India. The United States and Britain bargained away Korea's freedom to protect their own colonial presence from the rising power of Japan.

Although all these political problems were occurring elsewhere in Korea, things were reasonably normal in Busan, on the southern tip of Korea, where my grandfather Ky-Joon was born. He was blessed with physical beauty. Tall and muscular, with features similar to those of a Caucasian, he had a big, long straight nose, which was a sign of prosperity according to Korean beliefs. He might have been considered very handsome except for one detail: his left eyelid was closed, making him look as though he was partially asleep. My mother told me that when he was a little boy, he had tripped and fallen onto a stick. "It poked out his eye, and the black liquid poured out," my mother said.

His schoolmates teased him about his eye, asking if a bird had pecked it out. He got in so many fights that he finally quit school to escape his tormentors. But he vowed to make more money than any of them ever dreamed of having. Although my grandfather only attended school through the third grade, he could read Japanese newspapers and speak Japanese like a native. When he was eighteen, he got a job with the Japanese Electric Company, and after that, he set up his own rice refinery mill attached to his house, in addition to raising chickens and pigs. Milling machines ran all day, and everyone had to shout to be heard above the noise. Rice dust covered everything, and I never saw my grandfather in clean clothes. He worked daily at the mill and was always covered with yellow dust, even his eyelashes, his hair, and his face. As a child, I thought he looked like a yellow ghost.

My grandfather's mother died when he was nine, and his youngest brother, Ky-Young, was two years old. While four of his siblings sat next to his mother's body, wailing with grief, baby Ky-Young crawled over to her and pushed up her short *hanbok* jacket to nurse at her breast. When young Ky-Joon saw this, his own body shook with sobs. After that, he took care of his baby brother like a hawk cares for its young, feeding him and carrying him on his back wherever he went.

It was the unspoken obligation of the eldest sister to take charge of the household. The oldest child, Bok-Soo, was fifteen when her mother died, and she remained home to care for her younger brothers and sisters, not marrying until all of her siblings had grown up. But Ky-Young remained my grandfather's special charge. When he started school, my grandfather walked him to the classroom every morning. When Ky-Young was accepted to middle school with honors, Grandfather was overjoyed and paid all his tuition. This pattern lasted a lifetime—a bond between brothers that was unbreakable.

The baby brother, Ky-Young, was the intelligent one—the scholar in the family and an idealist who blazed with patriotism for his homeland. When he was sixteen, the Japanese captured many young Korean men thought to be working for the underground movement, and each mysteriously died while in prison. In 1919, when Ky-Young turned eighteen, exiled Koreans in Shanghai sent a representative to the Paris peace talks, and sent other representatives, including Syngman Rhee, to the Soviet Union, the United States, and Japan to seek support from the Korean students living there. On February 8, 1919, in Tokyo, six hundred Korean students led by Choi Pal-Young gathered at the Tokyo Korean YMCA and tried to present to the Japanese government a manifesto demanding Korean independence. But to no avail.

The Korean independence movement organized an international demonstration in support of freedom from Japanese rule that would draw world attention to Korea and bring pressure on Japan to give up her colonial rule, much as the Allied powers had recognized the rights of the European people to self-determination. The thirty-three signers

of the declaration of independence offered themselves to the Japanese
for arrest on March 1, 1919, the day of the funeral of deposed Emperor
Kojong, whom many suspected had been poisoned by the Japanese.
In a chain reaction, demonstrators marched into the streets, not just
in Seoul, but in every community in Korea. Waving national flags,
thousands of people who had come to Seoul for Kojong's funeral joined
in. In Busan, at Ky-Young's high school, a student leader announced,
"Today is the first day of Korean independence," while everyone
cheered. "*Mansei!*" Long live the nation! "*Mansei! Mansei!* A thousand
years of Korean independence!"

The students trusted that President Wilson would defend his
Fourteen Points at the peace conference at Versailles based on the
premise that governments derive their just powers from the consent of
the governed. They had confidence that he would not allow Japan to
continue to enslave our country. Soon the streets of Busan became a sea
of peaceful demonstrators waving Korean flags and marching toward
the police station demanding to be arrested. Ky-Young remembered
one old man shouting, "Finally, I can witness the freedom of my country
before I die."

The frightened Japanese police and soldiers tried to stop them
by threatening the crowds with bayonets, guns, and swords. Shouting
crowds of young and old charged, striking with their bare fists, and
the Japanese police and soldiers began shooting and killing the
unarmed people. Covered in the blood of the wounded and the dead,
the Japanese kept on. Standing that day among a thousand others,
Ky-Young and his friend Tae-Kook screamed and yelled, "A thousand
years of independence!"

When one line of people fell, the next stepped forward to take its
place. In that moment, each would rather have died than gone on living
without his freedom, and some of them did. Tae-Kook was shot and
killed. Thousands of others were arrested and tortured. The Japanese
hung even old people and children upside down from ceilings. They
burned people's fingers with hot irons, pulled fingernails out, poured
hot water or red pepper into their noses, stuck bamboo needles under
their fingernails, or pushed them into cramped boxes so small they
could hardly fit. Men were hung by the neck and displayed in public.
Despite this, the demonstrations continued for a couple of more
months while torture and killings occurred throughout every village
in the land.

In Kyung-Ki province, on April 15, twenty-three Christians were
herded into a church on the pretext of attending a meeting. Some
were killed outright with guns and swords. Others were left to burn in

a fire set by the Japanese military. Those who ran to escape the flames were shot on the spot. The Japanese then set fire to the whole village.

In another instance, suspected revolutionaries were arrested, and an entire village was ordered to watch while, one by one, the heads of the revolutionaries were cut off with a machete. The Christians were tied to crosses and killed by bayonet. The stories of the horror spread from the north to the south. A Korean leader was crucified outside the west gate of Seoul. "As a Christian, he can now go to heaven," the Japanese leader said, laughing at the women who came to weep and pray beside the dying man on the cross.

In another famous act of heroism, an eighteen-year-old schoolgirl named Yoo Kwan-Soon printed a thousand flags and led her entire student body into the streets in demonstration. Later, along with many other female students and women teachers, she was captured, tortured for days, and killed by Japanese police, who put a hose into her uterus and filled it with water.

These events forged in Ky-Young a fierce determination to sacrifice his life for the freedom of his homeland. After graduating with high honors from the Tong-Nae, the most prestigious high school in Busan, and finishing first in a nationwide marathon, Ky-Young took a job at the local Japanese bank. Many Koreans had already fled to the Kando area of Manchuria. Joining Koreans already there, they formed a strong paramilitary organization to resist the Japanese. But this force needed money to successfully offer a strong resistance, and learning this, Ky-Young planned to destroy the inner workings of a Japanese organization from within while at the same time funding the Korean independence movement.

One Sunday night in the fall of 1921, he went to the bank carrying an empty suitcase, the keys to the vault, and the combination to the safe. He filled the suitcase with stacks of bills and boarded the last train north. He had never left home before, and he thought of his brother Ky-Joon, for whom he had left a note. "*Hyung*, older brother," he wrote, "I am sorry, but you must understand that what I am doing is right. Someday, you will be proud of me."

Disembarking the next morning at the Korean border station, he set out on foot for the Yalu River, where someone was supposed to be waiting for him. The Yalu separates Korea from Manchuria, and the bridge spanning the river was very long. As he stepped on the bridge, half-dozen mounted Japanese military policemen burst from the trees and surrounded him.

"*Ma-tae!*" someone shouted. Stop!

He ran but was shot in the leg and shoulder. The suitcase flew out of his hand and over the bridge railing.

A ransacking of Ky-Young's home turned up a note meant for Ky-Young's brother Ky-Joon, who was taken to the police station for interrogation. He kept telling the police that he had no knowledge of his brother's activities, but they did not believe him and beat him. Later, he was fired from his job as a supervisor at the Japanese-owned electric company.

The Japanese police took Ky-Young to a local hospital and treated his wounds. Then they took him back to Busan, where he was put into solitary confinement. They brought him a watery porridge, which he refused to eat. The only thing he could do to pass the time was read the inscriptions of past prisoners on the walls. *"I am going to be executed today"* one said. *"I will kill every single Japanese man I see when I return to this world as a ghost."*

On the third day of his imprisonment, he was taken to a small room. One policeman held papers and a pen for Ky-Young to record his confession. "To whom were you taking the money?" he asked.

Ky-Young refused to answer. The police interrogator crushed his cigarette into Ky-Young's ear. "You need to be taught a lesson," he said, and he had Ky-Young put into a tiny cell jammed with several other prisoners. He could not lie down, and the stench was overwhelming.

The official torture began the next day. The police brought two rubber pipes and put one into Ky-Young's nose and other into his mouth. They lowered his head by yanking on his hair and then poured water into his lungs and stomach until he lost consciousness. He awoke in a cell where water covered the floor and insects covered his body.

The police repeated the pipe torture several times. He was beaten and kicked continuously. He was made to stand in one place for several days and nights. When he no longer had the strength to stand, they beat his head against the wall and floor. In his cell, he wrote on the wall, *"You might move the mountain, but you won't be able to move my soul. You might bend the iron bar, but you can't bend my heart."*

Ky-Young never revealed the identities of his contacts in the independence movement. After two months, he appeared in court, and his entire family was there as were several friends. Ky-Young looked like a skeleton draped with a white *hanbok*. He could hardly walk. A guard had to help him into the courtroom. Looking on, his brother, Ky-Joon, felt as though his heart was being cut out.

The verdict: Ky-Young was to repay the money he had stolen, and Ky-Joon was to secure the repayment.

After his release, Ky-Young was like a puppet without a soul. Bedridden for months, he never uttered a word; and for a long time after his recovery, all he did was sit in his room staring into space. In the family's registration file at the city hall, Ky-Young's name was slashed with red ink as a lifetime reminder of his criminal record. He could not obtain employment, so his older brother, Ky-Joon, looked after him and his family.

Ky-Young never told anyone of his hardship or bragged about what he had done for his country. To him, it was a duty any Korean would proudly have undertaken, and many God-believing, law-abiding Koreans like him made similar sacrifices for their country and offered their lives without hesitation.

As a child, I found one such story particularly haunting. In 1592, the Japanese invaded the Jinjoo province near Busan. A *kysang*—the Korean equivalent of a geisha—named Nong-Kae got a Japanese general drunk and took him to a pond. Holding him tight in her arms, Nong-Kae jumped into the water, and they both drowned. As a girl I imagined the devotion of that *kysang*. I saw their two bodies writhing beneath the water's dark surface, the *kysang*'s robe billowing out around her as she struggled against the general and her own instincts to break for air.

The Japanese notion that the Koreans were a spiritless people lacking the intelligence and energy to rule themselves proved to be untrue. In 1945, when World War II ended, Ky-Young became president of the Korean Independent Youth Organization; and when all the Japanese were "kicked out" of Korea and loaded on steamboats, Ky-Young became head of the inspection teams at the pier. He had the Japanese searched for valuable Korean antiques and other items that rightly belonged to the Korean people.

I have long pondered the lives of my grandfather and granduncle. I know that other men experienced equal or greater horrors. But these men's lives are special to me not only because they were my family, but also because they represent all I see in my people's heritage. Like bamboo, they bent but did not break. They took root and spread; the more they were cut down, the more fiercely they grew back again. They taught me what would also be required in my own life—the need to yield to the powerful and often harsh winds of circumstance while never breaking.

Nagai Eiki

East prince has come again
And every thing rejoices,
Grass and trees and insects
Every year return of life
Why is it that man alone,
Once he has gone cannot return?

—Park Hyogwon (1781-1880)

Life has its sorrows, as every rose has its thorns.

—Anonymous

In 1941, after my father's failed attempt to study in Waseda, my family returned to Busan, where our house had been broken into, and Father had no employment. Not long after, Mother had another baby boy that they named Tong-Kun; and that spring, when I was six, my father enrolled me in a Japanese elementary school. A child was usually enrolled in school at seven or eight years of age, but perhaps because of his deferred dreams of a law degree, my father wanted to give me a head start. Raised alone, he was not a warm person, and my brothers and I were a little scared of him. But after my enrollment, he bought me a Yamaha organ to celebrate and showed me the biggest book I had ever seen, a Korean dictionary, from which I would learn *hangul*, the Korean phonetic alphabet.

On the other hand, my mother was constantly involved in every aspect of my life then. The older girls who came to school wearing hand-me-down *hanboks* poked fun at me because I wore bright-colored knit dresses with intricately designed matching hats, gloves, and jackets that Mother had knitted for me. I was always sickly and a picky eater, so Mother sent our little maid with a lunch box filled with steaming, freshly cooked rice and delicious side dishes so that I wouldn't have to eat a cold meal like the rest of the children. Mother also instructed my teacher not to let me out for recess in the cold weather, and so I usually stayed in the classroom and watched the kids playing outside. My teachers knew that my parents were modern, young, and cared about my education. My mother often visited the classroom during the day when no other parents came. She helped me with my homework during the evening. On New Year's Day, my mother and I brought a big basket of apples, bananas, persimmons, and dates to my teacher's home. I became the teacher's pet in part because of her involvement at school and conferences with my instructors.

Although shy, I was a good student, too, which endeared me to my teachers. Once I learned how to read, I could not put down my books. They became an obsession, and I read constantly. During the lunch hour, my teacher had me read in front of the class while the other students were busy eating. I was proud whether children listened to me or not. On another day, Ms. Ishida teacher called me out of calligraphy class to follow a male teacher from the boys' class. He told me to bring my book and read it to the boys. They were so poor in this skill that the teacher wanted to shame them by showing how well a girl could do.

I also enjoyed going to the movies, dancing, and singing; and my parents often took me to performances. One day, my little maid came to school and told me that my mother wanted to take me to see Choi Sung-Hee, the only famous Korean dancer in the country.

"She said that you should tell your teacher that you have to go to the doctor."

I was so excited that I ran into my classroom, stuffed my books in my schoolbag, and ran up to my teacher, who was standing at the podium watching me, dumbfounded. I bowed quickly and gave her my excuse. That afternoon, after I saw Choi Sung-Hee's performance, I knew I wanted nothing other than to become a famous dancer and for the next three years was selected to dance for the school festival. My mother made my costumes, and looking back, it seems that history was unfolding year after year in the dances. For the first festival, I wore pom-poms and danced to Western music. The second year I wore a

Korean *hanbok* although we were not allowed to speak Korean. The third year I danced as a Japanese for the girls' Princess Day.

Every Korean had a Japanese name. Mine was Nagai Eiki. Like all other girls, my hair was cut with straight bangs in front and above my earlobes on the side. When we entered the school building, we took off our shoes and put them in individual boxes with numbers on them. When the teacher walked in, we all faced the Shinto shrine at the front of every classroom, bowed, and sang Japanese anthems as we were required to speak only Japanese in school and at home. To discipline us, teachers made disobedient students stand at the front of the class and, with their pointing sticks, beat their calves three times, waiting a few seconds between each blow. The students cried but remained standing straight.

Once a week, regardless of how cold it was, the principal, his upper body bare, stood on a platform with a back brush. Following his lead, we all had to brush our arms, chests, and backs as hard as we could until our bodies became as red as tomatoes. This was said to improve blood circulation. At the end of the day, we put our wooden chairs on our desks and moved them to one side. We swept the wooden floor, and on our knees, we wiped it clean with wet rags. To clean the windows, two girls sat on the windowsill facing each other to clean the glass with our breath, and we couldn't leave until our teacher came and inspected the room.

During summer vacation, we had to wake up at seven in the morning and go to a plaza nearby with grown-ups to do a one-hour-physical workout. We were given a card to be stamped each morning to make sure we didn't miss the exercise.

Every New Year's Day, all the students had to go to school for the New Year ceremony. In freezing-cold weather, we stood in the schoolyard and waited for what seemed be an eternity for the principal to come out and read a special message from the Japanese emperor. Holding a black lacquer chest to the eye level with both hands, the principal made his way from the building to the platform outside. We were told to bow our heads. The principal removed the scroll from the chest, opened it, and began reading out aloud. No one understood it. All we wanted was to go home where it was warm. We kept our heads bowed. We were taught that the Emperor of Japan was like God in heaven, so we dared not look up during the reading of his message. Many years later, I met Emperor Hirohito at a White House reception. He wore thick glasses, had a mustache, and stood in a corner like a puppet. As short as I, he looked as though his mind was far away, and I wondered how such a small, ordinary man could have struck such fear in everyone.

On December 7, 1941, Japan attacked Pearl Harbor; and by mid-1942, they'd driven the Americans out of the Philippines and the British from Hong Kong, Malaya, and Singapore. To celebrate the victory of the Singapore invasion, students were taken on a march into Busan with our schoolbags on our backs and little Japanese flags in our hands. It was a bone-chilling day. By the time we were dismissed, my face, hands, and feet were numb from the cold. Six years old, I stood in front of my school and cried. My desk mate put her arm around me and walked me home where I put my frozen hands under the covers on the hot *ondol* floor. My hands felt as if there were electrified.

I came to know the animosity of the Japanese toward their American enemies on the day I brought the yellow-haired, blue-eyed baby doll that my father had given me to show-and-tell. I left him with my teacher to be displayed on the bookshelf, but when I returned to class the next day, my doll's yellow hair had been colored with black ink. I couldn't take my eyes off him. When I went home and told my mother, she said, "Your teacher doesn't want a Yankee doll sitting in your classroom."

On another day, my teacher offered a couple of coupons for sneakers to the class. We couldn't purchase coveted sneakers without a coupon, and so all the children screamed for them with their hands up. I wasn't selected, but at dismissal, she called me back and gave me a coupon. As we all walked out of school, my classmates asked me what the teacher had wanted. I didn't know what to tell them. I was too young to know then that I was the teacher's pet, and that was the reason they pestered and teased me. Every day I went home crying and told my mother that I didn't want to go back to school. My mother went to the house of the older girl who was the leader of the group, scolded her, and then tried to bribe her to be my friend, but that didn't last long.

In art class, all the students drew pictures portraying the war. I was especially praised for one I drew of a bomb falling from an American airplane into the ocean and missing a Japanese ship.

The war grew worse. In the evening, there were blackouts and curfews, and we learned to cover windows with black cloth. All classes were ordered to paste strips of rice paper on the windows to prevent the glass from shattering in case a bomb was dropped on our school, and we practiced air raid drills daily, leaving the building and hurrying into underground shelters. We called our school lunches the "*Japanese flag lunch box*": white cooked rice in an oblong lunch box with a single *umeboshi*, a red pickled plum, stuck in the middle, to show that we were patriotic. When the outside of the plum was eaten, we kept sucking the seed because the rice alone had no taste.

All the Korean people were ordered to make a long cotton *sennin-bari*, or thousand stitches waistband, each with a thousand red stitches that had been sewed by a thousand women. I'd watched my mother and my grandmother putting the small dotlike red stitches on the long cloth. When the waistbands were done, they were sent to Japanese soldiers to keep them safe and to show that all the people were behind them. Recently, in the movie *Letters from Iwo Jima*, I saw how Japanese soldiers wrapped these cloths around their waists under their clothes.

We were also ordered to collect Korean rubber shoes, brass pots, dishes, chopsticks, and spoons for the munitions factories. Women were ordered to wear *monpe*, baggy pants that were pleated at the ankles, instead of the Korean full skirts. We drilled once a week, practicing how to put out fires.

With a shortage of books, two or three students ended up sharing one. Upset with the arrangement, my mother borrowed the teacher's books, copied them onto sheets of rice paper with a brush and black ink, bound them with thread, and made a book for my use. She told me I had better not misplace it the way I always misplaced my lunch box.

Although I never misplaced the books my mother made for me, I kept losing my lunch box, an expensive one, made of aluminum instead of stainless steel. My mother told my father to teach me a lesson. He told me to take my clothes off. Promising him I would never lose anything in my life ever again, I took my dress off, crying. He told me to take my panties off as well. Rubbing my hands together, I begged him to let me keep my panties on. "Please, please, please," I said. He told me to stop begging and keep my panties on. "Leave the house," he ordered. I obeyed and left the house. I was too ashamed to go out to the wide main street. Where else could I go except to my grandparents' house, a quarter mile away? I ran through the alleys, thinking I would have to live there for good. My grandmother gave me a *hanbok* that belonged to my cousin. After dinner, my mother came and held my hand as we walked home. When we arrived, I went upstairs, where the bedding had already been made on the floor and the mosquito net hung. I crawled under the comforter pretending I was asleep when my father came home from work. Mother told me that when I was a baby and my parents argued, Mother often ran off to my grandparents' house, taking me with her. Then Father came there saying that he just wanted Young-Hee back.

My father didn't have a job. One summer day when we were having
lunch, my father coughed out his food. As he looked at what he had
spit out, he turned pale. When my mother asked what was the matter,
without answering, he got up from the table, threw away his food in the
trash can, put on his shoes, and walked out of the house. My mother
went to the trash can to see what he had thrown out. His spoonful of
rice with lettuce was covered with blood.

My father had tuberculosis. For three years he lay in his small study
with his books, records, and radio/phonograph around him. He read.
No matter how cold it was, he kept the air vent open. He no longer
played his music or brought home boxes of fruit from work. No one
came to visit, and my father could only talk in whispers. My mother was
the only one allowed into his room. When she gave him injections in
his arm and buttocks, I peeked in through the partially open door. My
mother talked softly to him though my brother and I were not allowed to
make any noise. When we laughed during our play, my father knocked
on the door next to his head. We hated the sound of his knocking, and
whenever we heard it, we crawled underneath a comforter.

I have few memories of my father at that time. One afternoon, I
was in the yard when my father emerged from his room, his skinny
body draped in a baggy cotton *hanbok,* his pale white face against his
jet black hair. I froze and watched him move in slow motion across the
veranda and into our room. Although I was in plain view, he did not
look at me. He played the beginning of a song on my organ but did not
finish the piece. After a silence, my ghost of a father came back out of
our room, crossed the veranda, and returned to his own, sliding shut
the door. I stood there a long while, wondering if this brief glance was
the most I could have of him.

In the summer of 1942, our family took a trip to the country, hoping
that the fresh air would cure my father. Having heard that eating snakes
was a cure for tuberculosis, in his desperation my father caught them,
peeled off their skin, and ate them. Grandmother made dog soup,
which was supposed to be the best remedy for TB. When a giant snake
fell out of the ceiling of her room, she skinned the snake to make
soup for my father, though the neighbors whispered that the snake
brought good luck to the house and shouldn't be killed. My mother
also fed him soups made of chicken, ginger, and dog meat, but in the
end, nothing seemed to work. When we returned home, my father was
sicker than ever.

By the winter of the following year, my father was admitted to the
hospital, and we lived in more ease without my father's angry knocks

against his door or his figure silently moving about the house like a ghost. One evening as my mother spread out thick comforters, my two brothers and I rolled around on them imagining they were clouds. Outside, a cold wind shook the glass doors of our veranda, and from the street came the forlorn sound of a blind man's wooden clapper calling people to give massages. Chung-Soon, our maid, went out to answer a knock at the gate. It was Grandmother, who was staying with my father at the hospital. When Mother opened our bedroom door, Grandmother stood outside in freezing cold.

"The children's father wants you to come to the hospital," Grandmother told my mother.

"My heart sinks whenever you come for me," my mother said.

For the three years he'd been ill, I'd hardly been allowed around my father, and for his death, I was not allowed at all. Mother went alone to his *tatami* room in the hospital. He was breathing heavily, but his mind was clear. A nurse stood near, and the tag on her chest said her name was Kaneyama.

Between my father's heavy breaths, he said, "One more shot, please. One more shot, Kaneyama-san." My father told my mother in his hoarse voice to take care of his mother because she had lived a hard life.

When my mother told me of his last words, I wondered why he had never mentioned my brothers and me. Did he not love us? Did he not care? But my father was a man steeped in tradition. His first duty was to his mother as a responsible son. He left her alone on the farm after he left Yangsan, and he realized that his filial duty was not to be fulfilled because she was outliving him.

Buddha said life is *seng-no-byung-sa*—birth, old age, sickness, and death. But my father missed the chance to get old. He died when he was thirty-three, and his death changed everything.

My father was proud of his pictures he took.

Tong Ho, 2 and me, 4 yrs old.

Passport Picture
for Japan

In Japan with 3 uncles, my father,
Young Hee, Tong Ho, Mother

3rd grade on Japanese Princess Day
In back, 2nd from left is Naga; Eiki, me
my Japanese teacher, Hasegawa.

My Father, the Great Dragon

The Pine

When this frame is dead and gone
What will then become of me?
On the peak of Bongnae mountain
I shall become a spreading pine,
When white snow fills heaven and earth
I shall still stand alone and be green

—Sung Sam Moon (1418-1466)

It matters not how a man dies, but how he lives.

—Samuel Johnson (1709-84)

I remembered my father as the ghost he became while ill and only learned of him as he had been when young and strong through my mother's stories. When I asked her how my father, a poor farm boy, got it into his head to study at the most prestigious law school in Japan, she told me what my father had told her. My father was born in 1910, the year that Korea officially became a Japanese colony. He was called Chang-Yong, which meant "giant dragon." My father grew up in a poor family. His father died when he was a week old. His mother, who was named Haggi, sold lunches and drinks at her straw-roofed house, which was located near a bus station. Dust rose from the traffic on the unpaved country road in Yangsan, a small farming province on the outskirts of Busan. On March 1, 1919, when the whole country was in an uproar, demanding freedom and independence from Japan, the village of Yangsan was too far from Seoul for him to join in the demonstration; but my father, then nine years old, climbed onto the straw roof of his mother's house and planted a big Korean flag in its center. For this, my grandmother was taken to the police station.

Throughout his school days, my father delivered cables after school; and a few days before my father's graduation from elementary school in Yangsan, Mr. Wakamoto, the principal, called him to his office. He told my father that he was too intelligent, hardworking, and responsible to stay in Yangsan. So the principal had arranged with a friend in Busan, who was president of a Japanese wholesale fruit company, to employ my father.

Chang-Yong was fourteen, and his fate was sealed at that day.

With her only son moving to the city, my grandmother headed to *chang-nal* or market day to seek for a fortune-teller. He sat beside a birdcage and a small box stuffed with squares of folded paper. She told him the necessary information—that my father had been born on the second day of the first month in the year 1910, in the hour of the monkey, and that his father had died a week after his birth.

The fortune-teller began chanting to the bird as he opened the door of its cage. The myna bird hopped onto the fortune-teller's finger and pecked out a folded paper from the box. He took it from the bird's beak, then reached into his pocket for a few grains and fed them to the bird. Then he unfolded the paper and began to read.

"He has a good fortune," the fortune-teller told her. "He will succeed at whatever he chooses to do and be a rich man. It says here, 'Wealth will be gained by traveling, so take a trip.' I see a new beginning in store for this young man. In September, 'the fish in the pond will swim into the sea. You will find water when you dig in the earth. The earth will lead you to a mountain. The mountain is your conquest. Go south. You will find gold there.' *Ajuma*, this is a very good fortune. Let your son do whatever he wants."

"He is my only child," Haggi said as she lifted her skirt for the pouch of money to pay. "*Ajuma*, do not worry. If your son is strong and motivated, it does not matter where he goes. You know the saying 'Send a precious child away, and he will learn to hold his parents in his heart with deep appreciation,'" he said as he was putting his money in his pocket.

On her way home, the frogs in the nearby rice paddies croaked at each other as if in competition. Haggi listened and prayed to the frog with the loudest croak, telling him her son was going far away. "Would you please take care of him when he leaves home?"

After graduating from Yangsan Elementary, my father packed a small bundle, put on his *hanbok* and a pair of straw sandals, and went to the train station. As he sat on the train and watched the village and trees pass away outside the window, he did not know whether to laugh or cry. His mother's face appeared in his memory. Rain fell. The sound of the drops hitting against the window made him sad and made him think of his mother's face even more. "*Mother, be patient,*" he whispered to himself. "*I will take care of you someday soon. I promise to take care of you.*" Tears welled in his eyes. As the train sped along, Chang-Yong put away thoughts of his mother and began to wonder about his future. "*What will my master be like? Mr. Ishihara. Mr. Ishihara.*"

Busan was so different from my father's village. Chang-Yong joined the flow of traffic—streetcars, taxis, bicycles, and pedestrians. Everyone seemed in a hurry. Mr. Ishihara's house was not far from the train station. Chang-Yong walked up to the paved hill. The house was impressive, built on a high stone retaining wall with wide cement steps that led to a gate with "Ishihara Kajuo" engraved on wooden nameplate. A serving girl took the letter of recommendation from his principal to her mistress while Chang-Yong waited. As she scurried back into the house, her *getha* on the stone entryway sounded to Chang-Yong like the clapping of a horse's hooves against a cobblestone street.

When the girl finally admitted him, Chang-Yong felt as if he was entering to a new world filled with pine trees, red maples, and a huge pond with orange and white koi swimming. A breeze tinkled the long wind chimes that hung beneath the eaves. She took Chang-Yong to the largest room he had ever seen, with silk-covered sliding doors with painted cranes flying over snow-peaked mountains. A long scroll of calligraphy in bold black ink hung on the *tokonoma*, or alcove, above a single iris leaning against the rim of a bamboo vase. As Chang-Yong stood, admiring the room, he felt a longing that filled his imagination with visions of heaven that made his heart ache and his eyes well with tears.

As it turned out, Chang-Yong's daily household duties were to sweep the yard, clean the bathroom, feed the carp, and bring the paper in to the dining room. Mr. Ishihara told Chang-Yong he had better go into town with him the next morning to purchase new clothes and shoes. "We can't have you wearing straw shoes around here," he said and gave a kind laugh.

Mr. Ishihara had two daughters. The eldest was called Kyoko and was fourteen years old, the same age as Chang-Yong. Every morning as

Chang-Yong swept the courtyard, he noticed from the corner of his eye Kyoko's school uniform, a sailor top and a black skirt with straight pleats that opened and closed like a fan whenever she walked. Her hair was braided in two long pigtails, and her face was round like a warm bun. He loved to listen to her practice the piano. He did not know what she was playing, but the sweet melody affected him in much the same way that the house had when he first arrived. It filled him with a hunger to possess that which he saw and heard.

Kyoko constantly tried to seduce my father. She'd come up to him while he was on his knees working in the yard and say, "You see, I have this homework assignment. It needs to be completed by tomorrow morning, and I'm having an awful time with it." She'd touch the sole of his shoe with the toe of hers and ask him to come to her room to help her with her work. Chang-Yong always told her to leave the homework in his room, and he would take a look at it after his chores were completed.

Once when Chang-Yong was bathing in a tub of hot water up to his neck, Kyoko, with only a small rectangular towel covering her front, came in without knocking. Her braids had been undone, and her hair was wavy like kelp at the bottom of the sea. She approached the tub, sat on its edge, and let the towel slip out of her hand. He covered his face in his hands and begged Kyoko to not come in the tub. She giggled and told him that her family always took baths together. But he submerged himself, and Kyoko stuck out her tongue out and left.

His real attraction was not to Kyoko, but to Mr. Ishihara's music room. When Chang-Yong was alone in the house and done with his household duties, he went there because the melodies that had flowed out of it made Chang-Yong's heart tremble. The walls were covered with framed photographs of important people. Standing on the opposite side of the room was a tall radio/phonograph unit. One wall was covered with books, though he had no idea what they were about. He opened Fyodor Dostoyevsky's *Crime and Punishment* and, tracing the writing with his fingers, wondered what secrets such books held. Chang-Yong returned to the music room every chance he had and thumbed through records of Beethoven, Mendelssohn, Schubert, Strauss, popular Japanese songs, and popular American songs. When Mr. Ishihara played these every Sunday morning, Chang-Yong's heart ached.

My mother told me that my father, with the seed of his dream in his heart, avoided Kyoko, worked hard, and saved his money. Two years later, Mr. Ishihara—recognizing my father's intelligence, ambition, dedication, and good sense—sent him to an accounting school at night. My father worked the abacus like a machine and never made a mistake.

Eventually, he bought his own books to study and was later told to help himself to any he might be interested in from Mr. Ishihara's library.

As soon as my father graduated from accounting school, Mr. Ishihara hired him as an accountant for his fruit company. A year later, he was able to move out of the Ishihara household to rent a room of his own from a man named Ky-Joon.

His new life had begun. Ky-Joon had two daughters; Soo-Ok, the older one, and my mother Soon-Ok, the younger one. When Soo-Ok was seventeen, he wanted to ask her parents for marriage. But his friend Min-Sang, who was also renting a room, beat him to it. To make sure he didn't lose my mother too, he asked her parents for her hand when she was only fourteen years old. She called him Sai-sang, Mr. Song in Japanese, and she told me how she used to love to listen to all his classical recordings—Beethoven, Mendelssohn, Paganini, and popular Japanese songs—that he played on a small crank-up phonograph. Her mother thought my father was too rigid, but her father believed him honest and thrifty. So it was agreed, and Chang-Yong presented Soon-Ok with a 24-karat ring in the shape of a heart with a flower carved on it—the symbol of eternal love. Two years later, before my mother graduated, they were married. She was sixteen years old and he was twenty-three.

These stories of him were all that remained of the Great Dragon before he became sick. These and his belief that dreams must be pursued.

Yangsan

Small as you are, high in the sky,
there is nothing brighter than your beam.
Your light shines everywhere on everyone.
And though you see all, you never tell.
That is why you are my only one, my best friend.

—Yoon Sun Do (1587-1671)

Those who want much, are always much in need.

—Horace (65-8 BC)

During the war, my family was forced to defer any dreams in favor of survival. A few weeks after my father died, bombs fell from the sky, hitting the Cholyang district near my home. I was awakened in the middle of the night by my mother's screams and watched her frantically run back and forth like a wild animal between our room and the veranda. "*Aigo! Aigo!*" she wailed, clapping her hands. "What am I going to do? They're bombing us. What am I going to do?"

Sitting up on the mat, half awake, I saw her trying to lift the sewing machine. It was too heavy for her, so she abandoned it and continued to run aimlessly. While my two brothers slept, I scrambled off the mat we shared, still half asleep, and ran out to the veranda to see what was happening. Fire raged in the house next door, and the flames leapt across the narrow alley toward our home. I watched them dance with a thousand arms reaching toward the heavens. The heat made my cheeks, arms, and legs tingle. Although my grandfather's house was about a quarter mile away, he'd heard the bombing, and he ran to our home. "What the hell are you doing? Get the children out of the house," he said. We were scooped up to a neighbor's house, which wasn't directly threatened, and left alone on the wooden veranda while all the grown-ups stood in the street watching the fire.

After it was all over, the only damage to our house was some broken windows on the upper floor. The firemen had directed their hoses onto our stucco walls to prevent the fire from spreading. My father had made sure that our house was well built, and it had paid off.

Not long after the fire, a small rattling truck stopped in front of our house, and we loaded our household goods onto its bed. My mother, my brothers, and I were crammed into the front seat next to the driver like bean sprouts. Yul-Soon, my mother's cousin who lived with us, was squeezed in the back of the truck with the furniture. Once we left the smooth roads of the city, the truck rattled and shook so much that my cheeks and lips felt as if they were falling off, my whole body bounced, and my teeth rattled. Whenever the truck hit a pothole, everything flew into the air only to land in a different spot than before. We traveled so slowly that whenever other cars and trucks hurtled by us, we were covered by a choking cloud of dust. Squeezed between my brothers, I wondered if such a road could ever lead us to a beautiful home.

As we drove through the country, we passed by cabbage fields and rice paddies. Farmers, bending low to cut down tall crops, looked as though they were playing hide-and-seek with one another. There were no villages except for dust-covered mud-thatched huts that stood on the side of the unpaved road. *What kind of people lived in those helmet-shaped houses?*

As the truck struggled to climb a steep hill, I felt as if I wanted to get out and push the vehicle to the top. Finally, the truck stopped. Steam rose from its hood as if the engine was exhaling its last breath. We got out and sat along the side of the road, blinded by the dust of other vehicles passing us. The driver opened the hood and poked around while steam continued to hiss out. It seemed that we might be there forever. Finally, wiping his hands with a dirty rag, he murmured to himself, "I guess it's all right now."

When my father was ill and without a job or savings, he could not keep the house, and it was taken over by the bank. After the bomb dropped next door, Grandfather explained to Mother, "Every time the governor-general raises the *Kong Chul*, or quota for rice for the Japanese troops, it means there will be less for us in the city. You would be far better off in the country, close to Chang-Yong's paddies and away from the bombs. Besides, Kun-Yul said he would help you out with the farming."

A friend of my father's, Mr. Lee Kun-Yul, lived in Yangsan and had talked my mother into moving there after the bombing and my father's death. Since my mother had been engaged when she was fourteen and married to my father when she turned sixteen, she knew nothing about farming. But Mr. Lee told her that he would look after her needs. Besides, he was considered a rich and prominent man in his village because he had a tiled roof rather than the straw roof of most farmhouses.

We arrived at our new home at dusk after an entire day to reach our destination one hundred miles away. The farmhouse had no electricity. It had walls of mud and stone, a dirt floor in the kitchen, and two big holes in which to put our two metal pots. My mother yelled for Yul-Soon to hurry up and find the candles.

At daybreak, we awoke and began to explore our new home. Two wide paneled wooden gates opened under a roof connected to the main house. Tall dirt and stone walls surrounded the yard, with a well in the middle. The main building had three connecting rooms, with the all-purpose room next to the kitchen. We ate and slept in the all purpose room in the winter to save firewood. In Korea, all the rooms on the ground floor are called *ondol-bang* or warmed stone room. Under the floor ran a long, wide flue built of stone and mud that carried heat from the kitchen fire, which warmed the stones in the floor. Early in the evening when the fire from our supper was still burning, the floor would be very hot, and our bedding would be toasty. But toward morning, when the fire had died down, the room became cold, and we moved as close as we could get to the opening of the flue in the kitchen.

Next to the main house was a smaller structure with a room and a barn, built as quarters for a hired man and a cow, though we had neither at the time. The village was nothing more than a cluster of round straw-roofed houses that reminded me of giant clamshells. There once was a wide riverbed next to the village, and a steep levee had been built to protect the village from floods; but the river had dried up to a narrow stream on one side, and the rest was covered with cobblestones.

Although it was somewhat primitive, I could not deny the beauty and peacefulness of the village. After sunset, as the women of the village cooked their suppers, smoke rose from their chimneys like the ribbons of flying kites. Crimson clouds floated above three mountain peaks. The cowbells tinkled. The serenity made it hard to imagine that somewhere not too far away a war was being waged.

But I soon grew tired of the straw clamshell houses, the miles and miles of rice paddies, no markets, no stores, no bathhouses, no doctors, no hospitals, no cars or taxis, no song, and no dance. I grew tired of walking, grew tired of seeing—from sunup to sundown—the humped backs of the workers in the fields, their faces brown and their once-white *hanboks* tattered and gray from constant washing. When summer came, I went to the small stream by our village, took off my clothes, and swam along with the village children and the tiny fish, which were impossible to catch. When the sun went down, the other children, in dirty straw slippers, ran off to their parents' fields to help with the return of the cows that had been feeding all day on the grass. I watched the boys bringing them back on the ropes and wondered if cows had feelings too. I had no friends, no relatives. As long as Mother was home, I felt safe and happy enough. After all, I was a young child with no concept of the war. But when she went away to Busan, which was often, I felt abandoned and wondered why she did not take me along. I later realized that my mother, who was twenty-seven years old at that time, was also a dreamer and could not bear the thought of spending the rest of her days in Yangsan with no one but Yul-Soon, my brothers, and me.

During my mother's trips to Busan, I was left to spend hours playing my organ, reading Japanese storybooks, and dreaming as I paged through my mother's Japanese movie magazines. But the glamorous women with happy faces reminded me of just how unhappy I was. When I looked through my family albums and found photographs my father had taken, I wanted to disappear back into that time and place, to my house in Busan, my school, my music, and my father. No amount of rice could fill the hole in my heart. I dreamed of becoming a famous movie actress and singer like Deanna Durbin. I rode my bike and shook my hair in the wind, just the way she'd done in one of her films.

When it rained, I built a dollhouse with my father's volumes of Shakespeare's plays and filled it with matchstick people. I dressed them with my origami papers I had brought from Busan. One was the mother, the other one the father, and the two children lay in the middle. I also made myself a crown of flowers from the colored paper and danced and sang in front of my household of match-people as if they were a live audience.

The highlight of those days in the country was when the first-grade teacher asked me to select a child to dance at the school festival, and I picked the sister of a young and handsome teacher I liked. I choreographed her dance to "*Twinkle, Twinkle, Little Star.*" On the festival day, I stood next to the organ and sang the song while the little girl danced. I was ten years old and felt so grown.

But for the most part, I was a loner, finding solace and companionship in reading, singing, dancing, and playing my organ alone. At home, when Mother was away and there wasn't much else to do, I picked wild green onions or the vegetables called *sook*, or sagebrush. Sometimes Yul-Soon and I picked berries and persimmons. Once I stole and ate so many of the neighbors' sweet summer persimmons that I became constipated. Squatting in our outhouse, which was nothing but a gigantic earthen pot buried in the ground and surrounded by a straw fence, I eventually called to my mother for help. She brought out a thin silver spoon, wielding it like delicate surgical instrument, and removed—piece by piece—the source of my discomfort, mumbling the entire time, "*This is what it has come to in this godforsaken country. If you break a leg, where are you supposed to go? If you burn an arm, who will relieve the pain? No hospital. No doctors. Is this my destiny?*"

When my family lived in Busan, I was fed rice that was white and sticky. But in Yangsan, my rice bowl was filled with barley, the poor man's rice. Along with bowls of barley, we ate chopped chives mixed with vinegars, soy sauce, and ground red peppers, or dipped the hot green peppers we picked from our yard in bean paste. At dusk, when the whole family sat outside in the middle of the courtyard on a thick straw mat with a host of fireflies around us, my mother would put our dinner bowl—a mixture of barley, chives with soy sauce, and red pepper—in the middle of the table and say, "Okay, eat." It was the most delicious food I've ever eaten. She used to say, "*Hunger is the best appetite,*" and all of our spoons went into the big bowl like little shovels. That was our dinner. But we were happy because the dinner was delicious and Mother was with us.

But during the war, food was always an issue. For us to have eggs in Yangsan, my mother had bought a hen and rooster. They lived in a straw boat nest that our handyman, Mr. Park, had hung low from the end of the roof to protect the chickens from the snakes. One afternoon, my mother noticed that our hen was nowhere to be found. We spent the afternoon looking for the chicken, and after sunset, the rooster would not go into his nest. All night long, my mother muttered about the many possible fates of the missing hen. Our little hen must be lost in the bamboo field, searching for a way home while being stalked by snakes. Or the village children snatched her from the yard and ate every part of her. *Poor hen. Poor, poor hen.* As my mother moaned herself to sleep, I stared at the curve of her ear and wondered what in her heart made her feel such sadness for the hen that had gone away, and what in mine made me feel sadness for the rooster that had been left alone. I prayed to Buddha to let our hen come back to us.

The next morning, my mother called together all the village children and told them to look for our hen, but they returned empty-handed. During dinner, Mother repeated the same concerns. "*Poor hen, poor hen.*" But the following morning, the children came running and shouting, "We found her, we found her!" Chased by the boys, the hen strutted through our gate and into the yard, as if she knew we had been waiting for her grand entrance. The rooster, with one wing drooping to the ground like a feathered fan, danced around and around the hen. Then he jumped up and mated with her. The scene always stayed on my mind. "Even a chicken needs a mate," my mother said. That evening, as the two flew into their nest, I thought that more than some humans, chickens must have love and loyalty in their hearts.

About a week later, that same rooster saved my life. I'd gotten up early after a rainy night and slipped out onto the veranda. I wanted to wash my face at the well before Tong-Ho woke up. We only had one pair of sneakers, which was several sizes too big for either my brother or me, but we fought constantly over who was going to wear them. The heels were pressed down flat, which turned them into mules, the way many Koreans wear them because they constantly have to take them off and on. When I put my foot into the sneaker, something stung my toe. When I pulled out my foot, a huge scorpion (at least it looked huge to me) crawled out after spending the night there safe from the rain. I screamed. I cried. My mother rushed out from the kitchen.

"Now, calm down and go into the room while I go fetch the rooster."

When she returned, she explained, "Chickens and scorpions are bitter enemies, so the rooster will pick the poison out of your toe, purify the wound, and make it better in no time."

I sat on the *ondol* floor, stretched out my leg, and wiggled my toe at the rooster, who crowed and searched with frantic eyes for a way to escape. But after a while, he began to peck at my toe, and my toe got better. Besides scorpions, we had snakes. In the fall, we often saw their discarded skins lying behind the earthen pots. But one day, Yul-Soon came screaming and running out of the kitchen, her face as white as if she'd seen a ghost, after finding a live snake as thick as my arm behind the metal cooking pot that was hung on the flue.

Once, Mother took us up one of the mountains on the outskirts of the village for baths. I didn't know where we were going, but we kept climbing higher until we reached a place I had never been to before. It reminded me of one of the bedtime stories Mother often read to us. The story went like this: *One day, three angels came down from heaven*

and enjoyed their bath in a waterfall beneath a mountain. A man who had
come to the mountain to collect branches came upon the scene. When he saw the
angels' gowns on the rock, he hid one of them. When the angels finished their
bath and were ready to go up to heaven, one of them couldn't find her gown.
The two dressed angels didn't have any choice but to leave the naked one behind.
So the man took her to his house, and she became his wife. In a dream, a long
white-beard man appeared to the man and told him not to return the gown until
they had three children. But when she had two, her husband relaxed and gave
the gown back to her. She put it on, picked up a child under each of her arms,
and flew up to heaven.

On that mountain, in the middle of towering pines, a stream flowed between giant rocks, forming a pond. While Mother and Yul-Soon were shampooing their hair and scrubbing their bodies, my brothers and I swam and played in the pond. I never found out how my mother learned about this special place. Even now, I marvel at my mother's many voices and the complex person these voices revealed. She could yell, moan, complain, entertain, comfort, and confront. I loved the sound of her voice when she read Korean folktales and Aesop's fables to my brothers and me as we fell asleep. As we lay side by side with a tiny porcelain lamp burning over our heads, each story helped me escape reality and, in its stead, construct elaborate fantasies about the future. As Mother finished a story and blew out the lamp, rats raced on our paper ceiling, and I would whisper, "It is their racing time now."

We had lovely moments of storytelling and meals with her, but I was too young to be aware of how complicated and unprotected our lives were without my father, especially during a war. One morning she woke me early, saying, "Young-Hee yah, come on. We're going up to Book-Jung village this morning."

"Why there?" I asked.

"Never mind. You'll see."

It was early summer, and young rice plants lined the sides of the road, swaying back and forth in the breeze like waves in a wide green sea. After we had walked five *li* (a little over a mile), Mother stopped at the entrance of the village, a few hundred feet from a house with a tile roof. She began to shout.

"Hey, Hwang Jae-Young, do you really think you can eat up Song Chang-Yong's rice paddies without getting a stomachache?"

I sat on the ground as Mother paced up and down in silence and began to shout again.

"Hey, Hwang Jae-Young, do not believe for one minute that you are going to swallow Chang-Yong's farm that easily. As long as the dirt's not in my eyes, I won't let it happen."

She repeated her threats for about thirty minutes. When no one responded, she said, "Okay, let's go home now." We walked back along the deserted road to our own village in silence.

Years later, I learned that Hwang Jae-Young had been managing my father's farm while we lived in Busan. After Father's death, when we moved to Yangsan, my mother wanted the farm back, but Mr. Hwang refused to relinquish it. Since he considered himself one of the prominent men of the community, someone had told Mother that she should embarrass him in public so that he would lose face. When this tactic failed, she took him to the Japanese court in Busan. The final judgment was that Mr. Hwang was to manage the farm one more year and then hand it over to my mother. But one year later, the war ended, Korea was suddenly without a government, and my mother lost my father's farm.

In spite of these adjustments, we kept our traditions. The two most important holidays in Korea are *Solnal,* which is the Lunar New Year's Day, and *Chusok,* the Harvest Day, which takes place on the fifteenth day of the eighth moon of the Chinese year. During both holidays, we performed *chesa,* the ceremonies to offer formal memorial services for our ancestors. Quite naturally, my family's ceremonies revolved around our deceased father and grandfather.

A day before our first *Chusok* in Yangsan, Mother cooked all day while Yul-Soon polished the brassware with folded wet straw dipped in ashes. At dawn the next day, Mother shampooed her hair and took a hot bath in the laundry tub in the kitchen. As all Korean women must do for three years after their husbands' deaths, she dressed in a white linen *hanbok* and pinned a linen ribbon in her hair, indicating that she was a mourning widow. First, she placed a special, refined straw mat on the floor. In front of the screen, she arranged a big low dining table on which she organized the various foods to be used in the ritual of ancestor worship. She used the wooden dishes and brassware specially made for these occasions. Mother began by placing on the table a tall bowl of rice with a spoon stuck in the middle of the mound, then a bowl of beef soup with cubes of radish and bean curd. The vegetables were plates of seasoned spinach, bean sprouts, and ferns. Then she added a plate with two broiled pollack with their heads intact. Then she murmured to herself, "Those fish were served so our children could have as many children as the eggs of the pollack." After the table was set, my mother lined up the fruits and nuts, persimmons, apples, pears, chestnuts, and Chinese dates.

"Do you know why we serve persimmons?" she asked us. "A persimmon tree has a black core. Our parents had many heartaches and difficult times to bear in raising us. Their hearts were blackened like the heart of the persimmon tree."

Putting a dish of chestnuts on the table, my mother said, "Their flowers smell like a mother's breast when she feeds her baby. When the chestnut grows big and hard, it pops open and pushes out the nut, just as a mother pushes her child away from her breast when he grows strong and big."

She explained the meaning of the fish, the apples, and the other food. Kneeling, she placed a lit candle on a small dish next to a few sticks of incense. Then she rose and poured rice wine into a small bowl. Holding the bowl with her right hand and placing her left hand under the right, she moved the bowl in a circle three times over the candle while she prayed.

"We are all well. Stay in peace. Please look after Young-Hee, Tong-Ho, and Tong-Kun. Let them grow up to be safe and healthy."

My mother bowed three times, twice to the floor and once halfway. Sitting on the floor, she said, "Tong-Ho, yah, you're the first son of the Song family and the head of the household. Come and pay homage to your father."

"What about *Noonah*, my older sister?" he asked, pointing his chin at me.

"A girl does not have to do this," Mother said. "Someday she will marry and become part of someone else's family."

My seven-year-old brother stood up and tried to bow to his ancestors, but instead he fell flat on the floor with his two hands at his forehead. I giggled with my hands over my mouth.

My mother took a serving from each dish, put the food in a bowl, and told me to take the bowl outside and place it by our gate so that our father could share his food with his friends who did not have family to pay homage to their spirits.

Beggars and lepers came carrying cans and cloth bags, already partially filled with food received at other households. I had seen those people under bridges, some sleeping, some eating food out of cans, some talking to each other, some singing. "Remember, we were not born this way," I heard one say when I stretched my body over the edge of the cement bridge and looked down at them. They frightened me. I had heard rumors that some lepers killed babies and ate their livers as a cure for their disease.

After the ceremony, we had a rare feast for breakfast. Afterward, my mother put all the different dishes of foods onto a big wooden tray and told me to take the food to my grandmother's house, near my school, only five *li* away from ours. She covered the tray with a handmade patchwork table cover and placed it carefully on my head. Dressed in my new *hanbok*, I was glad to give my grandmother a chance to see me at my prettiest. Balancing the bundle of food on my head, I walked carefully, my chin level with the ground, moving only my eyes to watch out for rocks, puddles, and holes. As I crossed the bridge on the main street and was just starting down the hill, a group of children ran toward me from the opposite direction, shouting, "Fire! Fire!"

I carefully turned and saw black smoke shooting up into the sky. I walked back as fast as I could without dropping the tray, and when I came to the bridge, I saw that it was my house on fire. I asked one of the children to help me with my tray and sank down on the dirt path, praying that my beautiful organ would not be destroyed. It was my only friend—the only thing that helped me forget my loneliness.

The farmers of the village formed a bucket brigade, passing pails of water hand over hand as fast as they could from our well in the courtyard to the top of our straw roof. Soon the fire died, but water was everywhere.

The fifteenth night of the eighth moon of the Chinese year was the mid-autumn festival, held when the full moon was at its brightest and young women rode seesaws or swung high on swings. But because of the fire, there was no festivity for us that year. That night, as my mother, cousin, and brothers fell asleep, I looked up at the moon and thanked him for saving my organ from the fire. He smiled down upon me through our half-burned ceiling.

The following morning, the village helped my mother make a new straw roof for our house. Every year, all the roofs in the village were replaced with fresh straw directly after the harvest in the fall. But because of the fire, ours was replaced ahead of schedule and looked out of place among the other dingy roofs. I was thankful for the farmers of our village. Although they knew little about our family, they came out to help us without hesitation or expectation of a reward.

Our handyman, Mr. Park, lived in our house, and in exchange for his work, he was given a small room and a fraction of our harvest at the end of the season. He was tall, thin, and handsome. I did not know if he had a family or how old he was. His answers to our questions were either yes or no. He ate his meals alone in his room and left not one grain of barley in his bowl after he was done. This impressed me because my grandmother always said that grains were the fruit of a farmer's labor, and if I wasted any, God would punish me.

I used to visit Mr. Park after dinner and watch him make sandals for himself out of straw. Sometimes he made *jori* or flappers for my brothers and me. But those *jori* never lasted long after walking back and forth the five *li* to school. When it rained, walking on dirt road was worse. Mr. Park had too much to do to make my *jori* every other day. The only way I could have new *jori* when I needed them was to learn to make them myself. I asked him to show me how, and he said he would show me that evening. Excited, after finishing my dinner, I went to his room. When I opened his paper door, I saw that a white porcelain lamp, the size of my palm, with a burning wick the size of the tip of my baby finger, was placed in front of him. The straws were scattered around him. His big shadow was on the wall and ceiling that had no paper covering and the thick brown beams were exposed. He never said a word while working the straw pieces, and I watched intently as our shadows flickered like dancing monsters on the wall. Mr. Park first twisted two strands of straw into a long rope with the palms of his big, callused hands while holding their ends steady with his bare feet. Each time he added more strands, he spat on his palms. After he twisted a rope that was four times the length of my foot, he folded it into even fourths, hooked two ends on each of his toes, and wove the strands in and out from top to bottom. He then made a rope that was shorter and thinner, pierced the front end of the sole, and hooked it to form the thong of the slipper. Then he secured the loose ends on the sides, and one shoe was finished. I later made my own pair and proudly wore them to school. I had a hard time containing myself from lifting them up for the whole class to see.

Other events in the village showed me its harsher underside. One evening, shouts came from the other side of our dirt wall, and I climbed to the top to see over. Under the silver moon, a sobbing woman was surrounded by a crowd who were dragging her by her hair along the ground. Another woman ran toward her and began cutting off her hair as if she was cutting buckwheat noodles too long to eat.

"Do you know what we should do with a bitch like you?" one woman yelled. "We should burn you at the stake. We'll teach you never to do a thing like that again." The tirade continued as they dragged her out of the yard and past our house toward the outskirts of the village. "Don't ever come back to this village again," they said.

The women disappeared into the darkness. The angry voices, footsteps, and rustling skirts faded into the night. A dog barked.

Lying next to my mother that night, I touched her hair, which was tied into a tight bun. I remembered her telling me once that a woman's life was in her hair. What awful crime, I wondered, had the sobbing woman committed to have her life snipped away?

The next day, the whole village was buzzing with gossip. A neighbor woman visited Mother to discuss the incident.

"I thought she was acting strangely," Mother said. "Whenever she came to visit me, she seemed to be living in a different world. She lay down on the veranda and sang sad songs. I understand she has relatives in Busan."

"Her husband is such a sweet man," the neighbor said. "Poor soul. You don't need a law to get along with that man."

"I'm sure her husband feels sorry for her. They have a son. He would have forgiven her if the others hadn't gotten involved," my mother said.

Later, I learned that the sobbing woman had been having an affair with a married man in the village, and the lovers were caught in her house in the middle of the day. The punishment she received was common in the old days, especially in farming villages.

A year later, she sneaked back to Yangsan, came to my mother, and asked if she could wait at our house until her son returned from school. He was a boy about my age, and we sometimes walked home together. That day as he and I approached my gate, his mother came out and knelt before him. She grabbed his body, held stiff as a stick, and sobbed the same way she had the night she had lost her hair. "Sam-Dong ah, I missed you so much," she cried between sobs. I stood by, wondering if the boy would acknowledge his mother. Finally, I left them alone and walked the rest of the way home by myself.

Spring came, and the swallows built their nests under our roof. I climbed up to peek at the eggs, which looked like precious stones. Soon after, I saw chicks screeching to the sky for more food, their mouths open wide like little flowers in full bloom. Out of nowhere, it seemed, my mother gave birth to another baby boy. We named him Jinna, which meant "sweet baby." I held his tiny hands and feet, hummed lullabies to him, and watched him sleep as if he was my own living baby doll. But a few months after his birth, my mother disappeared without telling anyone where she was going. That night, the baby cried for his milk. Where had my mother gone? On the veranda, I carried him back and forth, singing as gently as I could and holding back my tears: Jinna would not stop crying, and I did not know how to feed a real baby.

The baby cried all night, and I didn't know what to do. At first I tied him on my back and tried to walk him to sleep, but he cried even more. Then I took him in my arms and rocked him back and forth. But still Jinna would not stop crying. I soaked a piece of cotton ball in some water and held it to his mouth. Jinna tried to suck it, but then he cried even louder. He screamed as if he was angry with me for trying to trick him. I could not bear his cry, so in desperation, I lifted my shirt, tried to give him my nipple. The baby searched with his mouth all around my flat chest, which only made him more frustrated than before.

Eventually I remembered that a neighbor woman had recently given birth to a baby. "Wait, little Jinna," I whispered to my baby brother. "Wait until the rooster crows. You'll get your milk when the rooster crows."

Although I was young, I didn't think it was proper to take my brother to her house in the middle of the night, so I waited for morning.

As soon as the sky lightened and our rooster crowed, I rushed Jinna to our neighbor. While I watched Jinna gulp up milk so fast that it looked as if he was choking on the woman's huge breast, I wondered what made my mother less than the bird I had seen on our eaves—feeding insects to her insatiable babies, taking care of them until they grew strong and were able to fly on their own.

Every day at sunset, I carried little Jinna on my back, walked over the bridge to the bus stop, and waited for my mother's return. When the bus arrived, I searched the windows looking for my mother's face. But only strangers stepped off, no one's eyes meeting mine, and the bus pulled away, leaving me to walk home in a cloud of dust, feeling as if something had died within me. When she returned a few days later, I overheard my mother saying that when you cannot stand the man, you cannot stand his baby. Mr. Lee had tried to talk my mother into exchanging her rice paddies for his. "If his were so good, why didn't he keep them for himself?" she asked. My mother wasn't a fool. Although Jinna's father was a seedy man, Jinna was not a seedy baby, and I loved him as if he were my full brother.

When Jinna was six months old, Mr. Lee came to our house and took him away, angry that Mother wanted nothing to do with him. I missed my brother. I did not trust Mr. Lee to take good care of him. The next morning, I walked to Mr. Lee's house in Book-Jung village to bring Jinna back home, but Mr. Lee was not at home.

"You cannot take the baby until the master comes home," one of the women said to me. Mr. Lee had several wives and several sets of children living in the same house. Jinna was sleeping in one of the rooms of the house. I held his hand and sang to him.

"In the black sky, there are three sibling stars, twinkling, twinkling, and smiling at each other lovingly. I do not know why, but one star is gone, and the remaining two weep for the missing one."

Mr. Lee returned home at sunset.

"Oh Young-Hee yah, you've come, huh?" he said as he entered his gate.

"I came to take Jinna home, but they wouldn't let me until you returned," I said.

"Ah, go ahead, go ahead. Take the baby."

Carrying Jinna on my back, I left the house as fast as I could, hoping Mr. Lee would not change his mind. When I lost sight of the village and was on the deserted road, I sang and skipped the rest of the way home. My baby brother was back in my care. But many years later, when I had my own child and was feeding him every four hours as the doctor told me to, I was haunted by the memory of what had happened to my baby brother.

Another incident I couldn't make full sense of until I was grown. I shared a small room with Yul-Soon. Some nights as I closed my eyes and began to fall asleep, Yul-Soon undressed me. With her saliva, she moistened my private places. Then she lay on top of me, chest to chest, stomach to stomach, triangle to triangle, and rubbed against me, quietly moaning into my ear. Our private parts were wet and slippery. A few minutes later, she wiped me with a towel and went to sleep. In American culture, such incidents would be dealt with severely. But in Korea's crowded conditions, we slept together, changed clothes in front of each other, and bathed together. Besides, she was like my own sister. As a result, I was more curious than anything else. A couple years later, my grandmother took Yul-Soon away and married her off to a Buddhist monk from her temple.

During the winter of 1944 to 1945, the Japanese were losing the war. The village of Yangsan suffered from a food shortage because of drought and because the government took our crops.

We were lucky if we had any grain to eat. The kids went up to the hill, broke up the pine branches, peeled off the outer skin and chewed the inner skin as if they were chewing gum. I tried but I couldn't eat it. By spring, our stock of rice was gone, and everyone was waiting for the barley to be harvested. The children's bellies were so swollen that they looked pregnant. Their faces were purple and swollen from eating too much poisonous grass. To make matters worse, my mother's former maid, who could not find work in Busan, moved in with us, adding to our household her husband and two boys, aged seven and nine.

With the coming of spring when I was nine, the whole village became busy and lively. The farmers cultivated the rice paddies, cows pulled plows through the fields, and the green rice plants grew. In May, when the farmers transplanted the young plants into water-filled paddies, everyone pitched in to help, including students who worked in the fields after school. In the slippery mud, the bundles were left here and

there to plant. One afternoon, feeling an itching on my leg, I looked
down and saw leeches slithering up my leg. I screamed and slapped
them off. Blood ran down my leg. I looked up at the others, thinking
they would run to my aid, but no one seemed to notice or care—they
were too busy working. After wiping away the blood, I returned to my
planting. At the end of each day, the sores on my legs were raw, and
the skin around my fingernails peeled off from the constant work in
the paddy water.

In the late summer, when the rice plants had grown tall and were
budding with grain, I sat with the other village children along a ridge
near the fields. We chased the birds away by pulling on strings attached
to scarecrows with noisemakers. When September came, the plants
hung low, swaying back and forth in the breeze. From a distance the
fields looked like vast shimmering seas of gold. *"The riper the grains,
the heavier its head,"* was a famous proverb, which means that the more
knowledge a person has, the more humble he should be, holding his
head low with the weight of many truths.

When the harvest came, the tall plants were cut and laid out on the
dried paddy until they dried completely. Then they were transferred to
the farmers' yards either by carts or A-frames and spread on big heavy
straw mats where the grains were separated from the stalks. The empty
stalks were tied up and used for the new roofs while the grains were
sent to the mill to be refined. For a short while after that, we could eat
as much rice as we wanted, and we ate a lot of new brown rice raw.

As I squatted in a corner of our kitchen, I watched Yul-Soon
preparing rice. She scooped grains into a basin and filled it with water.
Then with one hand, she washed the rice as she would dirty clothes.
After the impurities floated to the surface and the water became like
murky milk, she poured out all the water and did this several times until
the water ran clear. Then she put the washed grain into a big black metal
pot and added just the right amount of water, which she measured by
putting her palm in the pot. She covered the pot and waited for the
water to boil. When it began to bubble, she lowered the fire beneath
the pot and wiped the metal cover with a cold rag, thus reducing the
heat. The rice simmered slowly. The bottom layer, which became lightly
roasted, was made into rice tea and drunk after our meal along with
toasted rice. After the rice was cooked, she spooned the steaming grains
into small individual brass bowls with covers and stored them under the
comforter spread on the hot floor to keep them warm.

In the early summer of 1945, my favorite uncle, Min-Shik, came back
from Japan, where he had been studying, to marry the daughter of my

mother's friend. On the wedding night, my granduncle Ky-Young took all the children to a mountain, where my grandfather had bought a plot to build a temple for my grandmother after he'd taken a concubine. She lived there with a monk, and I used to stay there in the summers, praying in a big hall where all the beautiful golden Buddhas sat and looked down at me. There, Ky-Young reasoned, we would be safe from the bombing missions that still occasionally frightened the citizens.

The next day, the war officially ended. The date was August 15, 1945, the night of my uncle's wedding marking the end of our exile in Yangsan. When I returned to my old school in Busan, all the students freely spoke Korean, but for me, Japanese words were still alive on my tongue, and making the transition back to Korean took time.

The two years my family spent in Yangsan have had a lifelong effect on me. Looking back on that time, I realize that my loneliness was overwhelming, and my sense of maternal betrayal totally devastating. And because I was so young, I couldn't handle the pain. But I never defied my mother and never complained. In some ways, the adversity helped me grow stronger. My young and vulnerable mother also learned hard lessons of survival. Like bamboo, we both bent but did not break. Somehow both of us, each in our own way, lived through the Yangsan experience and became better for it. Seeing how some people had almost nothing but still lived their lives without complaint, I began to appreciate every little fortunate thing that came my way.

Busan

The war that kills everyone
Is it for the country?
Or is it to kill our boredom?
This hopeless war is no end in sight.

—Yee Duck-Ill (1561-1622)

All the world's a stage, and all the men and women merely players.

—Shakespeare

When World War II ended, Korea celebrated. For several weeks, the Korean people lived in a state of happiness and confusion, and for many, it was an emotional experience too deeply felt to be adequately described. Domestic political differences and the collision of the United States and Soviet Russia soon overshadowed their happiness, however.

Ordinary citizens desperately needed the basics to sustain their daily lives. Electricity and water were rationed. Our small stores had no goods to sell except old clothes provided by the American Salvation Army. We also received shipments of American rice. How strange their rice seemed—long and skinny, not round and fat like ours. We thought anything made in America was the best in the world. People would joke, "Even dung is good if it is American dung."

My granduncle and uncle worked at a pier where GIs were stationed. They brought us C-rations. The wax-covered cardboard boxes were filled with many different and wonderful things. When I first tried chewing gum, it was stiff, but it felt great in my mouth. I had never eaten anything so smooth, chewy, and sweet. We kept eating the gum, thinking it was some sort of American candy. Later when I learned that it wasn't to be swallowed, I worried that the gum had gotten stuck in my stomach. We never knew what we would find inside those boxes. It could be Spam. It could be chocolate cookies. Some items tasted strange, some delicious. But we were thankful for every mouthful.

While we struggled to survive, the Russo-American talks about the future of Korea continued. In the end, the unification of Korea was not to be, and Korea was divided at the thirty-eighth parallel—the north under Soviet rule, with Kim Il-Sung as dictator, and the south under the United States. We didn't realize it at the time, but this decision set the stage for Korea to become a pawn in the Cold War between the United States and Soviet Union, and many North Koreans fled to the south to escape Communist rule.

Again the old proverb was fitting: "*The shrimp's back breaks when the whales fight.*"

The new National Assembly elected Syngman Rhee, who'd fought for the freedom of the Korean homeland and returned after a thirty-three-year absence as the first president of the republic. On August 15, 1948, the third anniversary of liberation, the newly formed Republic of Korea was proclaimed to the world. Meanwhile, Communist agitators began to infiltrate the south, recruiting dissatisfied students to stir unrest and push for a united Communist Korea. Checkpoints were set up at every corner, and people without proper identification were jailed. In the south, the new government was having a difficult time. Communist-inspired strikes and riots were frequent, and so much money was spent maintaining public order that shortages of essential goods and inflation resulted. A majority of the assemblymen elected were without political party affiliations, a clear sign of public disenchantment with politicians. And the republic's armed forces, which possessed no tanks and no warplanes, were far inferior in strength to the North Korean forces.

I returned to Busan before my family moved back so I could start school. I planned to stay with my newly wedded uncle, Min-Shik, since I had no friends and no family. I was desperately lonely, and all I wanted to do was to be with familiar people. But because my uncle and his wife had just gotten married, they wanted to be alone on the weekends, and I was lonelier still. In the summer, I went to Grandmother's temple.

I often went to the main building, where all the Buddhas sat, and I prayed. I felt in peace.

I returned to school in Busan under my Korean birth name, Song Young-Hee, and when the rest of my family returned, we moved into an old house that my father had bought years ago as a rental investment. The house was over a hundred years old with a long courtyard in the middle, ten rooms, and its own outdoor kitchenette. The tenants were either young couples or single women. We were not rich, but we managed to survive with the small rent my mother collected from the tenants every month.

When I was accepted into Busan Girls' Middle School, I was given my first uniform, which consisted of a black sailor top, a pleated skirt, and black leather shoes. Delighted with my uniform, I did not want to take it off. At night, I placed my skirt beneath my bedding on the hot floor so that by morning the pleats would be nicely pressed. But every morning, getting to school was like fighting in a war. Most of the boys' and the girls' schools were located at one end of the city. A small streetcar came to Cholyang station every twenty minutes. If we were at the station before seven, we didn't have a problem. But by seven thirty, the place became total chaos. When the students swelled into the street, the bigger boys pushed each other to get into the little streetcars, ignoring the people who had come earlier and stood in line. When the frustrated conductor couldn't bring the situation in order, the tram took off with several boys still hanging on the door. All of the girls and the office workers stood watching the tram leave, like in the old Korean saying—"*A dog that is looking to the rooster that was chased up to the roof by the dog.*" Then we had no choice but to start an hour-and-a-half walk.

When I came home from school, I went and stood in line to carry water home from a faucet in the middle of our village that provided our water rations after three o'clock. When our turn came, our maid carried a tall aluminum water container on her head, and I carried two buckets in my hands since I was afraid that the heavy bucket on my head would make me stop growing. Then we went back and forth until our tall earthen crockpot was filled to the top.

Although the war had ended, I continued to read the Japanese books that our parents had accumulated in the old days. Serious Japanese literature was fascinating, especially the love stories, which I couldn't put down. One particular love story so gripped me that I could not wait until the next night to read it, so I took the book to school with me. During sewing class, which I found to be a waste of time, I hid my book underneath my desk on top of my lap and read the feverish tale while my teacher, Ms. Lee, showed the class how to sew. She was one of those people who had moved back from Japan after the war. Chubby and short. She wore glasses, and her hair was short and frizzy.

"Song Young-Hee," she called in the middle of her lesson. I was totally shocked to hear my name. "Bring your book to the front."

My teacher took the book from me and told me to meet her at the office during lunch. I did not care if she punished me, but I was afraid that I would never see my book again. At the door of my teacher's office, I peered through the window and saw that Ms. Lee, with unblinking eyes, was reading my book. When I walked in, she looked up and asked, "How old are you anyway?" She should have known my age since I was in the first grade of middle school, but my teacher found it absolutely unbelievable that I, a mere thirteen-year-old, was still able to read adult Japanese literature four years after the war had ended. She said that I deserved to be punished and have the book confiscated because I was not paying attention in class, but she would not do so if I promised her that I wouldn't bring it to school again, and I thanked God for my good luck.

I loved language as much as I hated mathematics, and English was my favorite class. It didn't hurt that my English teacher was a handsome bachelor. Over the years, it was a pattern of mine to fall in love with handsome male teachers. My mother was busy with her friends and I had no one. I had always been a lonely little girl, but my father's death left me even more so and thus constantly seeking someone to love me. I read later that fatherless women often seek the approval of men who are emotionally unavailable. But I didn't know that then. I was just a girl, daydreaming that my English teacher could be my prince.

I hardly had any friends. The other girls were silly and immature to me. My mother always said that I was mentally too mature, so my hours at school were spent daydreaming; and my hours at home were spent reading books, playing the organ, and singing. At school, I felt special and happy whenever I had to skip class to rehearse for a dance or play for the annual school fair. One year, we were to dance Brahms's "*Hungarian Dance No. 5*," Saint-Saëns's "*Swan*" from *Carnival of the Animals,* and Schubert's *Unfinished Symphony.* I brought all my father's classical records to the rehearsal room. But they disappeared, and I never got them back.

Although the students were prohibited from going to the movies and punished severely if caught, I sneaked into the theater whenever they showed foreign films. I loved the French movie *Carmen* with John Gavin, the English movie *The Beast and the Beauty* with Stewart Granger, and *Gaslight* with Ingrid Bergman and Charles Boyer. Seeing foreign movies was like living in my own fantasy world. When I came home, I acted out in the mirror the parts I had seen.

After I saw Deanna Durbin whistling and riding her bicycle, I was determined to learn how to ride a bicycle. I borrowed one from one of our tenants. In Korea, there was only one huge size of bicycle for men to ride as transportation, and bravely I tried to ride it, only to keep falling off and scratching my knees. I realized that it was a losing battle and finally gave it up. I also went to see the Korean opera. One day, I sneaked backstage after the show with the thought that I might talk to someone about the possibility of my joining the act. When I stepped up to the dark stage in the back, I saw a small dressing room next to the stage. Under the dim light, a lady with heavy makeup on was changing the diaper of a crying baby. It was winter, and the place was freezing. I turned and left.

During my second year of high school, a friend of my uncle Min-Kun, who was a student, asked me if I want to act in a play produced by the Busan Boys' High School at a local theater. In the part of the main character's younger sister, I was to wear my school uniform and perform a few lines. Although I had danced ballet and folk dances in school plays every year, I had never done any acting. But the thought of actually being in a play with boys excited me, so I agreed, although I knew the other girls at my school would frown upon me for performing with boys.

I was to perform on a Saturday and Sunday afternoon. So immediately after my Saturday-morning class, I hurried to the theater and removed from my sailor collar the two small plastic stars that represented the Busan Girls' High school. I thought I could justify performing with the boys by removing the stars because without them, the uniform no longer belonged to my school. Besides, the girls in my class didn't like me anyway, for never acting like or wanting to look like them. When the second-year girls were informally supposed to change their hairdos to parts in front, I kept my bangs. I was also content existing in my own world, reading, singing, and dancing in school performances, but my classmates saw me as aloof and conceited.

Whenever the boys sponsored an event, the girls attended, and I knew that the girls from my high school would see me perform, and think that I was impertinent. However, I didn't suspect they were planning revenge. After classes the Monday after the play, they held a meeting about my performing at the boys' high school. One after another they got up and berated me. "How dare you . . . who do you think you are? You put our school uniform on and performed with boys." I cried and shouted back at them, and we spent a good hour fighting.

Other events added unpleasantness to those years. Because of the constant threat from North Korea, all the schools did military exercises. A man in a military uniform stood on a platform shouting instructions while we marched like soldiers around the school grounds. I was curious to see the drill instructor's face, so one day as I marched past the platform, I turned my head sideways to glance at him. He leapt from the platform and slapped my face, knocking me to the ground. I fainted from the shock and for several days did not return to school. The instructor came to my house and apologized to my mother.

I especially hated school when my mother couldn't afford the monthly school payments and the teachers would send me back home right after I got to school. I felt shame and humiliation. So when it was time to pay, I neither got out of bed nor ate the whole day unless my mother gave me the money first.

Then on June 25, 1950, in the early hours of morning, without warning or declaration of war, the North Korean troops crossed the thirty-eighth parallel and swept down upon the unprepared south. The Republic's troops fought bravely but proved no match for the heavily armed Communists. The South Korean government was forced to move to Busan, and thousands of citizens fled before the advancing invaders. As the Communists closed in, as Busan was flooded with people, and the horror stories they brought with them, the uncertainty of our future paralyzed our daily lives. We spent our days wondering who had been arrested and tortured, or had disappeared. One of my relatives died in jail in Seoul because he was a community leader. The Communists kidnapped Min-Sang, my aunt Soo-Ok's husband, who was a well-to-do lawyer. One morning, a man Min-Sang knew came to the house and said he would like to talk to him. He went out with only the clothes he had on, and he never came back.

With all the horror stories the refugees told about their experiences in Seoul, the people of Busan were in constant fear for their future. Busan is located at the tip of the Korean Peninsula, and we had nowhere to flee to except into the ocean. But God was with us. United States troops arrived in Korea just before North Korean forces could take Busan. The U.S. troops were subsequently joined by troops from many other nations.

It was dangerous time for all the young men. At the time, my first boyfriend, Jae-Kyung, was my uncle's closest friend and a freshman at Busan University. We thought we would get married someday, but he was drafted and was trained in the remote countryside. After three short months of training, he was made a lieutenant and immediately sent to fight on the front lines. There was no mail during the war, so we could not communicate. Much later, Jae-Kyung was wounded, and found after several months near the North Korean border when General Douglas MacArthur made a surprise landing at Inchon, pushing the Communists out of South Korea and advancing into the North. Jae-Kyung was brought back to a hospital near Busan. He had survived by carrying the body of his young assistant on his back and running down the mountain, the dead body blocking all the bullets. Later, he told me how the small rice balls sent up from the bottom of the mountain to where the soldiers were fighting were frozen hard like baseballs by the time they were delivered. Once, Jae-Kyung's unit caught a North Korean soldier. They didn't realize it was a woman until they took off her hat. Knowing that their lieutenant was a man with compassion, the soldiers lied to Jae-Kyung, saying that the commander of the other platoon wanted to see him. When Jae-Kyung came back, he found that the woman soldier had been butchered to death, and both of her breasts had been cut off.

Although I was happy to see Jae-Kyung, my feelings proved too small and immature, and our time apart did not bring us closer. The war and the hard life made me grow up fast, and I was no longer the little girl I was when we met.

The city of Busan became a city of soldiers and refugees. Some of the smart people got contracts from the American military to collect the leftover food from the mess hall to open a soup kitchen. The men, who had to work on the street, lined up every day. A bowl of soup a day was all they could afford to eat, if they could afford that much.

When we went downtown, our bodies were literally moved along by the crowds. The once-beautiful hills and mountains were now covered with *hako-bang*, tiny houses constructed of cardboard and flattened beer cans. All the big buildings were taken over and transformed into military compounds. Almost overnight, schools became army headquarters, and the streets were lined with troops.

Ever since I was a little girl, I had been curious about Americans, wondering how they looked, smelled, walked, and talked. *What were they thinking? What did they eat? How did they sleep? How do they go to the bathroom?* I wanted to know if it was true that an American had the nose of an eagle, the eyes of a monster, and a huge mean mouth with corners that stretched from ear to ear, as I had seen in Japanese comic books. I remembered when we were living in Yangsan soon after World War II had ended, an army jeep carrying two American GIs made a brief stop in our village. Children ran from house to house warning everyone, "*Ko-jengee* is coming, *Ko-jengee* is coming." Big nose is coming. My mother had heard stories of American soldiers raping Korean women and told my cousin Yul-Soon, who was seventeen, to hide behind a pile of straw in the barn until the soldiers cleared out of the village. The tall alien-looking men came to our house, entered our courtyard, and my mother went out to meet them. All of us children stood several feet away from those strange-looking creatures. One of the GIs kept bowing and saying something to my mother, but she could not understand him. She bowed in return, and they bowed back. After a few minutes of bowing back and forth, the two Americans got into their jeep and drove out of our village.

In Busan, when I was riding the streetcar to high school, I used to see an American soldier standing guard at a tiny lot surrounded by barbed wire in downtown Busan. The lot was empty except for a couple of Quonset huts. He did not look anything like a monster, but he did look strange. The soldier was so skinny and so tall that I thought he could reach the sky. He had yellow hair and pale skin. When I first saw an American close up, I noticed that his eyes were like the blue marbles Korean boys often played with.

After the North Korean invasion, Busan overflowed with American GIs. At the end of every day, I saw soldiers sitting on a cement wall, shoulder to shoulder, swinging their legs and watching people walk by. This was an unusual scene for Koreans. I stared at them, and they stared back at me, both of us observing each other as we might be seeing an exotic animal. The Americans often carried big duffel bags filled with laundry over their shoulders. In Busan, there were no laundries. Everyone washed their own clothes, as not many people could afford the kind of fancy clothes that needed to be dry-cleaned. It wasn't long before laundries began popping up around the American military bases.

One afternoon, as I was walking home from my grandmother's house and about to turn into a narrow alley that led to home, I saw a GI carrying big duffel bag on his back, whistling a tune as he walked behind me. I turned my head and looked at him; he looked at me.

"Hi, *ahn nyung hasim nicka?*" He was asking how I was doing in Korean, and that made me smile. This man looked different from the yellow-haired, marble-eyed soldiers I was used to seeing. His hair was black. His skin was dark. I noticed wide patches on the sleeves of his uniform. I did not know it then, but learned later that his patches ranked him as master sergeant. Then he caught up with me. Walking next to me, he pointed at his bag and asked, "Wash? Wash?" I knew what he needed, so I eagerly nodded although I had not asked my mother about starting a laundry business. But I knew that she needed the money because she had been knitting so many children's sweaters and jackets to sell to her rich friends that her fingers and the backs of her hands were swollen.

One night, Mother woke me up. She was lying on the mat, moaning and saying, "Hurry, and get Grandmother and tell her I have to go to the hospital." She was hospitalized for appendicitis, and while she was too ill to knit, she asked me to help finish what she was working on. I tried, but knitting day after day on the same sweater was so boring. I thought my mother and Mrs. Chang, one of our tenants, could team up and start a laundry business. Mrs. Chang was a widow and a refugee with two children. Her husband had been a policeman. Soon after they had moved into our rental property, her husband had a heart attack and died. Mother said that he came from the north, and he died because he ate too much pork, which we never did with so much fish and wild vegetables available. The sergeant followed me to my house, and my mother and Mrs. Chang decided to give the laundry business a try, but no one discussed how much would be charged for the service. The American gave us his duffel bag of dirty laundry and left. My mother, Mrs. Chang, and our maid Ok-Ja got to work, washing piles of laundry by hand and hanging them to dry on the clotheslines in our long courtyard. They ironed and folded as fast as they could because they did not know when the American would return for his belongings.

(For Americans, it sounds odd that a poor house like ours had a maid. But at that time, many farmers were poor, and girls were sent to the city to work. Then they were fed and clothed and lived together as one of the family.)

A few days later, the sergeant returned to pick up his laundry. When he asked how much, my mother, Mrs. Chang, Ok-Ja, and I looked at each other blankly. My mother told me to tell him to pay whatever he thought was reasonable for the service. Pulling out his wallet, the sergeant did not look happy with the arrangement. He murmured to himself, "You have to know what to charge first." He handed me some American military money, and just when were to walk out, he caught sight of my Yamaha organ. He stopped to ask me if I played. I nodded. "Oh good. Why don't you play at our club?" I could not have understood the significance of his question at the time, but in that moment, my future was sealed. Looking back, I know somebody up there touched me to help me find a way for survival. I am sure the sergeant felt sorry for me. He never even auditioned me. I didn't know any American songs then. Mrs. Chang, holding half of what the sergeant gave us, murmured in a low voice, "With this kind of money, it's not worth it."

So began my first paying job. The club issued me a pass, which let me come and go as I pleased, and I felt important. All Koreans wondered what it was like inside of the compound. Every Friday evening, I played the organ at the Enlisted Men's Club, and I learned and practiced American songs from the Hit Parade music books, which the club received from the USO—songs like "*Wanted*" by Perry Como, "*It's Magic*" and "*Sentimental Journey*" by Doris Day, "*Sentimental Me*" by Ames Brothers, and Patti Page's "*My Happiness.*" A GI, who was a cook at the compound, lent me his small radio. Every waking hour, I listened to the Armed Forces Korea Network, singing along, learning by heart the American tunes and words.

During the day, when there was no activity, I rehearsed at the club or listened to the jukebox. But besides singing, there was apparently one other thing I had to learn.

"Hey, Song," a GI who happened to work in the club called out to me. He was a young man with blond hair. "Use your hands. Use your arms. Move your body. Don't just stand there like a stick." He tried to show me how to move. A little embarrassed, I tried to explain to him that Korean singers never used gestures when they performed. Shaking his head, he said, "No, no, you don't understand. When you sing, you have to sing like you're talking to an audience. Like this. If the song says, 'I love you,' you put your hand out in front of you, like you're saying 'It's you I love.' If the song says, 'I,' you press your hand on your chest, feel your heartbeat, and sing, 'I.' Get it?" He was not a singer, but he was an American, and he knew.

When I went home that night, I put a full-length mirror against the wall, and I practiced the gestures: "I love you, you love me."

They also showed American musical movies so that I could imitate the way they sang.

On Saturday nights, the club had a Korean floor show. Among all the others, I noticed that one particular floor show was booked regularly. They had a star singer who was tall and very pretty, and she wore a pale blue evening gown. I had never seen such a beautiful dress in all my life. Someone told me that she was engaged to the sergeant who was in charge of the club. He ordered fancy evening dresses from something called the Sears, Roebuck catalogue, and years later, I ordered a dress almost exactly like hers from Sears, Roebuck. She sang in English, but I could tell she did not understand a word and could not speak English. The sergeant was young, sloppy, and overweight. I could clearly see that the Korean singer did not love him. One afternoon when all the performers and the sergeant stood in front of the club to have photographs taken, the sergeant sat next to his fiancée. Frowning, the woman pushed him away, worried that he would sit on her beautiful gown.

Not long afterward, the military moved out of their compound. The Korean officials moved into the building, and I lost my first job as a musician. After the American GIs left, life for me became dull, and I wanted to follow them in pursuit of new adventure. At the end of the year, our new school opened in a makeshift building up on a hill away from where I lived, but my heart was already somewhere else.

Meanwhile, my mother fell in love with a nice man who boarded at our house and worked at an insurance company. I suspect he is the only man whom she loved. He was a gentle man, and we all called him Father. No one calls grown-ups by their first names.

But not all men were so kind, and my mother was swindled by a longtime acquaintance from Mr. Yum, whom we all knew for a long time. His daughter and I went to the same school. Then they had moved to Seoul and Mr. Yum worked as a head of a news paper company. One summer, he came to Busan with several reporters and stayed with us. A week after, all the reporters went back and he stayed behind. Little did we know his real motive. I was too young to know at the time, thirteen years old, but I learned later that he sweet-talked my mother to borrow money from the bank against our house in order to loan it to him. My mother was young and naïve. I remember she went up to Seoul to collect the money, but she never saw it again. While he was staying with us, he always talked to me sweetly, held my hand, and took me places, including a photo op where they took pictures of us together. No one had ever paid so much attention, and I felt as though I had a new father. But one evening, he tried to rape me, though I didn't understand what that was, and I was saved only because my mother came home and interrupted him.

After the repossession, we moved into a big house that my grandfather had built for his married son. His daughter-in-law, who did not want to live near her in-laws, had never moved in. My grandmother, who had lived in her mountain temple for three years, had a stroke and was brought down to the new house for us to take care of her. I loved this big new house as much as I hated the old house, which was eaten away by termites and infested with the giant red bed bugs that wouldn't leave us alone at night. Soon after we moved into a new house, Mother gave birth to a beautiful son. Again I loved him very much. But soon after he was born, he had smallpox. His mouth bristled with red sores, and he couldn't drink his milk or cry. Mother put big screen around her and her son to protect them from bad omens. Nothing worked and he died. Behind the screen, I could hear mother calling his name and crying, "Johnny-yah, drink your milk."

Regardless how beautiful the house was, my family needed money. So my mother, with Mr. Chang, her boyfriend, borrowed money and tried to go into the firewood business, which neither of them knew anything about. She would buy the wood when it was freshly cut. When the weather got cold and the wood was dried, it weighed less than when it was purchased. Since the wood was sold by weight, they never profited from the sales and were lucky not to lose money. Next, she opened a laundry near Haewundae Beach, which was located about twenty miles outside the city and lined with American military compounds. While my mother and Mrs. Chang lived there, I was left at home to care for my brothers.

Meanwhile, more refugees kept coming. My grandfather wanted to cash in by renting out rooms to the overflow of refugees. He told us to move out of his house. Every day he came to the house and yelled, "Where is everyone? Goddamn it! When are they going to move?" Whenever I heard him coming through the gate, I hid in a closet. I also hid whenever the old lady from whom my mother had borrowed money came by, yelling for payment. I decided to look for a job and was soon hired as a waitress at the Enlisted Men's Club. I was glad because I would now bring in some money, not only for food, but to repay the money my mother owed to the old lady. I saved and saved. The next time the old lady showed up, I asked her how much my mother owed her. I took out all my money and gave it to her without a word. She was stunned.

At the club one night after it had closed, I was walking up the stairs when a drunken GI slapped me across the face. I began to scream, and he knocked me unconscious. I woke up in the basement at the club. The room was dark, and I realized I was lying on one of the tables. A GI was fondling me. When I stood up from the table, he just walked away. Outside, more GIs were yelling at the drunk who had slapped me. After that evening, I never went back. Soon after that, Mother came from Haewundae and started to sell everything we owned. She sold my father's record collection, his books, the furniture, and my precious Yamaha organ. When I saw the two men taking my organ away, I felt as if they were carving out my heart with a dull dagger. But I did not speak, and my throat ached from the silence. I never wanted to return to the room and see the empty corner where my organ had once stood.

With the money she collected, my mother bought a small plot of land in front of my old school, which was then occupied by the American military, and built a small dirt house. The walls were made from mud over a lattice of bamboo and straw. The attached kitchen wall was made of thin plywood that didn't fit, and we could see out from between the panels. In the winter, the kitchen might as well have been outside. The three-room house had a small space in front facing the street, where Mother had planned to open a store, but by then there was not any money left. Ok-Ja, our little maid, went to Grandfather's mill, sneaked in, gathered up the broken rice chips from the machine, brought them home, and made rice gruel. My brother Tong-Ho, who was a teenager, yelled and tried to throw the rice chips away while Ok-Ja desperately hid them from him. I spent my days with a friend, who didn't have a mother, and ate meals there. Inflation was rampant, and the value of paper money grew less each day. People had to take a stack of money just to buy a few things at the market. Because of the sky-high inflation, the government changed the paper money, but this, too, was a disaster.

Mother received a deposit from a young couple who wished to rent one of our rooms, but later they changed their minds because they thought it wasn't a nice place to live since GIs were constantly in front of our house. Later, the man told my mother how sad he was when he came to ask for his deposit back and saw little children with nothing to eat but watered-down gruel for dinner. With nowhere else to turn for help, Mother went to her brother, who set up the English Institute and taught there. He gave her some money now and then.

On one rare occasion, my granduncle Ky-Joon visited our family and told me that I could find work at the dance hall where GIs were entertained. The owner was taking English lessons at the institute. He told my granduncle, who was working as an accountant at the institute, that he needed someone to keep track of lunches eaten by dancers. "It sounds like a very easy job," Granduncle said to me.

The dance hall, which was once an old warehouse near the railroad tracks, was not far from where I lived. I went down there one Saturday afternoon. The building sat alone in the middle of nowhere. I walked over dirt, stones, and railroad tracks. When I went up the cement steps and opened the door to enter the hall, I was almost knocked over by the blast of a trumpet. With bright sunlight from outside, I could see GIs in fatigues and combat boots dancing with Korean girls with painted faces and party dresses. I had never seen girls looking like this. After I entered the hall and shut the door, I stood for a few minutes, letting my eyes adjust to the darkness. There were a couple of windows high on the walls, but they were boarded up with plywood, and only a pencil-thin line of outside light shaped them. I felt as if I had stepped into a world very different from where I had been only a minute ago. I saw an opening across from the stage that was draped with a dirty, flimsy cloth hanging halfway to the floor. I saw that only girls went through that opening. As I stood looking around, an older man walked up to me, and I yelled in his ear that I had come to see Mr. Hwang. "Ah, you are the granddaughter of Mr. Choi?" he yelled back to me and gestured for me to follow him behind the flimsy cloth. The room was dark and dirty. The floor was wet and littered with cabbage peels and other vegetable debris. A couple of Korean ladies in dark *hanboks* were cooking under a naked lightbulb, and a couple of dancers were placing orders. All this was going on while the music blasted in my ears.

My job was to sit near the opening to the hall and write down who ate what, but it was impossible to concentrate while music from the dance hall blared. My ears followed the songs; my eyes were on the high-heeled shoes of the dancers and the booths full of GIs.

When the owner told me I would be paid three thousand *won* a month, which was about $15, I asked him if I could be paid daily because my family could not afford to wait a month for the three thousand *won*. Every day, around three o'clock in the afternoon, my brother came to the dance hall and asked for one hundred won so that my mother could buy rice for that evening's supper. I was embarrassed but had no choice but go to Mr. Hwang for my money. After a couple of weeks, I was fired.

Then my mother got another idea to use the empty space in the front of our house to open a bar. We were right across the street from the base, and she thought the GIs would come by for food, drink, music, and a good time. The location couldn't have been better, and the idea was good. But where could we get the money? My mother had two long wooden benches and a small counter made to hold a hand-cranked record player. Ok-Ja played records behind the counter. My father's distant cousin, a divorced woman, also joined us, but she was not much help because she was drunk much of the time. Ok-Ja had developed a system. When a GI ordered a beer, she would make him pay first, run to the store next door, buy the beer there, run back, and serve it to the customer. In between orders, she cranked the old record player with songs like Rosemary Clooney's "*Come On-a My House*" and Dinah Shore's "*Buttons and Bows*," the only American records we had. She played them over and over again.

We weren't making any money at all, but we kept going. Then one evening, everyone in the bar was arrested and loaded onto a quarter-ton truck along with prostitutes wearing heavy makeup and revealing dresses. All of us were taken down to police headquarters, but no one explained why we had been arrested. We were herded into a big office. No one came to take our names or lock us up in prison cells. I lay on the top of a desk all night freezing. That was our first and last adventure in the bar business.

Mother was pregnant again. She tried to lose the baby by rolling off the steps or falling from the hill, she told me. But nothing worked. When the baby was born, I helped the midwife delivering the baby. His father named him. Young Chang. He was happy baby and we all loved him.

Sentimental Journey

Why flowers blossom but fade away,
Why grass were green, but becomes brown
But rock, I know you will never change.

—Yoon Sun Do (1587-1671)

Most people go to their graves
With their song still unsung.

—Oliver Wendell Holmes, adapted

I knew a young man, Mr. Chung, who'd played the trumpet in the school band and now played professionally. I often visited his house to watch him practice, and I sang along with the songs I recognized. He was impressed and asked me where I learned all those songs no one else in Korea knew at the time. He asked if I would like to come and sing in the floorshow sometime. Could I? I wanted to jump up and kiss him, but instead, I shyly answered, "Yes."

Mr. Chung took me downtown to an old Japanese-style house and led me into a large room, the floor covered with straw mats. The first thing that caught my eye was the three beds standing side by side against the left side of the wall, the headboards facing the center of the room. Pink ruffled curtains hung between each bed and the front. Since Koreans slept on the floor instead of beds, I was perplexed.

I noticed three people sitting on the *tatami* floor. An old lady wearing a *hanbok* looked up at me. On the other side of her was a plain younger woman sewing what looked like sequins and beads. She wore no makeup and did not look up to acknowledge our entrance. In the middle of the room sat an older gentleman, studying pages of sheet music in front of him. A saxophone lay beside him. No one said a word.

When Mr. Choi, the manager of the show, strutted into the room, Mr. Chung introduced me as Ms. Song who knew a lot of American songs. I bowed, and Mr. Choi asked if this was my first time singing with a band.

"Do you have a family?"

"Yes, my mother and several brothers," I answered.

From the other side of the room, the old lady said, "That might be a problem."

I didn't know what it meant and I was worried. Ignoring the old lady, Mr. Choi pointed his chin to the old man with the saxophone and said, "Why don't you tell the bandleader what you're going to sing tonight?"

I told him "*Sentimental Journey*" and "*Sioux City Sue.*"

I wondered about rehearsals, but there was no mention of them, so I just sat there quietly. As time went by, three women entered. Suddenly, room became lively from chatting and laughing talking about their outings. A woman in her thirties with a moonlike face and permed hair turned out to be the second wife of Mr. Choi; a very pretty lady of about twenty-five was his third; and a very young and ugly girl with a radiant smile was the fourth Mrs. Choi. I learned that the old woman who was sitting in the room was Mr. Choi's mother, and the other plain woman was his first wife. Like most entertainers, they were refugees from Seoul and could not speak a word of English. They were owned by Mr. Choi, who provided each with one of the pink-curtained beds, in which he made love to them. I stared at the beds, wondering, *Did he go from bed to bed every night? Did the others sleep on the floor?* He made his living from them and had a big motorcycle, which no one else in Korea could afford.

A young man came upstairs and announced, "The truck is downstairs."

We all went down. Waiting for us outside was a military two-and-a-half-ton truck with a cover. Two American GIs helped women climb in to join the others there, and Mr. Choi called my name from the front corner in the dark. "Ms. Song, come and sit next to me," he said, patting the seat beside him.

We bounced over the city potholes. When the pavement stopped
and the dirt road started, the truck shook and the dust whirled around
behind us, blocking our view. No one talked, but a woman laid her
head on the shoulder of the man sitting next to her. Soon the truck
stopped. When we started back up, I saw that we had just passed a gate.
When we arrived at our destination, I saw the most amazing sight—the
shores of Haewundae Beach. Suddenly I was struck with a childhood
memory of walking on wet sand, twisting and digging my heels in search
of clams. I was a little girl then, with no worries in the world, protected
by my father and mother. I brushed away my thought and followed the
others. They carried makeup cases, musical instruments, a couple of
big boxes of costumes, lighting equipment, and folded stands for the
band. Everyone went into the dressing room located behind the big
stage. No one talked to me. The place was packed with American GIs.
In the dressing room, the women undressed except for their bras and
panties. Sitting on metal folding chairs, they put on their makeup,
drawing dark lines on each side of their noses in order to make them
appear long and high. Some dug their costumes from the chest and
hung them behind their chairs. Having neither makeup nor a costume,
I sat in a corner and watched as the band started to play.

The girls put on their costumes, stuffing their bras with handkerchiefs,
balls of toilet paper, or whatever they could find. Mr. Choi's moonfaced
second wife had dressed in a Hawaiian costume, her bowlegs in high
heels. Mr. Choi's third wife, a singer, wore a long Chinese-style dress;
the fourth, a revealing sailor suit. Another woman, who had not been
in Mr. Choi's room, wore a transparent Parisian costume that revealed
her navel, and a veil on her head.

The music had been playing for half an hour when I heard a
sudden drumroll. I thought my heart would jump out of my chest, but
I tried not to show my fears. I had no rehearsal. I had no costume. No
makeup. But the show was starting. First number was a tap dance. When
it was my turn, I walked onto the stage into the colored lights as if I
were meeting my death. Hundreds of faces looked at me. Dressed in
my simple red-white-and-blue flared skirt with a sleeveless white blouse
and a ribbon tied around my neck, I swayed under the spotlight and
sang, "*Gonna take a sentimental journey / Gonna set my heart at ease . . .*"
I was busy trying to remember what that GI had taught me long ago,
trying to sound like Doris Day, trying to move my arms, legs, and hips
every which way, trying to use every gesture and expression I knew. I
did not know if my timing was right, if my key was right, but I managed
to finish. As I bowed, the GIs went wild, clapping, stomping, whistling,
and shouting for more.

As I sang "*Sioux City Sue*," I hopped around and pulled up my skirt to show off my knees. I danced as I had seen the dancers do in all those American musical movies that I had watched at the military compound. At the end of the number, I bowed again and returned to the dressing room, breathless. As I gulped down a glass of cola, the audience stamped and yelled for more. The band tried to ignore the audience by bringing in the half-naked woman in the Parisian outfit, but the soldiers kept on until the band stopped and everything went quiet.

The bandleader rushed into the dressing room and asked me what other songs I knew. None came to mind. Then I blurted out, "*Sentimental Me*," and the leader took me back to the stage. "*Sentimental Me*" is a beautiful ballad, but the singer must know the intricate timing. After the first line, four bars must be counted before starting the second. But I moved on without waiting, and my singing moved in one direction while the band moved in another. I could not stop. I could not leave. I finally finished the number and walked offstage, hoping the band was not too upset with me. The GIs were quiet. After the Arabian night dancer, the third wife sang "*China Night*" in Japanese and "*Danny Boy*" holding her hands in front of her stomach that is typical for every singer in Korea. Then the second wife, wearing a stupid grass skirt, danced a Hawaiian dance in her high heels. But I had been the hit of the show. Later, I found out that those GIs were so wild about me because no other singers knew any American popular songs, or had any concept of how they were supposed to be sung.

At the time, everything was a cash-only basis. While Choi and his second wife went to the office and gathered money, we all waited on the truck. About twelve thirty, the truck dropped me off in the middle of deserted Main Street. I heard Mr. Choi say to me, "Don't forget to come early tomorrow, so you can rehearse."

The curfew was at ten, and not even a mouse was on the street. My house was up a steep hill, and fearing a ghost might grab me, I ran as fast I could. Breathless when I arrived, all of my family was sound asleep.

Early the next afternoon, I went to Mr. Choi and crawled after him into a small three-by-five storage space underneath the stairs. Bedding was spread on the floor, and someone must have slept there. A naked lightbulb dangled from the ceiling between our faces.

"Do you like performing?" Mr. Choi asked.

"Yes," I answered, looking down at my knees.

"I think you have potential. I think I can help you become a famous star."

Without lifting my head, I listened.

"Someday I'll send you to Japan, other countries, all over the world. I'll make you a famous singer," he said and paused. "Tell me something. If I asked you which is more important, fame or virginity, how would you answer?"

I lifted my head, looked him straight in the eyes, and answered, "Virginity, of course," wondering what that had to do with my singing.

"I knew you'd say that," said Mr. Choi. "Look, if you're going to be a famous singer, you need to work very hard. You need to be here all the time so you can practice with the band. And once you're famous, you'll have your family again. In the meantime, why don't you move here? You don't have to tell your mother where you're going. You don't need to bring anything with you. I'll give you everything you need."

Although I did not understand exactly what he was telling me, I agreed.

That night, I returned to the stage, still unrehearsed and unpaid. No one talked to me about money, and I did not ask. In Korea, children and young people did not ask about money because it was considered rude, so I assumed Mr. Choi would take care of me. The next day, I told my mother I was leaving home, going away on my own, and would not return for a long while. Pulling my arm, she begged me to tell her where I was going and what I would be doing. As I made my way out the door, I said I could not say. In the middle of the street, we held each other, crying, while the neighbors watched. Although many times I had considered running away from home to become an actress, when the opportunity presented itself, I could not go. I held my mother in my arms, felt her weeping on my shoulder. I wept with her and came back in.

A few months later, the moonfaced woman came looking for me, but my mother told her not to set foot in our house. A couple of girls who worked for Mr. Choi slept in the small room under the stairs and told me that in the middle of the night he tried to seduce them. Years after that, I heard a rumor that after all of his wives left him, Mr. Choi became a heroin addict and died penniless all alone under a bridge.

Eels

Bamboo and Pine

Peach and plum of spring time
Do not flaunt your pretty blossoms;
Consider rather the old pine
And green bamboo at year's end.
`What can change these noble stems
And their flourishing evergreen?

—Kim Yoo Ki (late seventeenth century)

What doesn't kill me,
Makes me stronger

—Albert Camus (1913-60)

After the surprise landing at Inchon, the Allied troops advanced back into the north, with some units even reaching the Yalu River. It seemed like unification between North and South Korea would be realized, but in October 1950, the Chinese Communist forces intervened, suddenly attacking the Allied forces in massive numbers. The United Nations forces were forced to retreat, and Seoul once again fell into the enemy's hands on January 4, 1951.

When my first boyfriend, Jae-Kyung, was hospitalized after being found in the mountains, he told me that it seemed as if the Chinese troops were pouring over the land like millions of ants. He was a commanding officer of an infantry unit, and all his men were killed during an attack. Separated from the main force, he had to dig a hole in the deep snow for shelter and lived on acorns and wild vegetables for three months. He was found and taken to a medical station soon after the United Nations forces regrouped, counterattacked, and recaptured Seoul on March 12, 1951. A stalemate was reached roughly in the area along the thirty-eighth parallel, where the conflict had begun.

Meanwhile, I was restless. My singing career with Mr. Choi was brief, but I could not put to rest my desire to perform. Now that I had tasted my destiny, the taste of ecstasy, there was no way I could give up. I kept talking to people, trying to find out how to find those entertainers.

I learned that there was a USO office downtown, which booked shows to entertain American GIs. I decided to go down there even though I did not know what I would do once I got there. With curlers in my hair and a scarf covering my head, I stood outside against a building, feeling lost and waiting—for what, I didn't know. I waited for almost forty minutes, hoping something would happen to me. Trucks from different military camps lined up in front of the building, picking up their assigned groups. Then a two-and a-half-ton truck without a top stopped with its engine still running. A man jumped off, came to me, and asked, "What do you do?"

"I sing."

"Good. Come on, we need a singer." Merely following him onto that truck was how I resumed my career in show business. I went to work for a dancer named Kay, who was a refugee from Seoul, living in a tiny room in Busan with her five-year-old daughter. For the finale of her act, Kay and her daughter did a Hawaiian number together. I would see the poor little girl asleep on a makeup table or a chair wearing a *lei* and grass skirt, waiting to go on stage with her mother.

I walked an hour every evening to Kay's place because she did not live on the main bus route, and besides I wanted to save the bus fare for other expenses. I could tell that Kay must have been pretty once. She was around forty years old, slender, and tall for a Korean woman, and seemed to be either constantly drunk or a little crazy. Whenever I arrived at her place, GIs were always there. One Sunday afternoon, a few days after I started to work for Kay, the girls were busy putting on their makeup and costumes when Kay stumbled into the dressing room, out of control. I was worried and wondered if I could do something for her. I looked at the others, but they pretended not to notice Kay's entrance. Kay mumbled something and went behind some long drapes. Her daughter held the drapes and stood guard nearby, not letting anyone see what her mother was doing. After about fifteen minutes, Kay stepped away from the drapes a different woman, took a seat next to me, took off her clothes except for her bra and panties, and began applying her makeup as if nothing had happened. As she smeared cake foundation on her hands, I noticed purplish spots on the backs of them and all along her arms. I became so distracted that I accidentally knocked over a glass of cola, which spilled onto Kay's cosmetics. Jumping to her feet, she exclaimed, "Oh my god, what is this girl doing to me?" She looked into a compact, and the expression on her face terrified me.

"I'm so sorry. I'm sorry. I'll replace everything," I said, offering to pay for whatever was ruined.

"Come on," she said angrily. "You're going to pay for this? You can't pay for this."

Later, I discovered that Kay was a heroin addict, and I had ruined her remaining stash.

There was also talk among the entertainers that there was a girl who danced while she sang, which was unheard of. My Western material and style got me noticed. One evening, a spotlight man named Mr. Lee came to talk to me in the dressing room after the show.

"Miss Song, do you know how to type?" he asked.

Wondering what typing had to do with singing, I told him that I had taken a typing class a long time ago but I was not confident I could type anything. "I work at a military compound during the day," he explained. "And my optical shop is looking for a typist. Nothing complicated. All you'll have to do is type names and ranks onto small cards."

I thought this job was the chance I needed. I didn't have the right dresses to sing in and often wished I could have some access to the American military post so that I could get a dress like that singer, who wore the beautiful blue gown from Sears, Roebuck. I'd bought an old black cocktail dress from the Salvation Army. It was short dress. I somehow made it long and slit the skirt all the way up one leg like the one Rita Hayworth had worn in *Gilda*. But I needed more and better costumes.

The optical shop at the 142nd Medical Depot was located near a few low-slung Quonset huts surrounded by barbed wire. I found the Quonset hut that said optical shop. When I went in, I saw several GIs wearing T-shirts busily working on the other side of the counter. A couple were sitting on one side, adjusting glasses under goose-necked lamps. A small radio was playing a country song. Across the room, two tall GIs stood sharpening lenses on the big wheels. A sergeant, wearing horn-rimmed glasses, greeted me; he reminded me of Harold Lloyd, an old comedian from silent movies.

"I'm Sergeant Cooper. I'm in charge of the shop," he said, shaking hands. He took out a three-by-five-inch index card from a file box and handed it to me. "See if you can type this."

I slid a blank card into the typewriter and looked at the one the sergeant had given me. There was a name, a rank, and one other piece of information about the soldier who had ordered eyeglasses. I placed both my hands on the appropriate keys just as I had learned, typed the first letter, looked back at the card, typed the second letter, looked back at the card. I felt my face burning. I thought time had stopped. When I finally finished, I handed the card to the sergeant, who perhaps felt sorry for me, and told me I could start work the next day. As I was leaving, I thought, *Well, at least I used all my fingers.*

Now I was a typist by day and a singer by night. As soon as the truck dropped me off after the show, I ran home and went to sleep for four or five hours without even washing off my makeup. At seven in the morning, I walked the mile to the main street and waited for the two-and-a half-ton truck. After my day at the optical shop, I hurried home, ate a quick dinner, walked for an hour to Kay's place, and was picked up for evening performing. I was never heavy, but I began losing weight fast.

Finally, I found a GI who would order some things from Sears, Roebuck. First, I ordered a pair of shoes. Since I didn't know what size my feet were, I put down size five, the smallest size. I sent it by parcel post, which took roughly a month. I counted every day. When the shoes finally arrived, they were too small. At night, I put the shoes above my head on the floor and, was hoped they would somehow get bigger in the middle of the night.

After several months of working for Kay, I found out that the other performers were being paid three thousand *won,* while I was getting only a thousand. When I confronted her, she told me it was because I was a beginner. But beginner or not, I was the only singer in her show and the most popular. Believing that she was pocketing part of my share to support her addiction, I left Kay and joined another group.

Mr. Park's entertainers were all young and inexperienced, but after watching my performance, he handed me four thousand *won.* He knew my worth. If not for the money I earned from typing and singing, my mother, my brothers, and I would have gone completely hungry, but what had begun as a love for singing had now become my family's principal means of survival.

Sometimes during the winter, I had to perform on an outdoor stage wearing only a skimpy gown. My tonsils flared up constantly. I came down with a high fever and was unable to eat or drink for several days. When I stayed in bed with fever, Mr. Park came to my house in a taxi and insisted I go to work. So I got out of my bed and left with him. Then my tonsillitis became so bad that I couldn't swallow even a drop of water. My mother took me to a doctor. I passed out in the examining room and later had my tonsils out.

When I recovered, I tried out with another group run by Ms. Cha. She was a dancer with short hair who looked and acted more like a man. Ms. Cha often yelled at and even slapped a tall singer named Ms. Kang, but no one spoke about it. On the truck, Ms. Cha always wanted me to sit next to her, and in the dressing room, she studied my body, sometimes touching my legs and commenting on my silky skin. I still didn't understand that she was attracted to me. But one day she came to my house when I was alone. It was winter, and I had my legs under the comforter, which was spread on the warm *ondol* floor. She put her legs under the comforter also. "It's nice and warm down here. Why don't you lie here?" she said, lifting up the comforter. In Korean rooms, we often put pillows on the floor, lie on them, and talk. So I didn't think anything of it and lay next to her. Then she started playing with my breasts and breathing hard. "I'll give you a good massage. Don't you like it?" Then her hand slid inside my underwear and went down to my stomach. I didn't know what to do. She was much older and was my boss. I was reminded of the time when I was in Yangsan, and Yul-Soon played with me. Now I was no longer a child, but I still didn't know how to stop her. Just then, my mother came home and called my name. Ms. Cha sat up, smoothed her hair, and left.

I kept out of Ms. Cha's way as much as possible in order to keep working and support my family during such difficult times. Surviving was the only goal. When Jinna was six years old, my grandfather told my mother to send the boy to his father in Yangsan. He kept telling Mother that we didn't need another mouth to feed. Also, Mr. Chang openly showed his dislike of the boy. Reluctantly, my mother sent Jinna to Yangsan. But every season brought her another set of worries. In summer, she said, "I know Jinna's sleeping with the farmhands. I just know it. They'll make him go out at dawn to feed the cow in the meadow, and he'll get bitten by a snake. He should have boots." When winter came, she said, "Jinna needs underwear. He needs warm clothes. He needs a notebook and a pencil, I am sure." Then she would say, "With all the children in that house, he probably can't keep any of his own."

Whenever she uttered these words, I tried to buy the things Jinna needed and get them to him. When Jinna was seven years old, I asked an American GI who had a jeep to take us to Yangsan. I was sitting at a small dining table when Jinna came into the room. Since we hadn't seen each other for so long, Jinna didn't know how to act except to sit in the corner of the room, his back toward me, and sob. It reminded me of when I had rocked him in my arms many nights ago when our mother had left for Busan and he had cried for milk. As I listened to him weeping, I wondered what sorrows and miseries his seven-year-old heart must have known to bring on such unending tears. I wanted to tell him we had come to take him home, but instead I told him about the things I brought for him. He knew that the gifts meant we would leave him behind again. When he pushed the things away, my heart broke, and I did not know what to do. As the jeep drove us away, Jinna stood by the wooden gate, sobbing and wiping his tears with his shirtsleeves. Years later, when he became sixteen years old, he got on the bus and came to Busan and never went back. I sent him to driving school, and later he became a personal driver for the president of an export/import company.

That day in Yangsan, when we drove down the street, we saw a lone woman walking toward us on the dirt road. As we drew close, I saw it was my grandmother. She was shivering in her thin white *hanbok*, and when she saw it was us, she started to cry. I didn't even have any money to give to her. I just told her, "Grandma, don't cry in front of this foreigner." To this day, I cannot forget that scene, and my heart never stops aching.

Once again, we had to leave the old dirt house. My mother never told us why, but my brother Tong-Ho, sixteen, and Tong-Kun, fourteen, moved into my granduncle's house. I moved into an upstairs *tatami* room at my grandfather's house, and Mother moved into a rental place downtown with Mr. Chang and Young Chang. After she found out that Mr. Chang had a young mistress, she thought she might able to mend the relationship without all the grown-up children around. But at the end, nothing worked.

Some nights in the winter, I came home from work and found my mother trying to warm my bedding. My grandfather's house, like all Korean houses, had no central heating except for the *ondol* floor downstairs. My room, being upstairs, got very cold, and my mother tried to be a human heating pad. I was heartbroken, knowing that all my brothers were living where they didn't belong. I was determined that we should have a place of our own so we could live all together once again as a family. I saved every penny I made and spent nothing on myself. In

Korea, there is no such thing as a mortgage. To buy a house, one has to pay the full amount in cash. Because of the inflation rate in the country, paper money was worthless; so whenever I saved enough, I purchased 24-karat gold bracelets, rings, broaches, necklaces—anything that I could get my hands on that would not depreciate. I always believed one of my favorite Korean proverbs: "*Litter can make mountains.*"

However, knowing that my mother was awful at saving money, I kept this from her and gave her only what she needed. She complained endlessly about how heartless I was, but her complaints to me were like the old Korean saying, "*chanting in a cow's ears.*" When I had saved enough, I brought out all of my gold and cash that I had hidden under my dresser and said, "Look, we can live as a family again." Stunned, my mother did not say a word.

Near the busy marketplace, we bought a small house with three rooms that my grandfather used to live in. My mother moved back from Mr. Chang's, and my brothers from my granduncle's. On that first night after we moved in, I came home late from work to see them all sleeping next to each other. Mother sat up with tears in her eyes and said, "Young-Hee ya, I cannot sleep tonight." Wiping her tears, she continued, "You, my most precious daughter, as little as a bird, sold your throat every night to support your family. I am ashamed. What kind of a mother am I?" she asked and quietly sobbed. "If your father were still alive, he would have sent you to the best school. You would have become a famous pianist. You would have married a good man. What kind of a life have I made for you?"

That night, my mother and I cried together, and it was good.

Meanwhile, the Russians called for truce negotiations, which finally began at Kaesong in July of 1951 and were transferred to Panmunjom in November of the same year. Suspended once, the talks dragged on for over a year before agreement was finally reached on July 27, 1953. Against the will of the Republic of Korea, it was agreed that each side should pull its forces back behind a demilitarized zone that was to follow the battle line at the time the armistice went into effect. Prisoners were exchanged, and a neutral supervision committee was set up to ensure that both sides abided by the agreement. The three years of struggle had resulted in nothing but loss of life and property for both sides, and unification had been rendered virtually impossible.

Taken and retaken four times, Seoul lay in ruins, as did most of the other cities of the south. More than half of all the industrial facilities were inoperable, countless roads and bridges were destroyed, and whole villages had been wiped out in many areas. But the gravest damage was to the Korean dream of unification that became only a minor issue in the Cold War.

The entertainment business slowly but surely moved back to Seoul along with the American military forces, including the 142nd Medical Department. I went to work at the 55th Quartermaster where I was picked as the woman with the most beautiful legs in the compound. My cousin Sue and I went to the main military post almost every night to catch up with the latest movies, and I was in heaven seeing *The Benny Goodman Story*, *The Glenn Miller Story*, *Annie Get Your Gun*, and *Love Me Tender*. Then we would go to the Enlisted Men's Club to eat spaghetti, which was the only dish we knew and liked. We danced the jitterbug to *"In the Mood,"* or slow-danced to *"I'm in the Mood for Love."* Now and then, I sang with a small group or with an American dance band that played mostly at officers' clubs until 1956. Singing for the dance band, without the spotlight and the screaming GIs, was boring.

However, as I was easing into my new life, I found myself coughing constantly. I saw a doctor while I was visiting my cousin in Seoul during summer vacation.

"You have a hole in your lung," the doctor told me, looking at my X-ray. I had tuberculosis. Remembering that my father had died at thirty-three from tuberculosis, I thought that I too was going to die young. On the train ride home, I saw the tall trees, the clear shadow creeks, and the rice paddies, and wondered if I wouldn't be in this world long.

I could not work at the base any longer because everyone had to pass a medical examination. In desperation, my mother tried to cure me with various soups: a revolting chicken and garlic soup made from a bird freshly killed at my house; a soup made of live eels, which she bought from the eel lady, who went from door to door with a baby on her back selling them from a large basin she carried upon her head: and finally, dog soup.

Although the idea of eating dog gave me nightmares, I was willing to try anything to get well. The thick black soup had the consistency of Jell-O and was eaten cold. Holding my nose, I quickly gulped it down while my mother, standing next to me, held a section of orange ready to put it in my mouth to wash away the aftertaste.

But after six months of drinking my mother's *koumkuck* (concoctions) and getting nightly shots on my *kungdungi* (buttocks), I was cured.

The casualties and damage inflicted by the war were heavy. The United Nations lost 150,000 lives, and suffered 250,000 wounded. In addition, 100,000 people were captured and taken to the north. Another

200,000 were missing, and millions were homeless. There were many thousands of war widows, more than 100,000 orphans, and thousands of unemployed, their numbers swelled by farmers leaving their land to seek work in the cities. Exact statistics are not available, but even by 1961 it was estimated that there were still about 279,000 unemployed, of whom 72,000 were university graduates and 51,000 were discharged soldiers and laid-off workers. Here was a powder keg of anger and resentment that waited only for a spark to set it off.

Seoul—Revolution

When a tree is dying, No one comes to sit under it.
When it was big and strong,
Everyone wanted part of it.
Now leaves are gone and the branches are broken.
Not even birds come and sit on it.

—Jung Chul (1536-1593)

When wealth is lost, nothing is lost, when health is lost,
Something is lost, when character is lost,
All is lost.

—German proverb

The war was over, but the aftermath brought South Korea much suffering. While the country was in turmoil, President Rhee nervously clung to power, refusing to let democracy take its course. A small group with political connections controlled the country's capital. President Rhee attempted to change the Constitution in order to preserve his power, but democracy in Korea seemed to be rapidly disappearing. The breaking point was reached with the elections of 1960. Realizing its unpopularity, the liberal regime used every means at its disposal, legal and illegal, to rig the elections in its favor. Demonstrations broke out almost at once, especially among students. The first occurred at Taegue on February 28, 1960, protesting political interference with schools. The most serious demonstrations were in Seoul. On March 15, election day, the students demonstrated against the elections, and this time the police fired into the crowd. In early April, the body of a student who had been killed by the police was found on the seashore at Masan. A riot followed.

Meanwhile, my family was safe, and I was working as a typist. In the summer of 1959, my brother Tong-Kun announced that he wanted to go to Seoul National University, which was the most prestigious school in Korea. Every year, thousands of students flocked to Seoul hoping for entrance, and there were stories of suicide among students who had been rejected.

After hearing of Tong-Kun's wishes, my mother came to me, expressing her concerns. "I don't know what to do. I told him he should try for Busan University instead, but he says he would rather not go at all if he couldn't go to Seoul. Why don't you talk to him? We can't afford to send him to Seoul. Where will we get that kind of money?"

My family, struggling to make ends meet, had not paid much attention to Tong-Kun's needs, emotionally or otherwise, but my brother was exceptionally intelligent, and his friends used to tell him he had a German-engineered brain. He was the quiet one, and I don't ever remember hearing his voice from that time. Popular among his friends, he kept deep inside the emotional pain and shame at seeing his sister in the company of GIs, which automatically labeled me a *Yang-kalbo*, Yankee prostitute, and so he built a wall around himself.

To Americans, unaccustomed to the Asian culture, it might seem strange for young women to support their families while able-bodied men sat around on their buttocks. But in Korea, not only were jobs scarce, but students, especially boys, were expected to focus only on their studies. Even now, young women have an easier time earning money in Korea than do men. The jobs available to women are mostly at bars and places where men are entertained. I was fortunate, though, because of my singing ability. Otherwise, I might have had no choice but to work at one of those places. I had my own hopes and dreams of going to school, studying music or dance, and becoming a pianist or ballerina, but I knew those were only my dreams. Though my income was hardly enough for our survival, I did as my mother had asked and spoke with Tong-Kun. "Do you really want to try for Seoul National University?"

"Yes, *Noonah*, I want to go to law school. I want to become a lawyer," he said with determination.

At the age of eighteen, with the train fare and money I had given him, my brother left for Seoul, on his own. If Tong-Kun passed the

entrance exams, I did not know how I would support him. As I waved
farewell, I reassured myself that the chances of his success were
remote. Since he had always excelled at school, Tong-Kun had been
overconfident and didn't study. After he learned he hadn't passed, he
came home dead drunk. I heard him throwing up in our backyard.
After that, he locked himself up in his tiny little room with only his
low desk, and he studied night and day. For a whole year, we hardly
saw his face. He didn't eat with us. He stopped seeing all of his friends.
The following year, he went up to Seoul to try again and this time was
accepted. He was beaming with pride, but there was no celebration.
Who would pay his tuition, plus room and board? I had no choice but
to find a way to help him. In April 1959, I went to Seoul in search of a
job and stayed with a violinist, Lee, who was a bandleader at one of the
many dance halls in the city.

I'd sung with his band when he'd played in Busan and once tried to
separate him and his wife during a fight. His wife had been crying, "Here
I am in this crummy place, away from my family and my comfortable
house . . ." and then she lunged at him and tore his shirt. The musicians
told me that Mr. Lee couldn't handle his strong-willed wife, and one
of his friends advised him to beat her half to death so she would know
who the boss was. "The 'training' has to be early in your marriage,"
his friend told him. So Mr. Lee did as he was told, and after she got
up from where he'd knocked her, she ran into the kitchen, grabbed a
knife, and came after him. "After that," the musician continued, "she
had him by the balls."

Another time Mrs. Lee and a friend kidnapped a woman who
supposedly had an affair with him. They took her to a small motel,
stripped her down, and pulled out all of her pubic hair. She wanted to
make sure the word spread and no one would dare touch her husband.
It strikes me as funny to think of the foreign men who believe Asian
women are docile. In Korea, we have the saying, "The fist is closer than
the law."

In Seoul, the musicians from Busan were now either entertaining
for the Eighth Army military bases or working at dance halls, which
were lavishly decorated. Mr. Kang, who used to play bass in our show in
Busan, was now working in one of these halls called Moo-Hwak-Sung,
which was located near Mr. Lee's house. I paid him a visit, and he asked
me to sing.

In Korea, dance halls are not only popular but they are all lavishly
designed with huge shining floors. I was a bit early. Many waiters with
penguin suits were standing here and there. I took a seat near the stage
and watched people dance on the glistening floor. My whole being

seemed to be melting away while I listened to the beautiful music—cha-cha, tango, and waltz—and I could hardly stop myself from dancing. Although I sang all the American popular songs, I couldn't remember when I'd last heard this beautiful music that I used to listen to long ago. When the band took a break, I went over to them and sat next to Mr. Kang. A waiter brought soft drinks for everyone.

"So what brings you here after all these years?" Mr. Kang asked.

"Oh, I don't know," I said with a shrug. "I came up to see if I could find a job."

"I'm sure you can," he said. "There are two big entertainment companies in Seoul now. But it's not like the old days. Almost all the dancers and singers are working for one company or the other. One's called Hwa-Yang, and the other is Universal. You should go and talk to them. You'll run into almost everyone you knew from the old days."

The big companies hired the performers, and the Eighth Army booked all the floorshows. Every three months, they had auditions and graded each show A, B, or C. The good shows never had a night off.

"So what are you going to sing tonight?" Mr. Kang asked.

"How about '*Tweedy Dee*'?" I asked. "*Tweedy Dee*" was a cute, jitterbug number I used to sing for GIs. It never failed to drive the American GIs wild.

"What else?"

"How about '*Seventeen*'?" another bouncy number, I suggested. As they played my song, I rushed up onto the stage and started to sing. "*Tweedy, tweedy, tweedy dee, I am as happy as can be, jiminy cricket, jiminy jack, I'm gonna be your honey tonight, tweedy, tweedy, tweedy dee.*" I hadn't sung like that for several years and felt as though I was a bird, flying to the endless blue sky. People dancing gathered around the stage to watch me. I was in heaven. When I stopped and bowed, everyone clapped wildly and would not go away from the stage. I sang a second number just as cute and wild as the first one.

When the band took another break, Mr. Kang said that the manager wanted to hire me starting the following month. When the club closed at ten thirty, everyone rushed out into the street and tried to catch a taxi to get home before the eleven o'clock curfew. Mr. Kang asked me where I was staying, and I told him I was staying with Mr. Lee and his wife.

"Why don't you come home with me tonight, and we can talk?"

I knew he was married, although I had never met his wife. But since I was planning to leave the next morning, I thought it might not be a bad idea to catch up on all the things I'd missed since they moved up to Seoul. We left the taxi at the main street and I followed Mr. Kang to the back alley. I noticed he was entering an inn. I am a different person now, but in those days, I never asked questions or sought details or suspected anything out of the ordinary. As it was almost midnight, I thought his wife must be sleeping and we would not be able to talk at his home, and so he'd brought me here.

In an upstairs room, he took off his clothes and crawled into the bed on the floor. The room was dark, with only a hazy light seeping through the window. I stood in the middle of the room and watched him.

"Why don't you come to bed?" he asked. It was after the curfew, and I had no idea where I was, and I was too embarrassed to do or say anything. I stayed dressed but lay next to him. All night long he tried to take my clothes off as I kept pushing him away. We wrestled like that for most of the night until he gave up and was quiet for a couple of hours. When dawn came, he got dressed and walked out. That was the last time I saw him.

Nothing like that had happened to me, and I just didn't know what I was supposed to do, especially with a person I knew for so long. Once I worked at an American-run club near the Busan pier. All the customers were seamen. One particular night, a Filipino man wouldn't leave me alone, and kept asking me to dance. A man named Tony told the man to leave me alone. The Filipino took the microphone from the stage and broke open Tony's head. As Tony, the manager and others tried to catch the Filipino, he ran around and around the club as if he were a mouse. Chairs were flying, and the club was in total chaos. The place had to close, and the manager of the club, an American, offered to drop me at my house. Instead, he took me to a dark place surrounded with bushes that was nowhere near my house and attacked me. I didn't know his action was rape since people didn't talk about those things in Korea. Besides, he wasn't a stranger. With all my might, I fought him. He finally gave up and took me home. I wonder if he would have killed me had it happened in America.

There was another occasion: A well-known Korean businessman called me one day. At the time, I was trying to establish my own company. He was handsome, vigorous, and sang classic songs beautifully. I liked him, and it is always good to have important contacts to do business. He said that he was on the way back from London and stopped in Washington to take care of some business. I was delighted and met him at a Chinese restaurant near the Arlington Marriott Hotel. After lunch, he said he had to go up to his room to make a phone call, and I should come up. As soon as we walked into his room, he threw me on the bed and was all over me. I was shocked, but I acted as if he was playing around and pushed him laughingly. The more I pushed him, the stronger he got. We struggled that way for a while. When I realized that he meant business, I yelled at him, saying, "If you don't get off, I am going to yell rape." He quickly got off me and sat down on a chair. As he looked at me with odd expression, he said, "Aren't you a frigid?" In Korea, those things are so common that most of women reluctantly give in, and men expect that. When a person is a friend, or someone you know well, women are usually embarrassed. Much later, when I saw him in Korea, I told him that he should learn something about how to persuade women.

A few days before I was to start working at Moo-Hwak-Sung nightclub, Mother and I came up to Seoul and found a small boarding house across the street from the dance hall. The house was not only filthy, but also inhabited by two small children who never gave me a moment of peace. But since it was only a temporary arrangement, I had no choice, though I was miserable the whole time I was there.

On the last night of my month-long singing job, Mother arrived again from Busan. She and the lady who owned the boarding house came to see my final performance. I gave one of my best performances that night, singing Paul Anka's hit song *"You Are My Destiny,"* stepping offstage to the audience at their tables. When I finished, the people went wild.

The next day, as I was eating breakfast in my room, the lady of the house came in and sat in front of me, staring at me as if I was a strange creature from outer space. I kept eating, never saying a word. She kept saying over and over, "I can't believe that was you last night. I can't believe you are the same person." Since she'd never heard me utter a word, she couldn't believe I could do what I did. Because of my insecurity and shyness in those days, I hardly talked to anyone, and I seldom smiled—Koreans never smile or start conversations with strangers. If we do, they think it's odd. Before I came to this country, I never struck up a conversation or smiled at anyone. The people who didn't know me well thought I was conceited, which was far from the truth. Because my persona on the stage was so purposefully alluring and sexy, people often misjudged who I really was in that area also.

In April 1960, during my walk home from the bathhouse, I came upon lines of people standing along the sidewalks, peering up and down the street. The street was deserted. No taxis, no buses, no noise. I asked a woman what was going on.

"There's a big student demonstration in town. The police shot some students near the Blue House." The equivalent of the White House.

"What students? From which school?" I asked in a panic. "Is it Seoul National?"

"Seoul National, along with students from other universities."
Where was my brother? How could I get to him?

Suddenly, an old truck rattled down the street, its bed filled with young students. One was holding up a bloodstained T-shirt as if it were a flag and shouting, "Citizens of Seoul! Citizens of Seoul!" Although his voice was strong, he sounded as if he was about to weep. "Citizens of Seoul! Look at what your government is doing to your children!"

With my hand covering my mouth, I began to sob.

Koreans now call this day the 4-19 Revolt, which changed Korean history. The citizens of Seoul revolted against the corruption of their government, the power-hungry president's lies, and the rigged election. That April, a police shooting of a student at Masan City angered everyone in Korea, and the students decided that they'd had it with the Rhee regime.

That evening and through the next morning, I looked everywhere for my brother. When I finally found him, I was overwhelmed with relief and joy. He had participated in the march and riot afterward, but miraculously he had not been hurt.

Despite his work to liberate Korea, President Rhee (or people who surrounded him) had become corrupt because of desire for power. He had failed to meet the needs and expectations of his people. In the middle of the night, Rhee and his Australian-born wife flew to Hawaii. The bloody bodies of Vice President Yi Ki-bung and his family were found in the basement of their luxurious home, where they had committed suicide. The students had led the first successful democratic revolution in Korea's history.

A new government was set up, but it was not strong enough constitutionally, nor were its leaders strong enough personally, to fill the gap created by the sudden ouster of the twelve-year-autocratic rule of President Syngman Rhee. The unhappy students again demonstrated and paraded in the streets. To make matters worse, the North Korean Communists, having recovered from their disastrous adventure of 1950-1953, seized the opportunity of internal disorder in the south to subvert whatever efforts the new administration could put forth. Elements with doubtful allegiance began urging for "peaceful unification," a familiar line of propaganda emanating from Radio Pyongyang daily at that time.

Before daybreak on May 16, 1961, the sound of sporadic rifle fire announced an uprising of military men. Battalions of soldiers, marines, and paratroopers marched into Seoul, occupying the capital city in a lightning coup led by Maj. Gen. Park Chung Hee. In the October of

1963 presidential election, Park Chung Hee, who had resigned from the army, ran for office, and was elected president. For Korea, that was a turning point. Under President Park's leadership, the human and natural resources of the nation were effectively organized for the first time in modern history. In June 1965, disregarding national anger toward his intention of normalizing relations with Japan, President Park put an end to the suspension of formal bilateral relations, which had been caused largely by the antagonism stemming from Japan's occupation of Korea from 1910 to 1945. Partly because of this action on his part, Korea's economy grew rapidly.

As for me, I started to work for Mr. Yang. He was funny, and I loved the way he choreographed. We were booked every night, with two shows on the weekends. Two years after I came to Seoul, I was invited to sing in Japan for two months.

Walker Hill

Do not do unto others, for your pleasure
Do not follow others, if it's not the truth
Live with dignity, and live with pure heart.

—Byun Ke Rang (1369-1430)

Keep the gold and keep the silver
But give us wisdom
          —Arabian proverb

Once in a blue moon, a few of the singers who had been famous in the old days were invited to Japan to entertain the many Koreans who had settled there after World War II and were homesick. My two-month tour in Japan was the first time in entertainment history that a singer who sang American pop songs was invited to sing in Japan.

When I returned from Japan, the promoters arranged a big welcome-home performance for me at Shi-Min-Kwon, one of the biggest theaters in Seoul. In front of the theater was a gigantic billboard that read, "WELCOME HOME SONG YOUNG-HEE FROM JAPAN TOUR." The American pop songs were very popular among young students, and when I sang, twisted, and danced to the tune, they went wild. Some of them jumped up on the stage to dance with me. But the military who worked at the theater took them away. After that performance at Shi-Min-Kwon Theater, I was invited to perform at every theater in Seoul, followed by many TV appearances and photo ops with magazines. But

I was unhappy. Every promoter wanted to book me, but I soon found out that they were all fly-by-night swindlers. For a five-day engagement with four performances a day, the promoter would bring me partial payment, promising me the rest as soon as the curtain went up and the tickets were sold. But I would never see the rest of the money, or the promoter. I was so new to the entertainment business that at first I worked for five whole days thinking I'd eventually be paid.

After I had been fooled time after time, I stopped performing when the promoter didn't pay me in full up front. But they didn't care after a couple of days of having the stars. On the other hand, I felt guilty, thinking I was disappointing the people who came to see me, though four performances a day took a toll on my health and my voice.

Once, after I'd finished my two-week engagement at the Grand Hotel, Mr. Lee, the general manager who'd hired me, would not pay me. I didn't know what to do, so I told my mother about it. Mother and I went to the hotel, and I sat next to my mother while she argued back and forth with the man, who was sitting in the corner of the hotel hallway. When she realized she wasn't getting anywhere, she grabbed the man's necktie and screamed, "You son of a bitch, you are worse than an animal, sucking the blood out of this little girl who is selling her throat to survive."

The next thing I knew, my mother was on the floor hanging on to his tie, and Mr. Lee was on top of her. Mr. Lee was panting hard and trying to loosen my mother's grip. I screamed for help, and people came and separated them. His face red as a beet, Mr. Lee straightened his tie, smoothed his hair, and hurried down the corridor. Mother screamed after him, "What kind of hotel is this to have a thief like you as general manager?"

We were so naïve that it never occurred to us to seek out someone higher in the hotel management. But I was getting disillusioned about the whole industry. My singing was my family's sole source of income, and I liked being paid more than the regular salary of bankers or officer workers for something I loved to do. But I hated the people that I had to deal with, and I hated not knowing whom I could trust. I had no one who cared for me or guided me. I didn't have any friends. I had to fight all the obstacles alone. In those days, I didn't know how to fight for my rights. Although I had been working and supporting my family for years, at the age of twenty-five, I was still a shy and insecure young woman. The thought of having to deal with wolves, who had no conscience and cheated innocent women who were trying to make a decent living, depressed me.

Not even singing on the stage lifted my spirits. I dreaded each day when I had to get up and start all over again. Yet what else could I do?

There was no such thing as an agent, and everyone had to figure out how to survive in the rat race. Other singers were aggressively promoting themselves, kissing up to songwriters and television managers or taking magazine editors out to dinner and giving them gifts. But I didn't want to. I was too honest and too proud to play those games. I stayed home and went to perform only when engagements came to me. Looking back, though, not appearing everywhere made me more popular. I didn't have much ambition. I performed because that's what I did the best, and it put the rice on the table for my family. Also, in order to make records, I would have had to sing Korean songs, and I had no desire to. I was never close to anyone, and no one knew my personal life. Everyone thought I had everything. But deep inside I was a scared little girl who was always worried about whether I would be able to continue working. And if not, what would happen to my family, who relied on me? The emotional strain was so great that I constantly promised myself that if I ever had a child, I would never burden him or her as I had been burdened.

Then, in 1964, someone from Walker Hill, the only fancy resort in Seoul at the time, invited me to sing there. I was ecstatic. Walker Hill! It was as exciting as being invited to sing in Las Vegas or somewhere in America. In addition, I would be paid monthly and wouldn't have to deal with middlemen, who, in the past, had cheated me so often. To be selected to perform there was every entertainer's dream.

Sitting on the outskirts of the city, Walker Hill, named after General Walton H. Walker, the first American general to serve in the Korean War, was built by the Korean government in the early 1960s to provide a quiet, exotic place for foreigners and foreign dignitaries to stay and be entertained. In the beginning, no Koreans were allowed to stay there, but this rule was relaxed when the government realized that in order to operate the huge place, they couldn't rely only on foreign visitors. However, only a few Koreans could afford or had the connections necessary to visit there.

The hotel was nestled on a beautiful hillside, overlooking the Han River. The winding stone-paved road leading to the hotel was lined on both sides with fancy plants and rocks. In the morning, veiled by morning mist, the mountain peaks stood as if they were protecting Korea.

The dinner theater was small but with a second balcony. Production numbers in the dinner theater were very elaborate, and the dancers selected to perform here were the tallest and prettiest in the country. Understandably, all were very proud to be working there.

I loved to sing at Walker Hill. It was the closest I had ever come to singing in an American musical. Fourteen musicians, all dressed in elegant black tuxedos, accompanied me. Every night, I was lifted up from below stage on a hydraulic elevator from the basement level to the stage, wearing my first wireless microphone under my dress, dancing and singing as I desired. Here it seemed my dreams had really come true. Now my repertoire became more sophisticated. I chose songs by Cole Porter, including "*Night and Day,*" "*It Was Just One of Those Things,*" and others from Broadway musicals. One of my favorites was "*I Enjoy Being a Girl*" from *Flower Drum Song.* The lyrics were so expressive that I could sing using every gesture to fit to the words.

I designed all of my own stage gowns. My favorite was a two-piece long gown made out of maroon brocade with a wraparound skirt. When I first entered the stage, it appeared that I was wearing a strapless long dress. After I finished my first number, which usually was a ballad, the tempo changed to either cha-cha or rock-and-roll. I would take off my wraparound skirt to reveal a pair of tight white pants attached to the maroon top. All around the pant legs were layers and layers of six-inch-long beads. Sometimes, I would use a top hat and cane. No one in Korea could sing the kinds of songs that I chose or imitate my stage performance. I even had my own star's dressing room, right next to the stage while the dancers used one big dressing room below the stage. The girls knew that several of the male dancers were gay and treated them as one of their own. In those days I weighed one hundred pounds and stood five feet and one inch tall. The world was going through its Marilyn Monroe phase, so naturally, I ordered padded bottoms and stiff, backless bras from Frederick's of Hollywood.

My daily routine was fairly simple. I listened to the radio all day in order to pick up new songs, and then left home at 5:00 PM for the thirty-minute bus ride to the hotel. When all the performers had arrived late in the afternoon, they all went to the hotel restaurant and ordered hamburgers. They signed their names, and later, the food charges were deducted from their pay. Meat was scarce and expensive, and there weren't many places where we could get a real American hamburger or cuisine. Not only did people love hamburgers, but eating them was considered chic. Although I was the highest-paid performer, I couldn't afford to eat anything other than my rice lunch box, which I brought every day. I was supporting three households: my mother with my two younger brothers in Busan, my brother Tong-Kun with his room and board and tuition in Seoul, and of course myself. My insecurity of not knowing when I'd be out of work never left me.

On payday when I received my monthly salary, the man who handed me my money (in cash) said, "Boy, it looks like Ms. Song is the only person who never eats at the restaurant. She is taking home every penny." Since the people didn't know how many lives were depending on me, they thought that I was frugal. Once, a man teased me when he saw me get off the bus, saying, "Don't you think a star like you should ride a taxi instead of a bus? What are you going to do with all the money you are saving?" I told him that I wanted to make sure that I was no burden on any of my family when I died.

One evening, a staff person told me that I should go to the next building, called Han-Kook-Kwan, or Korean House, between my performances. "President Park is entertaining generals from the Eighth Army," he said.

As I walked into the building, I saw a small combo playing in the big almost-empty room. Since it was a Korean house, everyone on the dance floor was in his or her stocking feet. The foreign men were dancing with Korean ladies, who were done up in colorful fancy Korean *hanboks* and boat-shaped white cotton booties instead of rubber shoes. I thought I should take off my high heels as soon as I walked into the hall, but I reasoned that since I was just going to stand next to the band and sing, I couldn't imagine myself standing in my stocking feet with my long gown dragging on the floor. Across the hall, there was a Korean room, whose floor was two feet above the floor of the hall. Many foreign and Korean men were sitting around a long low dining table, eating and drinking, with ladies in beautiful *hanboks* pouring the drinks and feeding them.

When I started to sing, a small Korean man, accompanied by a Korean lady, stepped down onto the floor of the hall. They both were without shoes and dancing toward me. Only then did I realize it was President Park himself. Suddenly he let go of his partner and came and grabbed my hand in the middle of my singing and pulled me toward him. I didn't know what to do. There I was, in high-heeled shoes, towering over the president of Korea in his stocking feet.

When we got to the middle of the floor, he asked, "Why don't you take off your shoes?" I tossed them to the band and kept dancing, dragging my dress all around the floor.

After that evening, he always called me to attend his parties. Sometimes they were held at one of the private villas on the hill. I learned that he loved female singers, and he often arranged for me to come and entertain him and his guests. When he was assassinated in

1979 in one of the rooms in the Blue House compound, a famous young singer, Shin Soo Bong, was at his side, holding him as he died.

Contrary to the perception that I led an exciting life with a well-paying job and lots of men fawning over me, my life was very lonely and sheltered. I didn't go anywhere, and I didn't have any friends. I was always very particular, and if I couldn't have loyal friends whom I could trust, I preferred not to have any. If I can't open up my soul, what is the use of having a friend? I am still that way. I also didn't like the men in my field. They were shallow and seemed not to care about anything other than playing their instruments every night or drinking *Jin-Ro* (a Korean drink) and chewing on the legs of dried squid during the truck ride home after a show, or playing *Hato*, a Korean card game, in their spare time. Besides, most of them barely survived. There was no shortage of musicians, and the country was still in a shambles. I was like a drop of oil in water. I neither belonged to the life that was essential to my survival nor to the lives of "normal" people. Girls called me now and then when they were in town and seemed to be always surprised to find me at home. Because of my life in the limelight and my wild and sexy persona on stage, people usually had a completely inaccurate perception of my character. Even now, people seem surprised when I tell them that I hardly went out. I loved my career, but I was not happy with everything that was associated with it.

In the 1960s, Korean entertainers didn't get rich no matter how good they were. Everyone was trying to survive and make quick money. The entertainment industry in Korea was still in the crawling stage, nothing was organized or established, and most entertainers barely made enough money to live. Moreover, I didn't like the public's perception of artists as strange creatures with empty heads.

Recently, this line of thinking was expressed by an acquaintance. The person forgot that I was a singer and said of his mother, a violinist in the National Symphony Orchestra, "I love my mother dearly, but she is an artist, and she was a nut." Then he realized what he'd said and apologized. I told him I knew what he meant, and in some respects, I agreed. Artists are often gifted people. Normal, to them, is boring, and to live under restrictions and structure is like asking them to stop breathing. To be creative, they have to have free spirits, like the birds that can fly wherever their wings take them or the fish that swim anywhere they desire. I never wanted to be like "others," and I still don't want to be. When I told a woman I know, Ms. Shin, that I was a singer at the time Ron married me, she laughingly said, "How in the world did a man like Ron Nessen married a showgirl?" Nowadays, it's a different story, but in days when Korea was in a shambles, being called "showgirl" was like being called "Jap" or "nigger." Ms. Shin was a retired woman, and must have left Korea when Korea was still struggling. Although she said it half-jokingly, I knew she meant it

Getting tired of both my work and my personal life, I also had to think about my marriage prospects. I loved when I was on the stage, but I knew there was nothing else I wanted more in life than to be someone's wife and have a family. My singing made my blood run and made my heart beat, but the bottom line was I was a woman's woman. I wanted to have babies, be a good mother, teach my children wisdom, watch them grow, and be proud when they grew up and contributed their good deeds to society. But how would I do this? I couldn't go out at a normal hour with normal people. I was sad when I had to work at night, especially on holidays, seeing everyone having a good time. No prominent Korean family would have a singer as a daughter-in-law, and no "normal" Korean man would consider having me as his respected wife. No matter how famous I became, for me, nothing would bring ultimate happiness except becoming a wife and a mother. But as long as I was an entertainer, I was afraid that would never happen.

A very well-to-do businessman asked me out and brought another couple along. He had a car, a luxury most people couldn't afford, and drove out of town to a beautiful lake surrounded by mountains where I had never been before. We went on a boat ride and had a very nice time. When the sun started to go down, we headed back, and halfway to the city, this man complained about being ill. He parked on a mountain road and told me that he couldn't drive all the way back home. It was obvious that the men wanted to take us two women somewhere for the night. After thirty minutes, he gave up and drove us home. I never saw him after that.

Incidents like this convinced me that I had to accept reality; I would never be able to marry a Korean man, as most of them considered a woman who worked every night a plaything, but nothing else.

One day, I saw a blonde American woman rehearsing on the stage with the band. Someone told me that she was a new striptease dancer. Once a month they booked some interesting foreign entertainers, mostly singers. *A stripper?* I thought. She was young, but she was so fat and so unkempt that it was disgusting. I watched her rehearsing, thinking her act might surprise me. Instead, she did nothing but walk on the stage and slap a long leather strap on the floor while the band played the theme song from *Peter Gunn*. That evening, she shared my dressing room, and I learned some of Joanny's history. She was only twenty-one, and her parents had divorced when she was young. She'd been shipped back and forth between Hawaii and the mainland, where her parents lived. Her current family turned out to be a Russian wolfhound and her Filipino dog-sitter, and I couldn't believe the dog was as big as a little donkey and bigger than the dog-sitter.

She'd quickly learned that her blonde hair and her body intrigued Asian men. She had neither talent nor imagination, but strippers usually didn't have to do anything special except show their naked bodies. She was in the Philippines before she came to Seoul. One night after her performance at the nightclub, a gang kidnapped her at gunpoint and took her to a hotel. After they tied her to the bedpost, they gang-raped her. She took out a small handgun from her purse. "I always carry this with me now," she said. I felt sorry for her and had a sudden urge to help her in some way, though these urges usually brought me pain and disappointment.

Joanny had been working at Walker Hill for about three weeks when she changed her routine to one involving a big old-fashioned American bathtub on the stage. Joanny was busy giving instructions. "Put the makeup stand here, the bathtub there . . ."

As a man passed by me, I heard him saying under his breath, "Damn it, where are we supposed to find bubble powder?"

It struck me as funny because we never had anything like a bubble bath. That evening, I stood behind the curtain and watched Joanny's routine. She was dressed in a short see-through lime green nightie that barely covered her rear. Underneath she wore bikini panties. First she walked around the stage. Then she sat in front of the makeup table, brushing her hair and looking into a hand mirror. Then she repeated her walking routine while she took off her jacket. Her breasts were pushing out every which way while her fat stomach hung over the top of the bikini. I looked out at the audience. People were whispering and giggling. The bandmaster was looking at her with a disgusted expression. It was so pathetic that I couldn't watch any longer. When I saw her put her feet into the bubble bath, I went back to my dressing room.

The music ended to weak applause. I was sitting in front of the dressing mirror when she walked in, and I saw her figure in the mirror. She was shivering, wet and dripping, with a towel around her body. Her face was ashen as if she'd seen a ghost.

"Oh my god, oh my god, what am I to do, Song?" She was hysterical.

I just sat there.

"Oh, Song, I just found out I'm pregnant."

I wasn't sure if I had heard her correctly.

"What are you talking about?" I asked.

"I'm pregnant, damn it. Oh, I'm going to die." She was shivering even more than before.

"No, wait a minute," I said. "Sit down here. Calm down. Let's start from the beginning. How do you know you're pregnant?"

"I felt it."

"Are you sure?"

"Yeah, I'm positive. I felt this baby inside of me, moving."

I just sat there, frozen.

"Song, please, you have to help me."

"What are you going to do?"

Now I was scared. Abortion was illegal in Korea, but it was secretly accepted as the only available method of birth control. What if something went wrong? But I couldn't ignore her predicament either. I told my mother, and she told me where I could take Joanny. She was already six months along.

After the abortion, she acted as if nothing had happened, and was happy as usual. She had her room, her "family" with her, and free meals every day. I am sure that when her first three-week contract was terminated, she renegotiated and got a fraction of her original monthly salary, but she didn't seem to care. She wanted to stay as long as she could. Sometimes, she made extra money by having sex with Korean men. But I heard most of them were disappointed because she never dressed decently and ran around barefoot.

After three months at Walker Hill, Joanny was terminated and needed a place to stay. I was renting a couple of rooms at one of the huge houses, so I brought her "family" there. She had one *ondol* room, and my mother gave her some Korean bedding. She ate with us. This American girl, who often acted more Korean than a Korean, intrigued me. She sat on the floor cross-legged and ate whatever I put before her. She ate her rice with chopsticks like the Japanese do. She spoke some Japanese. All three of them—Joanny, the dog, and the dog-sitter—slept in one room, though Koreans never bring dogs inside, especially not a big dog like Joanny's. The girl would go to the marketplace and buy a big piece of beef. Then she would cut it into pieces, open the dog's mouth, put the cut-up meat in one piece at the time, close the mouth, and wait until the meat went down its throat.

Seeing this strange ritual every day, my mother kept saying, "Look at that crazy woman, stuffing that dog with meat that people can't even afford to eat."

I took her and her Filipino maid to a bathhouse. She didn't want to go to the communal bath, so we went to a private one. She was still very heavy. I was soaking in the tub, and when she joined me, water spilled all over the edge of bathtub. When I looked at her, she said, "Oh, shut up." We all had a good laugh.

A month after she moved in with us, she moved out, not telling me where she was going. When she had shared the dressing room with me at Walker Hill, I noticed she always went down to the dancers' dressing room. She followed around an older woman who was a dancer and the choreographer. After she moved in with us, she kept calling the woman on the phone and taking her expensive gifts. Looking back, she must have wanted her to teach her an act or two. I never asked her for money while she was with me. Yet she never once said thank you or gave anything to the little maid who cooked for us. After she left us, she never called.

She was a child without guidance. She lived like a stray dog, never having learned how a decent human being should behave toward others. This experience made me promise to myself that I would bring up my own children in a secure, two-parent family so that they would never behave the way Joanny did. But as Koreans say, until you are buried under the ground, never talk big.

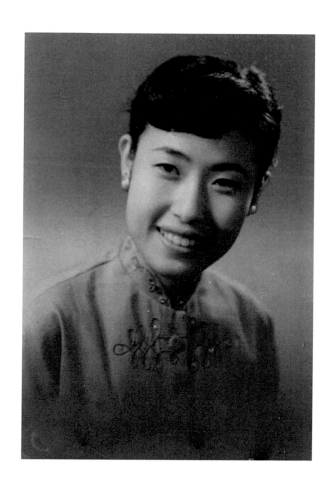

Teenager

Optical shop, 1955

Cindy, Mr. Yang Chul, Amy

I wanted to look like Rita Hayward in *Gilda*.

1962
Performing in Japan with Mr. Kill Ok-yoon

Singing in Japan

Performing in Japan

1962—Japan

Singing for the 8th Army

Walker Hill, Promotion pictures.

Walker Hill

1962, In Japan. Me at the left.
Mr. Hyun Inn, the singer

Walker Hill

Walker Hill

Walker Hill

The Tour—Bangkok

Why is the mountain always green?
Why does the river run forever?
If people work as endlessly nature does
We could rule the world.

—Lee Hwang (1501-1570)

To different minds, the same world is a hell, and a heaven.

—Ralph Waldo Emerson (1803-1882)

In 1964, a couple approached me about going on tour. Madame Chang wore a stylish maroon suit of light wool and a white silk blouse. Her black leather bag was obviously a designer brand that most women could not afford. On her finger was a big diamond ring. "For several nights now, I have been coming to Walker Hill to see the show. I am forming a group to take on a tour of East Asia. I've already chosen two dancers from Walker Hill, and I would like you to join us.

"The tour is for six months," the woman said. "I'll provide round-trip tickets, room and board, and all costumes and musical arrangements for two thirty-minute shows. I am paying dancers $100 each. I will pay you two hundred."

The man glanced at me. I didn't know how much $200 was worth outside of Korea, but again, negotiating money was difficult for young Korean people, especially when speaking with their elders. I knew I had a special singing style, and there were hardly any other singers who knew what they were singing when they sang in English. In Korea, singers sang and dancers danced. No one did both at the same time as I did.

I quickly figured that the money the woman offered was more than I was earning at Walker Hill. But little did I know it was nothing outside of Korea. I agreed. We had no written contract, but a verbal one. That is mostly how it was then in Korea.

"Okay, then, it's settled," she said as she stood up and picked up her handbag. "We have to start rehearsing and get costumes made."

In the 1960s, Korea was still in a bad economic situation. To stop people from spending hard currency, which the country needed badly, not many were allowed to leave the country except for official reasons. There were rumors that one or two groups had left Korea for tours, and all of the entertainers left behind envied them. Of course, I was flattered to be chosen.

Madame Chang, a widow in her forties, had grown up in Shanghai and spoke Mandarin fluently. She owned a tearoom in the heart of downtown Seoul, which proved she was well connected. I often wondered how she became involved in the entertainment business, but slowly figured it out. Her connections with the government official who helped get authorization for her entertainment business came about as an excuse for bringing hard currency from abroad and a cover-up for a black market business smuggling in expensive goods from Hong Kong, such as jewelry and furs, which were impossible to buy in Korea legally. Rich people would pay any amount for the expensive products, and it was a well-known fact that if you gave enough money to the right person in Korea, anything was possible. She had to have someone high up who would allow her to bring them in without inspection at the airport, and her connection was the man whom she was always with.

August was set as the month of our departure, and I wanted to take some new sequined dresses on the tour. An American or British businessman who lived in Hong Kong came to see my show at Walker Hill whenever he was in Seoul on a business trip. I asked him if he would bring me sequins in three different colors—red, green, and royal blue—from Hong Kong. As soon as they arrived, my mother, our maid, and I sat on the floor night and day for four months sewing the sequins onto my three dresses and three pairs of shoes to match. By August, the dresses and shoes were packed in my bag, and I was ready to leave Korea.

The weeks before our departure were packed with rehearsals, photo shoots, and fittings. I wanted a new name. Song Young-Hee worked in Korea, but for other countries, I wanted a simple and easy name people would remember. I went through the alphabet: Amy Song, Barbara Song, Cindy Song, Debby Song, and so on. I finally decided to call myself Cindy—Cindy Song. The name had a nice ring, and I loved Eddie Fisher's song, "Cindy, Oh Cindy." The other two girls decided they needed new names too. One called herself Nana. She was married and had two children. The other picked Mimi. Nana was short but had a very sexy face, and she tried hard to behave that way too. Mimi was tall and had curly hair, which was unusual for a Korean. She performed Korean folk dances beautifully.

Our first song-and-dance number was "*Arirang*," which was one of Korea's most famous folk songs. We wore *hanboks* made of pink transparent material with layers of underskirts made of white netting. The skirts were full and attached to the jackets so that we could easily slip in and out of them wearing the next costumes underneath. The three of us danced the first verse together, and then broke up for the second verse. While Mimi and Nana danced, I sang. After the opening number, Mimi performed a Korean drum dance. Then I sang again. Then Nana danced in a bikini. For the finale, I sang and threw off my skirt toward the end of the number, breaking into a rumba called "*Mañana*." Mimi and Nana returned to the stage, joining me for the finale, dressed in red bikinis with turbans on their heads.

In August, all three of us, Mimi, Nana, and I arrived in the airport dressed in white sleeveless dresses with matching jackets designed by Madame Chang. With our families there to see us off, we girls felt as though we were going up to heaven, or maybe like an Olympic team on our way to competition with Madame Chang as our coach. She was not pleased that our first engagement was in Bangkok instead of Hong Kong. Other than my brief tour to Japan a couple of years before, the three of us had never really traveled outside Korea, so we depended on Madame Chang's authority and experience. During our layover in Hong Kong, she suggested we go into town and shop instead of waiting at the airport. So we put our carry-on bags in airport lockers and took a taxi to downtown Hong Kong. Madame Chang took us to the back streets of Kowloon, where cheap goods were sold. In the 1960s in Korea, there were no imported goods like clothes and household products—or domestic goods, for that matter. In the back street, shoes, sandals, and handbags were spread from one end of Kowloon to the other. We knew they were cheap goods, but we were starving for anything, and to us, they looked as though they had been dropped from heaven. Since we knew we couldn't take the time to see everything, we raced from one place to another looking and buying. Although I brought extra money with me, I only bought one pair of sandals and a hand massager, since I wanted to do my shopping on our way back home. We lost all track of the time and rushed back to catch our flight.

The Kai Tak Airport looked deserted. A few workers dressed in navy blue uniforms stood near the gate. We went to the lockers, took out our carry-on bags, and hurried to the gate. Madame Chang handed our boarding passes to the agent, who looked at us, and, in English, said, "Your plane has left already." Madame Chang and the two dancers did not speak English, and they looked at me for the translation. When I told them what was said, Madame Chang's face dropped.

"Oh my god, what are we supposed to do?" she said with panic in her voice. What happened to our luggage, our costumes, and the drums? How would we get to Bangkok?"

Mimi, Nana, and I looked to Madame Chang like three lost children.

"You can catch the next flight," the agent said. Seeing all of our shopping bags, he told us that we had to pay $50 for any additional carry-on. We had makeup cases, handbags, a bag of music arrangements, which weighed a ton, and shopping bags, everything Madame Chang had told us to bring on the plane with us so that she didn't have to pay additional fees. When I told her what the agent said, Madame Chang's face dropped all over again. "Oh my god, what are we going to do? Tell her we brought all these things from Korea."

The agent replied, "Yes, but you've bought more things here."

After I translated for Madame Chang, she looked at Mimi, Nana, and me as if directing us to pay our share. But the three of us stood there, dumb, frozen, and embarrassed, looking back at the woman who was supposed to be our coach, the woman on whom we depended. She spoke loudly to us in Korean, but when Madame Chang realized that none of us was going to pay the extra fee, she turned her back to us, making sure we would not see the inside of her wallet, peeled out a $50 bill, and handed it to the agent. Without having traveled much, we had no way of knowing whether the airline agent was taking advantage of the situation, but I am almost positive that we looked naïve enough for this to be probable. On the plane, no one talked. All the day's excitement had disappeared in one minute.

When we arrived in Bangkok, it was dark. A driver from the club at which we were to perform picked us up from the airport and dropped us off at a shabby house in the middle of a residential area. The house was dirty, empty, and, because of the tropical climate, there were no windows except openings in the walls. There was nothing to eat and nothing to cook with. And when Madame Chang saw lizards crawling over the walls, she decided there was no way she would stay in that house. The next day, we moved to Chani Château, the club where we were to perform. The owner was a Japanese man, but we were never introduced.

The upstairs had several rooms with window air conditioners, but Madame Chang refused to stay in an air-conditioned room saying our blood would dry up. "Don't you know that air conditioners dry up your blood? Don't you know?" The three of us, without any objection, meekly obeyed her wishes and took a Japanese room with *tatami* floors and a fan. Westerners might wonder why grown women would follow Madame Chang like children never questioning. But in Asia, we were conditioned from day one to obey and respect older people and to never question their authority. Because of mosquitoes, a large, room-sized net was draped in the room that reminded me of my childhood. Madame Chang gave each of us an allowance of $2 a day for our meals until we got paid at the end of the month. How could we pay for all three meals with such a meager amount? Were we to suck our thumbs for breakfast and lunch?

Mimi, standing in the middle of the room, held her $2 in her hand and asked, "Now, what can we get with $2 this morning?" Nana and I were lying on the floor in our bras and panties. We had no idea where anything was.

As I began dressing myself, I said, "Well, let's go out and see what's out there." But Nana was too depressed to get out of bed. So Mimi and I went out looking for something to eat. We knew we could not afford to dine in a restaurant, so we went into a small convenience store, which sold cans of sodas, and candies we had never seen before. We bought a package of crackers and canned meat.

Much later, but not until we arrived in Hong Kong, I found out that the club gave performers the choice of taking two of their meals at the club or being paid $5 each day, a dollar and a half for breakfast and three and a half for dinner. Since Madame Chang was not a performer, the club would not pay for her meals. She took our money, gave us $2 each, and pocketed the rest. Not only was she determined to get a free ride from our hard work, but she also made sure she got back her $50 from the incident at the airport.

Mimi and I came from the southern part of Korea, and our diet consisted of vegetables and fish, so we were able to get by. But Nana, whose parents were from the north, was used to eating meat. The half starvation we were experiencing was just too much for her, and sometimes she was too weak to dance, but she went on stage and worked anyway. Even with such cold-hearted treatment, no one had the courage to confront Madame Chang. We just stopped talking to her.

After making such a fuss about air conditioners, Madame Chang ended up staying with a friend of hers who owned a Korean restaurant called Arirang. Besides, the mosquitoes were so vicious and so many, even during day, that they bit through our pants. We felt trapped and frustrated. About a week after our arrival, a man from the club told me that someone was asking for Ms. Song. I wondered who in the world could have known I was in Bangkok. When I went out in front of the club and found John, the businessman from Hong Kong who had brought me the sequins, I nearly fainted. Although I hardly knew him, seeing a familiar face brought me such happiness. "I've just arrived in Bangkok on a business trip," he said with a big smile. "I was taking a walk and was surprised to see your picture here." He pointed at a display case in front of the club, and for the first time, I saw our picture. The club had three acts: a magic act, a male vocal trio from the Philippines, and of course ours—*Cindy and the Apples.*

John took me to a small restaurant, where I ordered a basket of fried chicken, not knowing what the other dishes on the menu were like. The half chicken I was served was so small and so skinny that I couldn't tell which one of us was the more starved, the chicken or me. But I ate hungrily as if someone would take my chicken away if I didn't hurry, tearing at the meat with my mouth, chewing, sucking the bones, and finishing the basket in five minutes. There was an old Korean saying that would have described me perfectly: *She was so hungry that she would not have known if death fell in front of her.* When I finished, John was looking at me in dismay, but being a gentleman, he did not ask any questions. If I had been more open and knew a little more about life, I would have told him about Madame Chang and how she was nearly starving us, but I was not sure then what was considered appropriate behavior with an American gentleman. If I hadn't been so shy, I would have ordered several more baskets of fried chicken.

For a few days while John was in town, he took the three of us sightseeing, which lifted our spirits. We saw exotic golden temples. We went to the Erawan Hotel, where John was staying, and he took pictures of us in front of a mauve sunset and a pond with a surface that looked like glass. Wherever we went, people turned their heads to look at us because we were dressed in long colorful *hanboks.*

The next day, John took us to a dock, where we were to take a boat to a small island on which a famous building stood. The water was low. The man in the boat extended his hand to Mimi. As she held it and tried to step in, the boat began to drift back. While we stood frozen, as if watching in slow motion, Mimi fell into the dirty canal. Not many Korean women know how to swim, and I was sure Mimi would drown. We all stood on the dock, not knowing what to do next. But immediately, her head surfaced, and she was shouting, "Oh, my eyelashes! My eyelashes!" She desperately tried to grab her false eyelashes, which were floating in the murky water somewhere. We looked, but no one could find them. Luckily, her very thin dress dried quickly as we all got in the boat and made our way to the island. That incident reminded me of a similar incident when two showgirls went to a Busan beach with a couple of GIs. One of the showgirls was all dolled up in a sexy bikini. When she went into the water and started to swim, her sponge falsies floated out of her suit and into the sea. When she started to scream, one of the GIs dove into the water and retrieved them.

Another day in Bangkok, we walked around the hotel and found jewelry stores. I bought a couple of rings for my mother and a Thai doll for me. But when our four-week engagement at Chani Château came to a close, I promised myself that I would never return to Bangkok and its vicious mosquitoes, which bit us day and night. Little did I know that I would come back as rich tourist soon. On the plane, the three of us hoped the next stop would be better than the first. Our destination was Singapore.

The Tour—Singapore and Saigon

White egret, do not laugh at the raven for being black
He may be black outside;
Does that mean he's black inside?
And perhaps snow-white plumage can conceal
A black heart. Could that be you?

—Ye Jeek (1362-1431)

Love is the whole history of a woman's life,
it is but an episode in a man's.

—Madame de Stael (1766-1817)

Driving from the Singapore airport, I was speechless. The streets were clean, the sun was warm, the breeze was cool, and I had never been in such a beautiful city. Our arrival at the first-class Hotel Singapura, where we were to perform for two weeks, made us forget the four hellish weeks in Bangkok. Seeing it, our spirits rose, and we felt as though we were there on vacation.

As soon as we arrived, a local paper interviewed us; and the next day, pictures of Cindy and the Apples, along with a lengthy article, appeared in the paper. The three of us shared a suite, and we could eat whatever we pleased in the breakfast room. Madame Chang, not wanting to pay for her own meals, told us to sign for hers as well.

As soon as we arrived, I had boil on my top lip. It only got bigger and bigger, and not only couldn't I open my mouth, but I could hardly sing. It never occurred us to seek a doctor. One evening, after the performance, Mimi said that she could fix it if I let her. I was afraid, but what else could I do? She told me to lay down on the bed and told Nana to sit on top of me. Then, she went to work. She held a small bath cloth on each of her hands and squeezed the boil with all her might. I saw stars falling in front of my eyes and I screamed bloody murder. Afterwards, I sat on bed and cried my eyes out. I am not sure when was the last time I felt such a pain.

The Olympic-sized swimming pool in the hotel was very inviting, but we only saw Westerners sitting around the pool. None of us were swimmers, but the three of us bought bikinis, stuffed our tops with sponges, and lounged about near the pool. We saw a handsome young man walk toward the diving board, leading a baby by the hand, who wore a pair of little navy blue briefs and appeared no more than a year old. Mimi, Nana, and I, not used to seeing Caucasian babies, were going crazy over him. The man took the baby onto the diving board and, without warning, threw him into the water.

Mimi, Nana, and I, our eyes like saucers, covered our mouths with our hands and stopped breathing. The baby popped his head out of the water and began swimming toward the woman. When the woman lifted the baby up out of the water, he bawled out loud. We were so relieved; we clapped our hands and laughed. When the baby heard our laughter, he stopped crying, looked our way, and gave us a big smile. I assumed the man, woman, and child were Americans because who else would be daring enough to throw a baby into the water?

Our two weeks in Singapore went by too quickly. Madame Chang and the girls shopped. They bought handbags made of alligator skin, but I was still holding on to my money. I knew there was nothing here that I couldn't buy when we got to Hong Kong. On some evenings, we dined by the pool. Malaysian girls in their native dresses served us *satay,* which was a local barbecue dish prepared with skewered lamb. In two weeks, Mimi, Nana, and I had not only gained our weight back, but our skin glistened like marble from the improved nutrition and the peaceful nature of our time in Singapore. As we left the country, we hoped that our next stop would bring us just as much comfort and happiness.

Every time we left one place for another, Madame Chang would sigh and say, "Wouldn't it be great if we could go to Hong Kong?" As

if Hong Kong was the Promised Land. I never knew who lined up our
itinerary or how Madame Chang went about booking our shows or even
made phone calls, for that matter, because she did not know a word of
English. She never asked me for help, trying to conceal her contacts.
Once in a while, she would whisper to me, saying, "When we get to Hong
Kong, you and I will stay together." When Madame Chang announced
Saigon as our next destination, I felt uneasy because I had heard that
Vietnam was having troubles. I did not know how serious it was until we
went to the Vietnamese Embassy to fill out forms for our visas. When
I saw pictures of the war zone—tanks, guns, and dead bodies hanging
on the walls—I told myself I had already seen too many wars in my life.
Did I need to see another? A line in the visa application said, "Write the
name and address of those persons who should be notified in case of an
emergency." *No other country had this question on its visa form. What kind
of an emergency? Would I meet my death in Saigon? For what and for whom?
Madame Chang and Cindy and the Apples?* As I stared at the application,
I wondered if I should get on a plane and go back home. Home, where
I had already survived two wars, where my mother and brothers waited
for me, where I might fall in love with a nice young man, marry, and
start a family of my own. Forget Hong Kong. Forget seeing the world.
Forget singing. I did not want to die in Vietnam.

Nevertheless, along with Madame Chang and the Apples, I boarded
the plane to Saigon. As the captain told us to fasten our seat belts
for landing, I looked out the window and saw camouflaged military
vehicles, military equipment, tents, nets, and guns, announcing the
war in Vietnam. What was I to do?

Saigon was hot and humid. As we were driving along the streets, I
saw women riding motorbikes wearing *ao dai*, their long dresses, which
were fluttering in the wind. The Vietnamese women looked tiny, fragile,
breakable, as if they were twelve or thirteen years old. Their dresses,
with the high-neck collars, the side slits running up to their hips, and
the silky, loose trousers underneath, were made out of thin satin like
material that showed their panties beneath. They wore high-lacquered
sandals that showed off their long manicured toenails. I thought the
women were very exotic and sexy with their long black hair. With their
triangular straw hats hanging upon their backs, flapping like wings,
the women floated up and down the streets of muggy Saigon like silent
angels with no message to deliver.

As soon as we checked into our room, Madame Chang announced
that we had to make a courtesy call to the Korean Embassy. There
weren't any Korean visitors in Vietnam, and the consul general and
the others seemed delighted to meet us. Madame Chang seemed to

know Consul Kim and said he was a friend of her husband, but I had the feeling that she knew him either from one of her previous tours, or that he was a friend of her important contact in Korea. We were sent the following morning to the Canal, which was near the hotel, to greet the battalions of Korean soldiers arriving in Saigon to fight in Vietnam's war. When we arrived at the Canal, little paper Korean flags were handed to us. As I held one between my fingers, I remembered my first year in the Japanese school, when I nearly froze, parading around the city to celebrate the invasion of Singapore.

A ship was docked on the canal, and the young Korean soldiers standing eagerly on shore reminded me of my first boyfriend. As I watched huge numbers of Korean men arrive, I sadly wondered how many would die fighting on foreign soil, so far from their homes, so far from their families.

The Korean newspapers printed pictures of us in our *hanboks*, waving our paper flags, with Korean soldiers standing in the background. My mother wrote to tell me how happy she was to see me in good health.

After two weeks at the Majestic Hotel, there was still no word on another booking. During our wait, the Korean Embassy arranged for us to perform at a Chinese restaurant and nightclub called the Van Canh. The night before our performance, the owner of the club prepared a feast for us, and I watched Nana devour everything from turtle soup to stir-fried lemon crabs. She ate as if she had not eaten for years. I thought that was how I must have looked when I ate that skinny fried chicken in Bangkok with John. As I mentioned earlier, it seemed that Nana could not survive without eating a heavy meat diet, and when she saw the Chinese dishes made of lamb, pork, and beef, she ate as if she were stocking up for the future. She also loved tropical fruits, and stuffed herself with mangoes until her face broke out in a rash.

The owner of the restaurant provided us with an upstairs room in an old house, and a Chinese *amah*, a maid who cooked our meals and took care of our needs. She did not speak a word of English, and we did not speak a word of Chinese.

On our first night in the old house, the three of us lay in one big bed, ready to fall asleep, when we heard a loud booming sound in the distance. I held my breath. Another *boom*, then another. If I had been a child, I would have guessed that rice was popping in a hot cloth bag. A few minutes later, I turned toward Mimi, lying next to me, and I asked, "Did you hear that?" She had her eyes wide open.

"Suppose they push down into the city, just like the North Koreans did?" I asked.

We all got up. Facing the headboard, folding our knees under our bodies, lacing our hands beneath our foreheads, we began to pray. I didn't know what else to pray for except to ask God to help us leave Saigon alive.

The next morning, I jumped out of the bed, went to the veranda, and looked up and down the street. Everything was as it had been. The rickshaws, the young women on their motorbikes going wherever they were supposed to be going. Every night after that, when the artillery went off, I would say, "*It's bed time, our lullaby is playing.*" It was a different kind of lullaby than when I was a little girl in Yangsan, falling asleep, listening to the rats race above the paper ceiling.

The embassy arranged for us to perform for General Nguyen Cao Ky, commanding general of the air force and later the prime minister of Vietnam. He wore an orange scarf around his neck, dark sunglasses, and carried a riding crop. It was big news among the American reporters when his beautiful wife, who once was an airline stewardess, had plastic surgery on her eyes to make them look Western.

That night we were supposed to perform for the general and his guests, but I had a high fever. By the time Consul Kim and his assistant came from the embassy to pick us up, my whole body had stiffened like a board, and I couldn't move or talk. Consul Kim, together with Mimi, massaged my feet and hands. I was in a lot of pain, but no one knew what to do. Madame Chang never attempted to come near and assist. As the Korean saying goes, "*Whose dog is barking?*" which means "Who cares?" This mysterious sickness lasted about thirty minutes and then miraculously began to lessen. As the stiffness disappeared from my body, I felt as limp and lifeless as salted cabbage. I encouraged everyone to go on without me. Consul Kim was the only one who asked me if I was sure I'd be all right.

After everyone left, I felt as though all my strength had slipped right out from my body. Talking rapidly in Chinese, the concerned *amah* brought me some soft-boiled rice, but I couldn't even lift my hand. I was drifting in and out of a black tunnel. After this incident, the Chinese *amah* protected me and took care of me as if I were her own daughter. If I could only have talked to her and told her how much I appreciated her.

Finally, the news arrived that we were going to Hong Kong. Madame Chang was exuberant, but our own anticipation and enthusiasm were muted. Because of the incident with my illness and the way Madame Chang had treated us in Bangkok, we weren't happy being on the tour any longer. Madame Chang tried sweet-talking me, saying that I could stay with her. But I am a straightforward person, and nothing could corrupt me. As an old proverb says, *"Don't go if it's not the road."* On the plane to Hong Kong, Nana said, "I hope we don't have to be anywhere near her." We all vehemently agreed.

The Tour—Hong Kong

Even though the sky is high
Be careful what you reach for.
Even though the ground is firm
Be careful how you walk.
The high sky and the firm ground
Have the ability to deceive you.

—Joo Ue Shick (dates unknown)

Cherish your yesterday; dream your tomorrow;
And always live your today!

—Author Unknown

When I looked out the plane's window and saw all those high-rise buildings standing side by side like little Korean matchboxes, I became excited. Hong Kong, the jewel of the Orient, the place where one could purchase anything under the sun. I had often dreamed of Hong Kong and what it would be like. When American GIs went off on their R & R trips, they all wanted to go to Hong Kong; and the girls at the military bases, of course, wanted them to bring back raincoats, slips, material, shoes, you name it. Once I even asked my mother what to ask for.

"Tell them to bring back some material made in Macau. It's the best."

When we arrived in Hong Kong, we checked in at a place called the Hoover Guest House on Nathan Road. The tall building was right next to the pier, the Star Ferry, on the Kowloon side of town. Hong Kong is divided into two sections, with a channel between them. One side is the Kowloon Peninsula, which has the stores, nightclubs, and poor people; the other is Hong Kong Island, which has all the rich people, as well as the beautiful beach called Repulse Bay.

For the first two days, we were busy window-shopping, trying to figure out what we might want to buy when we left for home. On the main street, where we were staying, the jewelry stores lined up one after another for our inspection. After a while, looking at all of those diamonds, jade, rubies, sapphires, emeralds, tiger-eyes, and pearls, I felt numb. Then there were the tailor shops, which guaranteed to make anything for you within twenty-four hours. Other stores were filled with every fancy material imaginable from all over the world. When we walked down the street, a man from each store would try to talk us into entering. Not an inch of space was wasted. I saw hundreds of sampan, where people actually lived. They washed and hung their clothes on lines on the boats. With babies on their backs, women rowed tourists to the Aberdeen, the boat restaurant.

At the back-street market was a menagerie of animals. Every variety dried bird, snake, dog, and monkey was there, not to be sold as food. Chinese druggists displayed twisted roots, dried sea horses, powdered pearls, deer antlers, and big glass jars of pickled or dried snakes, desiccated leaves, and every type of nut. Someone once told me that the Chinese eat live monkey brains while the animal is trapped on top of the table. I was horrified and hoped the man who told me that was only trying to shock me. But the Chinese told me it was true.

Other times, we went up to the Tiger Balm Pagoda, a tacky monument advertising the health benefits of this all-purpose medication. Like the country tourists, we posed for pictures in front of the "pagoda," which was a sculpted concrete vulgarity. The hills rose behind us, as if we were standing in the midst of paradise. I also saw hundreds of billboards advertising Japanese products. Since the Korean economy was still in bad shape in the 1960s, looking at those billboards upset me.

Almost all of the high-rise buildings near the harbor had guesthouses on every floor. Ours, the Hoover, was on the ninth floor. When we got off the elevator, we would walk through a long, narrow dining area. Four or five rooms were lined up on one side. In the middle of the wooden floor, there was a long table, large enough to accommodate nine or ten people. The owner of the Hoover, Mr. Wang, and his wife and two children were from Shanghai. Mr. Wang did all the cooking, and his wife did the other household work. The children were so well behaved and quiet that we hardly ever noticed them. When Madame Chang asked us if we were going to eat at the Hoover or take the expense money, we unanimously agreed that we wanted to eat at the guesthouse. We did not want Madame Chang to steal our meal money again, and besides, Mr. Wang was an excellent cook, and we had a variety of delicious meals every day.

We were to perform three shows at three different places every night. The nine and eleven o'clock shows were on the Kowloon side, and the last show, at one o'clock, was on the Hong Kong side. By the time we reached our guesthouse, washed up, and got ready for bed, it was never before four in the morning. I have no idea if Madame Chang pocketed our share of the room and board, but we were ordered to share one room with two small single beds. I usually shared my bed with Mimi, and Nana slept by herself. She was very friendly with one of the Philippine drummers and sometimes came in later than we did. When the light was off and we were ready to sleep, we often heard Nana playing with herself. Since Mimi and I were so naïve, we would giggle and poke each other at the noises Nana was making.

Hong Kong was a paradise for entertainers. They could work for months without going to any other country. Another good thing was that, unlike in Saigon, where she was on our tails every minute, Madame Chang was staying at another guesthouse, and we never saw her. Once in a while, we would bump into each other on the street or see her picking her teeth after leaving a restaurant.

After our shows, we were often invited over to tables to sit with various businessmen. On one such occasion, a few nights after we had started, we were asked to a dinner party where there were about ten businessmen from Hong Kong, all British. One cute one named Tony asked me out. When the day came, the three of us went down to meet him. Tony was waiting in a red two-seater sports car, and was surely surprised to see three women when he'd expected one. We three girls looked at the car and then at each other.

"How are we going to go in this little bitty thing?" Nana asked in Korean. Being an English gentleman, he quickly got out of the car.

"There's really no problem," he said. "With the top down, two of you girls can sit on the top of the back, putting your feet inside the car, and you can sit in the front with me," he said, looking in my direction.

We were still somewhat reluctant. I didn't know anything about the car, and beyond that, the arrangement just didn't sound right.

"Come on, Mimi and Nana," Tony urged. "Don't worry. You'll love the ride."

Finally we agreed to try it, and so we arranged ourselves according to Tony's plan. When I got into the front seat, Tony gave me a big wink, and off we went. Mimi and Nana were not too happy about their carefully coifed hair flying around in the wind. The next thing I knew, we were on a vehicular ferry. We were fascinated to see that the vehicle was piggybacking on the boat crossing the harbor. We got out of the car and stood by the railing, not caring what happened to our hair, and watched the city all around us. We were each absorbed in our own world. When we reached the Hong Kong side, Tony *zoomed* his little car up steeply winding roads to the top of the hill. At the Peak area, he parked his car. Looking down at the spectacular view of the whole city and sparkling ocean beneath us, we were all speechless. I had a hard time containing myself. I wanted to yell at the top of my lungs, "Hey, out there, I am at the top of the world." The girls forgot all about their uncomfortable ride. We posed to have our pictures taken, sitting and leaning on Tony's car.

Tony seemed to be at all the banquets, and he always brought his guests to our performances. When we were invited to one of those dinner occasions, we were seated at a large table for twelve, and the food never stopped coming. The huge restaurant was filled with those big round tables, all occupied by people. The sound made by the dishes and bowls as people served and ate seemed like a strange concert.

Tony invited all three of us girls to his posh flat overlooking all of Hong Kong. The sea was sparkling, the sampans and houseboats soundlessly moving. Looking around this beautiful flat, I couldn't help but wonder why some people have so much and others have so little.

Others were already there. The men were mostly British, with a few good-looking, long-legged Chinese girls wearing their beautiful *cheongsame* and jade jewelry. Music was playing, and finger foods were placed on the table. An elderly Chinese manservant went around and refilled the glasses. Tony was sitting on the couch and talking to a very distinguished-looking silver-haired British gentleman. As I sat quietly next to them, I heard this older gentleman spelling out a word instead of speaking it. My ears perked up. What secret was this man trying to relate to Tony?

"I am envious of your y-o-u-t-h," he said.

I turned to the gentleman and said, "Well, you had that too sometime in your life."

They both looked at each other with dismay. They did not expect a Korean showgirl like me to know English so well.

Tony told me that he was engaged to a girl in London and was planning to get married as soon as she graduated from school. He was a wonderful dancer, fun to be with, and I enjoyed his good friendship as long as we were in Hong Kong. I also saw John, the businessman who took me out when I'd been in Bangkok. He brought his wife to see our show one evening, but except for that occasion, he never called me. His wife seemed so stiff and hard, and I guessed that he was too well-known in a small city like Hong Kong to be seen with showgirls.

One day, I received a long letter from Mother. It began, "*Dearest, Young-Hee, I was not going to tell you this since I did not want to worry you, but as you know, you are more than a daughter to me. You have always solved all of our problems, and now I wish you were here to do so once again. Your brother Tong-Kun has been in the hospital for almost a month.*" Then my mother wrote to explain that my brother had been hospitalized for a simple appendicitis operation. The hospital had evidently used bad blood in a transfusion. A week after the original operation, they had to cut out most of my brother's liver, and a week after that, they had to remove part of his large intestine. Tong-Kun had just graduated from Seoul National University and had been preparing to take the bar exam. My mother's letter ended, "*Young-Hee yah, I am taking care of Tong-Kun day and night. I understand that there are special pills for liver ailments, and these pills are made in Japan. I wonder if you could get this medicine for your brother. He is lucky that he is still alive.*"

I sat on my bed, dumbfounded.

My brothers were like my own children. I still remember when I was only eight, when the teacher handed out some cookies, I saved mine and brought it home and gave it to my baby brother Tong-Kun. I had always done everything I could for them to ease the pain of our poverty. Now Tong-Kun was fighting for his life, and I became consumed with the thought of getting those pills for him. An equally confounding problem was how to smuggle the medicine, since nothing foreign-made was legally allowed into Korea.

One evening, as if He had heard my prayers, God sent me an angel to solve my problem.

After our second performance on the Kowloon side, two American men asked us to have drinks with them. Of course, none of us drank, so we just had Coke and left to go to Hong Kong for our last performance.

"Can we come along and watch your last show?" they asked, and so we told them the name of the nightclub, not taking them seriously.

While we were dressing for the last performance at one o'clock in the morning, a waiter brought me a note.

"We'll see you after the show," it said. I didn't know who sent the note, and I really didn't care. We got such notes all the time.

"Why don't you go and see them after the show," Nana suggested, "and we'll see those officers whom we met in Kowloon." Because I could speak English, I always dominated the conversations. Nana, who was very pretty and sexy, must have wanted those officers for herself, which was fine with me. I was tired, and all I had on my mind was my brother's illness and his need for those liver pills.

When we left the club, I figured I would go back to the Hoover by myself if Nana and Mimi wanted to go somewhere with the officers. When the taxi came, one of the officers pushed me in the taxi and the other soldier pushed Mimi in. It meant that four of us were jammed in the back of the small taxi while Nana had to sit by herself in the front. The atmosphere was getting stuffy. No one said a word.

We went to the Victoria terminal, and took the last ferry, *Walla Walla,* back to Kowloon. Except for a couple of Chinese men, the ferry was empty. We all sat on a long wooden bench. The water was sparkling, and other than the noise of the engine, there was no sound. When we got off the ferry, the two officers asked Mimi and me if we would like to have a bowl of noodles. I felt bad for Nana, but we left her, went to a back-street noodle stand, busy despite the hour, and had a bowl of Chinese noodles.

"How long are you guys staying in Hong Kong?" I asked.

"We're leaving tomorrow," Gary said. Tall and handsome, he was the one who'd sat next to me in the cab. "Too bad we didn't meet you sooner," he went on. "We've been here two weeks on R & R."

"Where are you staying in Japan?" I asked.

"In Okinawa. We're flight officers."

Suddenly I couldn't concentrate on anything else.

"Yes?" I said, thinking as fast as I could. "Gary, I wonder if you could do me a little favor."

I told him about my brother's illness and asked if he could find the necessary medicine and somehow get it into Korea.

It sounds unrealistic to me now, writing this, but at the time I was only focused on helping my brother. Besides, as I thought it out, being a pilot, he must have been able to take his plane anywhere he wanted to go. Amazingly, he was very sweet about my request.

"Sure, I suppose I could arrange that," he said with a big smile. I wanted to hug and kiss him right there. I didn't ask how or even offer him money. Then I became skeptical. I'd seen too many GIs promise anything just to get what they wanted, and afterward, the girls never heard from them again. Nevertheless, I gave him the name of the pills in Japanese, my home telephone number in Seoul, and we exchanged addresses. I really didn't believe that he would help me despite what he'd said.

A week or more later, I got a letter from my mother, saying that some Korean man who worked at Kimpo Air Base, a U.S. Air Force base in Seoul, had brought two bottles of pills for my brother. I was stunned. Gary had kept his word. Obviously, he could not fly to Korea himself, but he had made an arrangement with one of his Air Force buddies to get the medicine to us. This incident made me reconsider my previous prejudice against American men and restored my faith in humankind. After that, Gary and I kept in touch through letters until he moved back to Kansas and I left Hong Kong. He became more than just a pen pal. I grew very fond of him and tried to find him for a long time, but I never succeeded. More than anything, I wanted to thank him in person, and maybe someday, I will still be able to.

Mother wrote and told me that Tong-Kun was ready to be discharged, but that she didn't have money to pay for the hospital stay. He must have stayed nearly a month. Again I wrote a letter to a long-time American friend in Seoul to help me. Mother told me that Nick sent a man with money, and Tong-Kun was discharged.

After about three months of performing in every nightclub in Hong Kong, it seemed that we were running out of first—and second-class venues. Now we were being booked at dirty Chinese theaters without microphones, or even a band, which left us lip-syncing to taped music. We even performed at a tawdry place called the Wan Chai. It was in the district where the sailors hang out. The famous book and movie called *The World of Suzie Wong* was based on a bargirl who worked at the Wan Chai. I was certain that we could get bookings in other countries, but Madame Chang was determined that we stay in Hong Kong until the last day of our scheduled itinerary.

The final performance date in our contract was nearing. We wanted to stay behind, work for ourselves, and make some money to take with us when we went back to Seoul. We knew, though, that Madame Chang would not permit us to do that, and she held all of our passports and plane tickets. In anticipation of going home, I started buying records and clothes for my brothers and sending them back to Korea.

Nevertheless, we girls talked about how we could perhaps stay behind. Being smarter than Mimi and me, Nana thought we should go on strike and not work at all unless Madame Chang gave us back our passports and tickets. I, who was still very naive, felt guilty but went along. Sure enough, the very next day, the tickets and passports were delivered via a Mr. Cho, a Korean man who ran Madame Chang's errands. But Mr. Cho came back a few days later and said that he had to take all of our passports to the Korean consulate in Hong Kong to extend them, and we had no choice but to give them up.

I found out from Mr. Cho that he, in fact, had done all the bookings for Madame Chang with a Chinese booking agent named Benny Tung. I thought I would jump out of my skin with joy. I talked to Mr. Cho about taking me with him when he went to pick up the passports since he was anxious to come to the United States and that he had something of a crush on me.

"You know how we have worked for Madame Chang for almost nothing," I began. "We just want to stay behind for a few months so we can make some money for ourselves before we go home to Korea. You have to help us."

So we went to the consulate together and got our passports. He also told me that Mr. Tung had booked us in Taipei on the way home. I went to see Mr. Tung and told him that there was no way that we were going to Taipei to perform for Madame Chang under any circumstances. I told him that our contract was over, and we had no further obligation to work for her. "But we will go there if you let us work on our own."

He didn't care for whom we worked, as long as we worked, so he gave us the airline tickets. Only then did I learn that we would get $350 a week with room and board and airline tickets, whereas Madame Chang had paid all of us together less than that per week.

"We're getting out of here. Hurry up and pack," I told the girls. We caught a taxi and went off to the airport. My heart was pounding like a drum. I thought we would be caught at any minute, and imagined a big hand grabbing the collar of my shirt and dragging me to a police station. Even on the plane, we looked around at every face as if we were thieves. Even while performing in Taipei for two weeks, we expected Madame Chang to suddenly appear and drag us back to Korea. Even when we returned to Hong Kong, we were still worried that she would be waiting for us. But she had already left Hong Kong, and we were free at last.

There is an interesting footnote to this part of my life. Years later, in 1969, I went back to Korea right after my marriage, and I saw Madame Chang in a nightclub. She was sitting across the dance hall, staring at me as if she was going to drill a hole in my face. I looked back at her just as ferociously, though I am not sure if she recognized me as Cindy Song.

A few weeks after we girls returned to Hong Kong from Taipei, I received a phone call.

"I am from the Korean consulate," a man's voice said. "Are you girls working in Hong Kong now?"

"Yes," I replied.

"We had a call from the government of Korea saying that you girls are just bumming around Hong Kong without working. If you are not working, we have to send you back."

We knew that Madame Chang had connections, but little did we know how well connected she was until that moment. The whole picture of our tour came into focus at last. The man she was with in Korea must have been in the KCIA (the Korean CIA), the most powerful organization in Korea.

"Actually, I would like to invite you to come and see our show tonight," I told him and gave him the name and the address of the club where we were engaged. I assumed that Madame Chang did not know about my contacting Benny Tung.

An older gentleman from the consulate did come that night, and we went out to meet him after our performance.

"That was a very good show," he said. "Well, it seems that you girls are doing fine, earning dollars for Korea." He paused. "You are sending your money back to Korea, aren't you?"

"Oh yes," the three of us said as if in one voice. "You know, Consul, we are working to help our families. We send back every single penny we make."

"Okay then," he said. "I will report this fact back to Korea."

He left, but with Madame Chang's vindictiveness in his wake.

After six months of doing more or less the same routine, I realized that not only was I bored, but we had performed at every nightclub in Hong Kong, which was why contracts were always for six months. We weren't considered "new faces" any longer, and Mr. Tung paid us only $250 instead of $350. We toyed with the idea of going back to Korea and returning with a new act, but we didn't have the capital, and there would be no guarantee that we would be allowed out of Korea again. We knew that Madame Chang would do everything in her power to stop us. But our bookings in Hong Kong were dwindling, and we had to do something.

Nana decided to go home. She was the only married woman, and she wanted to see her children. Mimi and I decided to stay on a little longer. Mr. Tung said that he could send us to the Philippines, but I declined when I remembered Joanny. I was not that desperate to venture into a country where everyone carried guns. For the moment, we decided to go back to Vietnam. That final trip to Saigon was the beginning of the most significant time of my life. A miracle was preparing itself in ways that would astound me.

Back to Saigon

I'd like to take my heart
And make it into a moon.
It would hang a thousand miles up in the sky,
Find my sweetheart and shine on him.

—Jung Chul (1536-1593)

It is sad not to be loved, but it is much sadder
not to be able to love.

—Miguel de Unamuno (1864-1936, Spanish poet)

Before I left Hong Kong, I sent a cable to Consul Kim at the Korean Embassy in Saigon regarding our arrival, and he arranged for a cheap hotel in Cholon, the Chinese district. The hotel was an old building with thick walls that looked as though they had not been painted since the hotel was built. The front had no door, so anyone could walk in and out, like a mall. The small reception area near the entrance had no furniture except for a small desk pushed into a corner, where a Chinese woman in long black pajama pants and rubber slippers was on duty to answer the telephone. The guest rooms were all on one floor, which was like a maze. We washed in a communal bath with a cement sink and no hot water. Our room was huge with a high ceiling, but the windows were covered by dust-laden heavy drapes so that we couldn't tell if it was day or night. No one there, including the guests, spoke English.

We had a week or ten days to kill before we were to start work at the Van Canh restaurant. Mimi and I decided to go into town. In a café on Tu Do Street, we ordered a couple of French pastries and Chinese jasmine tea. As I sat sipping my tea, a man asked, "Aren't you the singer from Seoul?"

I looked up, startled, at a small Asian man with fair skin. In Korea, when I went to the market or a bathhouse, I would sometimes hear young girls whispering to each other, "That's Song Young-Hee, the singer." But I was surprised to be recognized outside of Seoul. "Yes, I am," I replied in English.

"Then you are a Korean," he said in Korean. "I remember seeing you on TV in Seoul."

The man's name was Mr. Shim, and he was working as a soundman for NBC News out of the Saigon Bureau. He was coming on to me for a date, but even without asking him, I knew that he had to be married, because all Korean men were married, and my rule was never to go out with a married man.

A couple of days later, I received a call from him. "Ms. Song, what about dinner tonight?"

I tried to put him off, but he insisted and suggested that I bring Mimi. I relented, rationalizing that I could use a good meal after the meager dinners we cooked on the portable stove in our hotel room, or the cheap rice noodle soup eaten at the dirty restaurant next to our hotel. I thought bringing Mimi would prevent any undesirable after-dinner activities.

After our meal in a fancy Chinese restaurant not far from our hotel, Mr. Shim suggested that we have a drink in the bar.

"I want to go back to our own hotel," Mimi whispered to me.

I wished that I could go with her, but I didn't have the heart to say good night right after such a good meal. Mr. Shim and I took a tiny taxi to the Caravelle Hotel, where all the foreign reporters were staying. A Vietnamese security officer was sitting at a small desk next to the elevator with folding metal doors. After signing in and leaving my ID with the officer, Mr. Shim said, "You should leave your handbag in my room before we go up to the bar."

Although I understood his intentions, I was too shy to make him lose face. After we left my bag on his bed, we went to the top floor where the bar was located. Not a drinker, I ordered a small crème de menthe, and we sat against corner of wall facing the bar where several foreign men were drinking. An Asian woman and a middle-aged American man waved and joined us.

"This is Ms. Song," Mr. Shim said, introducing me all around. The woman's name was Michico, she was Japanese, and her husband, Syd,

worked at the NBC office in Saigon. Soon after, a handsome Western
man walked in to the bar, and with a glass of the Vietnamese beer
Bar-Bour-Bahe (33) in his hand, he too came over.

Looking at me from the corner of his eye, the young man sat down
beside me.

"Ron, this is Cindy Song, a singer from Korea. She'll be performing
in Saigon. Cindy, this is Ron Nessen, a NBC news correspondent. Ron
just arrived from New York."

Mr. Shim asked how long Ron would be staying in Saigon, and Ron,
still looking at me, said two months. I calculated that would be sometime
in November, about the time when we might be leaving. I snuck glances
at him. He had dark hair and big brown eyes and was wearing an old
faded shirt with half-sleeves and an old beat-up watch.

Mr. Shim asked where he'd go after that.

"I think London," Ron said, putting his cigarette on an ashtray and
exhaling the smoke. As he poured the rest of his beer, he was peeking at
my thigh, exposed in the slit of my pink lace cheongsam. I was getting
a little headache, so I put my hand to my forehead.

"Are you feeling okay?" Mr. Shim asked.

"I just have a small headache from the drink."

"Do you want me to bring you some aspirin?" Ron asked, putting
out his cigarette. "My room's right next door."

I told him I would be all right.

Since the curfew was at eleven, at ten thirty, the bartender called out
for the last round, and everyone finished his drink and signed his own
bill. As we walked out of the bar, Ron asked, "Do you guys want to see
my room?" Number *805* was a spacious suite with a sofa, a few chrome
armchairs, and a shiny marble floor. Then we all squeezed into the tiny
elevator, though I didn't know where Ron was going in the middle of
the night. I hated that Mr. Shim had made me leave my handbag in his
room. What would everyone think when I got off on the fourth floor
with him at almost curfew? As I grabbed my bag and made for the door,
Mr. Shim held my arms, pleading with me to stay.

"Mr. Shim, I am not that kind of girl. If you don't let go of my arm,
I will be very angry."

He apologized, but in front of the hotel, he climbed in my taxi
with me and continued to try and sell himself to me. "I'm going to be
in Saigon for a while, and we can have fun. You can go to Hong Kong
with me on vacation next month."

I wasn't listening. Instead, I was wondering how to see Ron again.

Since I knew Mr. Shim wouldn't give Ron my number, the only thing
for me to do was to call Ron when I got back to my hotel. Mimi was

sitting on the bed and was fixing one of her costumes when I returned to our room. I told her I'd just met the most handsome man and was going to call him. I threw my handbag on the bed and ran out to the front desk. Ron wasn't in, but I left a message.

I told Mimi while I was undressing that Ron had just arrived in Saigon to cover the war, and I wanted to get to know him. "I wonder if he is married."

Mimi lay on our bed with only a bra and panties on, staring at me.

The next day, around noon, the Chinese lady at the front desk yelled, "*Teng Hwa.*" Telephone!

I ran to the front desk and answered tremulously.

"This is Ron. I just got your message."

I was thinking frantically of something to say. "Hi," I managed finally. "I just called you because you looked like someone I knew in Seoul." This was partly true, but not the real reason.

"Look, I'm on my way to cover a story out of town. Can I call you when I get back in about five days?"

In the week before our engagement to perform at Van Cahn, I stayed in my room counting the days and worrying.

"Mimi, suppose something happened to him?" I said. "His face line doesn't have a long life."

Mimi and I were lying on our bed, wearing practically nothing, and the ceiling fan was whirring over our heads. At about five o'clock in the afternoon, the Chinese woman yelled, "*Teng Hwa!*" and I ran out of my room while trying to put my arms into the sleeves of my robe.

"I'm back," Ron said. "Can you meet me at my hotel around seven? Bring your friend, too. I'll bring someone with me."

I ran back to my room and told Mimi to hurry up and get dressed. At the Caravelle Hotel, Ron introduced us to an older man named Jack, who was an NBC bureau chief, and we went to a huge posh nightclub. A Vietnamese girl singer performing with the band reminded me of myself when I used to sing at a nightclub in Seoul. Since I had never been to a French restaurant, I didn't recognize much on the menu and ordered the only foreign dish I knew—spaghetti and meatballs. Ron and Jack ordered appetizers, but I didn't know what an appetizer was. When the waiter brought their first course, Ron was served snails and picked one from its shell to give me. Remembering the snails I used to pick in the slimy rice fields of Yangsan, I couldn't believe how delicious it was, and I ended up eating most of them.

"Boy, you really like snails!" he exclaimed.

Of course, the truth was, I was half-starving. I ate my spaghetti as fast as I could. Ron asked me to dance. He danced wonderfully, even the cha-cha and jitterbug. Most American men didn't dance very well, and I thought what fun he was. He wasn't wearing a ring, but I knew some men just didn't wear rings, and I didn't want to ask him straight out. Instead, I reached for his left hand.

"Let me read your palm," I said, opening his hand.

"Yeah?" he said as he looked at his palm. "Do I have a long life line?"

I studied his marriage line. The two lines between his forefinger and his thumb were wide apart, which meant an early marriage wouldn't survive.

"You have a bad marriage line," I told him. "You should not get married at a young age."

"Hey, look at this girl! She really can read my fortune." He seemed genuinely impressed. "You're right, Cindy. I should never have gotten married. But I'm divorced now."

I learned later that he also had a nine-year-old daughter.

When our singing engagement at the Van Canh finally began, I invited Ron to see our show. Mostly Vietnamese came to this club, but Ron brought his friend, another NBC correspondent named Dean, and Dean's girlfriend, Jill, a photographer (she later became the wife of Kurt Vonnegut, the famous author). She took many pictures during our performance, and after my first song, "*Around the World,*" in swing, I asked Ron to come up on the stage for the next number, "*It's Been a Long, Long Time.*"

"Can you help me?" I asked him.

"I'll try," he said.

So I curled up against him and started to sing.

After my line, I handed him the microphone, and he sang, "*It's been a long, long time.*" Off-key.

"*I haven't felt like this my dear, since I can't remember when,*" I sang in turn.

"'*It's been a long, long time,*'" he repeated, and at the song's end, I gave him a big kiss on the cheek, we both bowed, and he returned to his seat. Dean and Jill were laughing and kidding him. Then Mimi came out and pulled Ron up onto the stage to dance the twist with her. We probably should have paid him for all the help he gave us that night.

Unfortunately, I had to leave the next day for an engagement at a military base near the coast in Nah Tran. The whole time I was gone, I thought of nothing but Ron. In Nah Tran, Mimi and I walked the beach, and it reminded me of the Busan beach, which seemed like another life and another world. I sat on the sand and looked out at the endless ocean, wondering what was on the other side.

"Mimi, did you ever love someone? I mean really love," I asked Mimi, who was lying down next to me with a little handkerchief covering her face to prevent it from getting brown.

"No, not really. When I was younger, I thought I would get married someday and have a family. But after the war and after my father died and his business went bankrupt, I had to work to support my family by dancing. And now I don't know if I will ever get married."

I thought, how sad the fate of most Korean girls. Almost everyone at the time had a similar story.

"You like Ron a lot, don't you?" Mimi asked.

"Yeah, so what? He'll be leaving in a short while, and so will I. Besides, I promised myself I'd never love again. The pain this man has caused me is enough to last my lifetime. Meanwhile, I'll have a good time, right?"

In 1960, soon after I moved to Seoul, I'd met an American man named Nick. He was a general manager for the Post Exchange that served the whole north part of Seoul. He was so jealous of my lifestyle, singing every night for GIs so that we could hardly be together; he literally made both of us sick. First, he ended up in the military hospital with a mysterious high fever, and then I ended up in the German hospital with a bad ulcer. We talked about marriage before I went on a two-month tour to Japan. When I came back, he'd become a totally different man. He wouldn't call or see me. Since I didn't know what the problem was, I was literally going out of my mind. Then there were rumors about how he picked up prostitutes in front of Bando Hotel, one of the well-known hotels in Seoul City. When we were together, he told me all about his difficult childhood, when he was abandoned by his mother and lived in several different foster homes. But to me, it was all a foreign language. Then he joined Army at eighteen and shipped out to Japan. There he found that he could sleep with any woman for the price of a pack or a carton of Lucky cigarettes. Later, he went to school and became an officer. Then he was discharged and got a job at the Post Exchange. Obviously he had "problem" which he knew but didn't confide in anyone. I was rescued from going out of my mind when Madam Chang asked me to join the tour. I promised myself I'd never come back to Korea as long as he was there.

In Hong Kong, I knew a nice older single retired American gentleman who used to live in the penthouse floor of the fancy hotel that was next to our guesthouse. We weren't romantically involved, but he often took us out when we weren't working or came with us when we went shopping. Before I left Hong Kong, he asked me to marry him. I asked him, "Why me, when there are so many beautiful Chinese women in Hong Kong?" His answer was that they only cared about jewelry and money. I guess somehow he knew I was different. I thought about how nice it would be not to ever worry about money, never worry about a man cheating on me, and how nice it would be to live in Hong Kong where I could see my family as often as I wanted to. But the bottom line was that I didn't love him.

When I returned to Saigon, Ron and I saw each other almost every night when I was not working and when he was in town. When we went out for dinner, he was always with his boss. He asked what he could get for me from the PX, but I never asked for anything—using him to get me things never entered my mind. Other times he told me how much more money he was making while he was in Vietnam. Although I was always poor, somehow those subjects never interested me. In Saigon, when we went out with other reporters, they ate, drank, laughed, and argued while I sat, ate, and listened. I was a singer in foreign country with foreign men. I did not care about the war or the news. Their world seemed so far away from where and who I was. Every night I stayed at his hotel, came back to mine the next morning, and then went back to his hotel the next evening.

Sometimes, they had fancy parties on the roof of his hotel. I didn't know who the guests were, but they were all reporters, and pretty famous ones. At one party, I wore a pink lace *cheongsam* and silver stage shoes with a white-and-silver shawl around my shoulders. Beneath the plate-sized moon and the stars sprinkled across the velvet sky above, a candlelit table was set with a gorgeous flower arrangement like a scene out of a movie. Men and women stood around talking and laughing, and I thought how strange these American women seemed, side by side with men, holding their drinks and cigarettes, acting just like them, a scene we would never see in Korea. At dinner, I was introduced to an artichoke appetizer. It looked like a big green flower to me, and I had to watch others out of the corner of my eye to see how to eat it. I was struck by how far away the war seemed from this new part of my life.

Soon after, I came down with the same strange fever that I'd had before, but this time my bones ached, and I was burning up. When I couldn't take the pain any longer, I asked the hotel to send me a masseur in the middle of the night. A small stooped blind Chinese man came to my room. No matter how hard he pressed his fingers on me, I could not feel anything.

The next day, Ron came with an NBC car and took me to a Vietnamese doctor. The doctor poked me here and there and came up with no diagnosis. "Are you pregnant?" he asked. I felt like saying, "Are you stupid? Why don't you shut up if you don't know?"

The fever continued for several days. Then, without my taking any medicine, it slowly subsided. But my palms and the soles of my feet itched like crazy. I scrubbed them with my stiff hairbrush as hard as I could, day and night, but the itching persisted for several days. To this day, I don't know what I had, but it must have killed all the bad germs in my body because after that I never got sick again.

I was beginning to appreciate how sweet Ron was to me. He took me to his NBC office and introduced me to everyone. When Mimi received a letter from home saying that her mother had passed away, she cried over not being able to go home. "What's the use? I won't be able to see her anyhow." When I told Ron, he gave her $200.

Our month-long engagement at the club was coming to an end, but I didn't want to leave Saigon until Ron did. I asked him when he was leaving.

"Well, I think I might stay for a while longer," he said. "What about you?"

A group that I knew was organizing a tour of Europe, but I told them that Europe seemed awfully far from Korea. The truth was I wanted to stay in Saigon with Ron as long as he stayed, and whatever fate had in store, I did not want to control it. *"Follow the stream instead of going against it,"* Confucius said. A few days later, Ron told me that he was staying on in Vietnam indefinitely. Fear overcame me. I had not planned to love Ron, but I knew that I had happiness that I had never experienced before and that with him, all my pain, my sorrow, and my fears seemed to leave my soul. We never spoke of love. But what I felt for him was greater than I could express in words, and I knew then that I would be there for him as long as he needed me.

December came. I saw a small skinny tree sitting on the side table. During the day, on Ron's small record player, I listened to Barbra Streisand's song *"Why Did I Choose You?"* over and over, trying to memorize the words. The song seemed personal to me. With the hot climate and war going on, there was nothing to remind me of Christmas. But early Christmas morning, Ron got up and dressed quickly. "I'll be right back," he told me.

When he returned, he brought a little flat-nosed puppy, a shih tzu, a Chinese dog about the size of my hand. I had often talked about how much I'd missed my Pomeranian, Bobby, who I'd left back home, and I still carried Bobby's picture with me everywhere. I was touched that Ron had found the perfect gift to ease my longing.

With more GIs being sent to Vietnam, Mimi and I had more jobs, sometimes working two or three places on weekends. Then Ron invited me to a black-tie party for New Year's Eve, the busiest payday of the year for entertainers. "Would you come with me?" he asked.

I was torn. That was the one night I could demand more money. I didn't say yes or no right then. A few days later, we were in his office watching one of the pieces he'd taped earlier. I sat behind him, rubbing his back.

"Did you decide what you're going to do about New Year's?" he asked.

"Yes," I said.

"Well?"

"Didn't you give me an order to come with you?" I said, laughing.

To be honest, I was afraid Ron would take someone else if I said no. In February, he asked me to accompany him to Bangkok. In November, he'd gone to Hong Kong on vacation alone. I'd been secretly excited that he might ask me along, and I thought it would be nice to do some shopping. Also, I wanted to bring back the suitcase that I had left behind with Mr. Williams, the older gentleman, because I didn't realize I would be away so long.

"Can I go with you?" I'd asked.

"No, you can't come," he replied.

I had read one of the letters from a woman in New York that mentioned something about her trip to Hong Kong in November. I knew he was meeting her there and that she was one of the many women with whom he had affairs before he left the United States. I was hurt, and tears welled in my eyes. From Hong Kong, he sent me postcards saying that in the future he would not take his vacations without me, and when he returned, he made sure that the NBC driver took me to the airport to meet him.

For our trip to Bangkok, I was worried about the airfare. I didn't know how much Ron was making, and I couldn't afford to pay for my trip. But he traded the first-class ticket that NBC provided for two economy-class tickets. I, of course, remembered my last trip there with Madame Chang. This time, instead of being half starved in a dingy, shared room, I stayed at a fancy hotel. One day Ron wanted to stop at a bank to withdraw $3,000 in American currency in order to exchange the currency on the black market because there the rate was higher.

When Ron asked for $3,000 in cash, I saw a few men in the back of the bank talking with serious expressions on their faces. I whispered to Ron, "They probably want to know why you need all that money in cash."

Ron looked worried. "What should I tell them if they ask me?"

My brain started spinning. I whispered, "Just tell them that you borrowed the money in cash, and you have to pay it back in cash."

Still looking at those men, Ron said, "I'm glad you are here with me."

When they handed him the money, we ran out as fast as we could. I think they were trying to get together all the money they had. It reminded me of an old proverb: "The thief trips over from his own foot." We saw the floating market that sold everything imaginable from boats. At the Golden Temple, Ron took pictures of me clowning around and imitating the Buddha statue. He bought Thai silk for his mother and Thai royal dolls for his daughter's collection. When not being tourists, we sat around beside the hotel pool, and I taught him how to interpret dreams, good and bad. "If you dream about fire or a pig, you'll obtain some money, but if you see women or money, that means trouble."

I told him that one should never give a handkerchief or shoes to his lover.

"Why?" he asked.

"Because they both mean good-bye. With the handkerchief, a lover will wipe her tears. With shoes, the lover will walk away."

Everything I told him about Asian proverbs or customs, Ron jotted down in his notebook.

I dreamed about my father while in Bangkok, the first and only time I ever saw him in my dreams. He was on a boat, which was leaving me behind on the shore. The dream woke me, and I cried. Why was I seeing my father? Was he telling me that he was leaving me because now I was in good hands, and I no longer needed him to watch over me? I had worried about supporting my family so intensely for so long that I'd lived in a permanent state of tension and had never been able to experience such a vacation free of worries. For the first time in my life, I was with someone who cared about me and who seemed to want to make me happy.

One day we decided to see an American movie. In front of the theater, a line of stands selling roasted dried squids hung on the line. I had not seen squid since I'd left Korea, where it was considered a delicacy and very expensive, and I felt as though I had run into a family member. More excited about the squid than the movie, I bought one and sat in the theater chewing happily on the squid. I didn't care what was on the screen. Years later, in Washington DC, Ron revealed how disgusted he'd felt that night, watching me sucking on the smelly squid.

I wish that he could have joked about it or teased me, but we were so careful not to say or do anything to hurt each other's feelings then that the resulting gap in communication later became a great source of problems between us.

Two months later, in April, we went to Kuala Lumpur in Malaysia, since correspondents in Vietnam got two-week vacations every two months. Ron's birthday was May 25, and I wanted to buy him a nice watch to replace the old one he wore. Koreans do not give small gifts; to do so is considered humiliating. I only knew of the brands Omega and Rolex and didn't have a lot of money, but I wanted to get one that he would like.

"Between an Omega and a Rolex, what kind of watch do you think is nicer?" I asked.

Ron just looked puzzled.

I went shopping by myself, and it quickly became obvious that I couldn't afford a gold Rolex, so I settled on an Omega made of stainless steel. When I came back to the hotel, Ron presented me with a small gold Rolex lady's watch, so I gave him the stainless steel watch before his birthday. Each of us realized the gifts were important symbols of how we felt, and Ron showed off his watch to everyone.

My pledge that I would never *"let the sleeping tiger awake again"* was not quite working. I was afraid. I was happy with Ron, but he was often away, and I was constantly on edge worrying about his welfare. I gave him a good-luck charm, a tiger tooth on a chain, to protect him. After watching me carry my dresses back and forth between his hotel and mine every day, Ron asked me to move in with him. Mimi and I were working less and less, since I was the one who lined up our bookings and my time was totally consumed with Ron. I felt guilty at first about Mimi, but she kept herself busy socializing with Korean soldiers and other friends while waiting for me to decide what we were going to do.

When Ron was out of town, I stayed in his room, reading his books: James Michener's *Sayonara* and Richard Mason's *The World of Suzie Wong*. He often said I was between Suzie Wong and Lucy from Charlie Brown comic. When I read Grant Wolfkill's *Reported to Be Alive,* about his experience as a captive in Cambodia, I feared that the same thing might happen to Ron. I also read all the letters he was receiving from Washington, including one from his mother that warned him to be careful because I might be a Vietcong. Most of the letters were from women who gushed about how handsome he looked on TV, but I was particularly interested in reading the letters from his girlfriend in Washington DC, who had been the cause of his divorce. She talked about his coverage from Vietnam on the *Huntley-Brinkley Report.* I had no idea what or who *Huntley and Brinkley* were or how famous Ron was. All I knew was that he was the sweetest man on earth, and no one had ever treated me as he did, and I couldn't do enough for him in return.

I pampered him when he was in Saigon, laying out his underwear and socks when he took a shower, soaking his hairbrush and washing it every day. Korean women treat their men something between a little child and a king. Ron praised me, saying that American women were unhappy because they thought of themselves and their careers instead of only their men. He told me that I was a "real woman" who believed that the one thing that would make me happy was giving my life to my man.

I never said "*I love you*," as many American women do, but I believed that actions spoke louder. When I was fourteen years old and in high school, I wrote a poem called "Love." I don't remember the exact words, but it went something like this:

> *What is love?*
> *Love is something we cannot feel with our touch,*
> *we cannot see with our eyes,*
> *we cannot smell with our nose,*
> *we can't cut it with a knife,*
> *but it is tougher than iron,*
> *more beautiful than any flower,*
> *smells better than any fragrance,*
> *and it is fearless against any threat and it can conquer the world.*

For our July vacation, we went to Hong Kong, our favorite place, and stayed at the Grand Hotel. We went out with staff people from the local NBC bureau—once on someone's big yacht from which I even tried waterskiing. Another evening we took a sampan, a boat rowed by a woman with a baby on her back, to Aberdeen, the houseboat restaurant. Inside a square metal cage underwater next to the restaurant, we scooped up our own fish and lobster to be cooked. One day, we went together to a jewelry store in our hotel and picked out a simple—1-karat—but flawless diamond ring.

We went to a small Chinese restaurant and climbed the narrow staircase to the first floor, which, like most Chinese restaurants, was partitioned into private rooms. With a pair of tongs, a waiter handed us hot towels smelling of disinfectant and then he poured hot tea. I held out my left hand and admired my ring, turning it this way and that, watching the sparkling stone under the light while Ron watched.

"You know, this ring is just to see if everything will be okay," he cautioned. Since he had just gotten over a bitter divorce, he was apprehensive about commitment. But having never even married, I had no idea what he meant, nor did I care. I wanted the ring, engagement ring or not. I was happy that I could show it off to the people in Saigon.

When we were alone, I asked everything, and he told me the details of his life—his childhood, his affairs with different women, his painful divorce, how much he missed his daughter, and how he still mourned a son who'd died at five from cancer. I didn't care what he had done with other women, or how many women there were before we met. I just wanted to understand who he was. He told me I was the only person he felt comfortable with, and I liked him best when we were alone because he was relaxed and not trying so hard to be someone he wasn't. He never asked anything about me.

A couple days after we returned from Hong Kong, Ron left on assignment, and I was getting ready for bed around midnight when Jill knocked on my door. She sat down on the couch without saying anything.

"Cindy, come and sit down," she said.

Puzzled, I sat next to her.

"I have something to tell you," she said nervously. "Ron was hurt . . . don't worry, he's okay, but he was hurt."

I went numb. The very thing I had been dreading had come to pass.

Jill explained that at about four thirty that afternoon, the military had notified NBC that Ron had been wounded. Ron Steinman, the new bureau chief, called Jill, and being a strong American woman—Korean women wouldn't think of doing what Jill did for me—she demanded that NBC arrange to fly me to Pleiku field hospital, where Ron would be treated. NBC worked on it all afternoon, calling every important person in the United States Army, I imagined, and finally getting permission. I'm not sure they would have arranged this if I hadn't gotten a ring from Ron.

"Dean and I will come and get you at four tomorrow morning," she said. "The NBC car will meet us in front of the hotel. Meanwhile, I want you to get some sleep and pack something for Ron."

Somehow I couldn't cry. But I was shaking like a rice paper door in the cold winter wind, and my teeth chattered as I walked from one room to another like a person who had lost her mind. I was trying to imagine what had happened and, of course, was prohibited from knowing anything. John S. Lang, a New York Post correspondent, later described the incident in an article.

At 13:30 hours on July 12, 1966, Nessen was with the 101st Airborne who were firing into the jungle on the far side of a scummy stream in the delta. They only wanted to fill their canteens, but tactics required that they do a reconnaissance fire to see if the enemy was waiting in ambush. Nessen watched the maneuver, vaguely bemused by the awful noise of the weaponry. He remembers seeing leaves flipping back toward the Americans and thinking that someone was returning fire. There was something like a playful finger-thump on his chest. And then his world went black. His throat filled with blood, and troopers were preparing to give him a tracheotomy with a penknife when he had a convulsion that cleared the obstruction. The nearest aid station was three miles away, too far to reach by foot. But a colonel, with whom he had breakfast that morning, happened to hear of his wounding and came for him in a helicopter.

Four o'clock next morning, Jill, Dean, and I sat at the stairs of the hotel waiting for the NBC car to arrive. While Jill curled up to Dean, I sat next to them like a sack of rice. I wasn't really there. My thoughts were with Ron. Would he be alive when I reached him? Would he be conscious?

A car with a Vietnamese driver came, and we went directly to the Tan Son Nhut Airport. In contrast to the black inside of me, the place was splashed with the early sun coming through the windows and packed with GIs. I met a new correspondent, Lem Tucker, who was supposed to accompany me. I moved like a wooden toy someone had just wound up, and we boarded a giant cargo plane filled with soldiers, sitting against the wall among the GIs. A voice over a loudspeaker said something about the procedures to follow if the plane was hit, but I barely listened; the thought of dying before I reached Ron was only a vague distraction. When we arrived at the field airport, a jeep drove us to the hospital—a Quonset hut in the middle of nowhere.

"Why don't you wait here for me," Lem said. "I'll go and find out whether Ron is here. They might have flown him back to Saigon."

He came back within a few minutes and took me to the nurses' quarters to rest while he tried to find out more information. A young nurse by the name of Joan Rogers gave me her bunk and said that I should lie down. I was tired, but all I could do was sit on the end of the bunk and stare into space. About thirty minutes later, Lem rushed back and told me that a plane had just landed and that we should go and see if Ron was onboard. We ran back to the Quonset hut. Many GIs were standing or sitting outside, all in fatigues. Inside, beds were lined up on both sides. Every bed was filled, and everyone looked the same. I started from the first bed, walking down the row, examining their faces. Then I saw Ron. He was pale like the others. He was still wearing his army fatigue pants, socks, but nothing on top. Tubes were hooked up to him everywhere. He wasn't aware of me until I touched his foot. "What are you doing here?" he asked. Later, he told me that after he'd been shot, his only fear had been that he would die before having the chance to marry me.

Soon Ron was moved to an intensive care hut with one other soldier, who was tied to his cot and unable to speak. He had a hole in his throat, and an air pipe was attached for him to breathe. It would be blocked when he wanted to speak. Doctors and nurses were always around him. A nurse, sitting at his bedside, read him a letter from his wife. Everyday, she read the same letter over and over. A few times each day, they removed the air pipe from his neck, flipped him over, left him in that position for ten minutes or so, flipped him back up, and put the pipe back in.

One day, after the man was flipped down, all the nurses and a doctor ran out. A few minutes later, the men's arm was flapping up and down. He wanted something, but what could I do? Then a nurse came back in, calling, "Sergeant, are you alright?" No response. She kept calling. Then she ran out and brought more people. They flipped him over and pumped his chest calling his name. Finally, he was back. That scene always stayed on my mind, wondering whether he ever made it back to his family. Ron stayed there for five days with me at his side. I slept on one of the empty cots, and after three days, I was able to help him walk to the latrine; the following day, I helped him wash his hair. When it was time to fly him back to Saigon on a military plane, I sat next to him on the stretcher, holding his hand. All the while he worried about his job. I didn't understand why he was so concerned about a job when he had almost died. But I eventually understood that a correspondent's job is as insecure as a singer's, and without a renewed contract, there wasn't any guarantee of work.

Ron was taken to a military hospital near the Tan Son Nhut Airport. He still hadn't heard from NBC. He didn't know if he was going to be sent back to the States, and while waiting for a visit from his boss, who never came, he was quite irritable. He was asking everyone if they'd heard anything from New York, especially what was going to happen to his job or where he would be stationed. He even yelled at me. I was hurt, and I didn't go to see him the following day. When I went back next day, he gave me a handwritten letter that said how he had waited and waited and when I still hadn't come at the end of the day, he thought he would have been better off if he had died when he was wounded.

Finally, a few days later, word came that Ron was to fly to Washington and be admitted to Walter Reed Hospital. He was brought out on a stretcher and loaded into an ambulance. "I'll write you," he said.

But I believed that was the last time I would ever see him. As the ambulance drove out of the gate, I never knew that the noise of an engine could hurt so much. I walked out crying, and once inside my cab, I screamed. In the empty hotel room, I lay on the bed and cried more. The details of our eleven months together flashed in front of my eyes like a movie. I remembered the last scene from *Love Is a Many-Splendored Thing*, the true love story of an American correspondent and a Eurasian doctor. Before the main character was killed in the Korean War, he wrote a last letter to his girlfriend. In it he said, "*Suyin, God has been so good to us. Somebody once said that it is a 'tragedy not to be loved.' We have not missed, you and I, we have not missed the many-splendored thing.*"

I stopped crying then. Had God been good to me? Yes, I had loved. I had loved with my life, and even in death I would love. Yes, I would go on loving him as long as there was a soul within me.

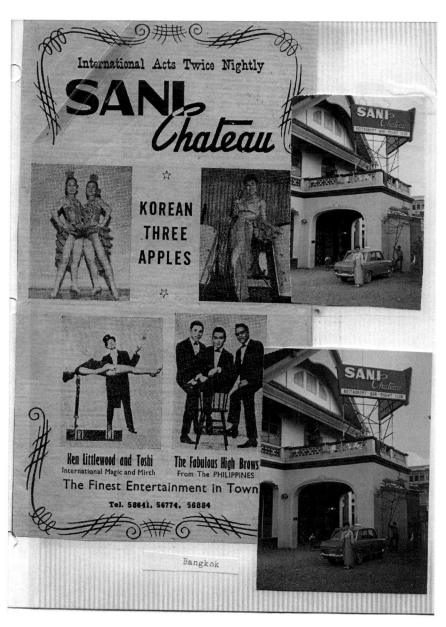

1st night club in Bangkok

Modeling, 1955
Below, when I started my singing career

My first blue gown from Sears Roebuck

Opening number, Arirang

1964 Opening number, Arirang

Cindy on the left while Mimi is on the right

Finale, Hong Kong

Performing in Hong Kong

Nana, me, Mimi

Hong Kong

Hong Kong on Tony's sports car

Saigon with Mimi, Nana and me

Saigon 1965

Bangkok

1964 Bangkok
Mimi, Nana and Cindy

1964 Singapura Continental, Cindy, Madam Chang, Mimi,
Nana waiting to go on stage

Korean Embassy staff
welcomed us with flower.

Saigon

On a tricycle

Ron dancing the Twist with Mimi at Van Cahn

The picture was taken by
my photographer friend Jill Krementz"

1965 I am singing to Ron at Van Cahn night club in Saigon.

This picture also taken by Jill Krementz.

First vacation in Bangkok

1966 Vacation in Malaysia in my bikini

Entertaining Korean troops in Saigon

Singing to the Korean troops in Vietnam

1966 Last vacation in Hong Kong, on sailboat.

New York

Shall I die and forget him,
Or shall I live and keep longing for him?
It is hard to forget:
Yet hard to keep longing.
Only if you tell me how,
I can decide which path to take.

—Me-Hwa (famous kisang, geisha)

Once a woman has given you her heart,
You can never get rid of the rest of her.

—Sir John Vanbrugh (1664-1726)

I could not be in Saigon, where everything reminded me of Ron, so I decided to go back to Hong Kong with Mimi. Looking out the plane's window, I kept asking myself why. Had I committed a crime in my previous life? As I closed my eyes and leaned back, scenes from *Love Is a Many-Splendored Thing* kept flashing through my mind. Many of my ideas about life and love had been influenced by Hollywood, but this particular film seemed to speak directly to my situation. The Eurasian heroine tells her correspondent lover that in China, people hide their happiness out of fear of angering of the Jealousy God. I had never been happier than those last months in Saigon with Ron. Had I angered the Jealousy God?

Mimi and I checked into the Hoover Guest House, where we had
stayed the year before, and our agent, Mr. Tung, booked us at the clubs
where we used to work. Because we'd been away for almost a year, we
could pass as a new act. But between shows I could neither eat nor
sleep. Ron promised he would write before he left Saigon, but no letters
came. *Had he already forgotten me? Was he still alive?* I didn't know an
airline strike was preventing me from getting his letters. Then finally,
they arrived in bunches. The typewritten words looked like black ants
covering the pages from one corner to the other, and Ron sounded
just as depressed and distraught as I. He thought I wasn't writing and
begged me to respond. Not knowing where I would be, he'd also sent
copies of his letters to Saigon. His letters, like his diary, contained every
detail from morning to night; his daily breath therapy for his injury,
how he discouraged all of his former girlfriends from calling because
he was now an engaged man, how he couldn't sleep at night from
thinking about me and had to take sleeping pills. Being away from me,
he wrote, made him realize how people who are in love feel everything
with such great intensity, both the pain and the happiness. He wanted
to see how he felt without me but finally realized what a mistake he had
made by not bringing me with him to the United States. He told me
to get a tourist visa and come. But because we'd traveled everywhere
together while we lived in Saigon, he had no idea how hard it was for
an Asian to get a visa to the United States. He thought perhaps the
NBC bureau chief and his Chinese office manager, Kenneth, might
be able to help.

Reluctantly, I went to the American consulate in Hong Kong with
Kenneth. I signed in at the desk, and as I sat waiting to be interviewed,
scenes from another of my favorite movies, *Sayonara*, came to mind. In
this film, an American GI falls in love with a Japanese girl. To break up
their relationship, the army orders him back home. He wants to marry
her so he can bring her back to America with him. When the army
refuses, they both commit suicide. The Jealousy God strikes again, and
it was strange how my life was beginning to imitate movies.

The consulate waiting room was packed with Chinese. *Did the
entire population of Hong Kong want to go the States? What if I was rejected?*
I grew more nervous and felt like a criminal about to be questioned
by the police. *What if I said the wrong thing? What was the right thing to
say?* My palms began to sweat, and my heart started to beat like Mimi's
drum.

After what seemed like an eternity, a man behind the counter
beckoned me over.

"What kind of form do you want?" he asked.

My mind went blank. Finally, I blurted, "I . . . want a visa for the United States."

"I know that," he replied impatiently. "But what kind of visa? Do you want to emigrate?"

"Can I?"

"That depends. What nationality are you?"

"Korean."

"I don't know if there's a quota for you," he said, leaving the counter.

Quota? What's a quota? I wondered. A few minutes later he came back.

"No, you cannot emigrate," he told me.

"Then I want a visa to visit," I said.

He handed me a form for a tourist visa, and I went back to my seat. The form asked me to state my reason for visiting the States. *Should I say that I wanted to go as a tourist or that I wanted to visit my fiancé? Perhaps if I told them that he was wounded in the Vietnam War, they might sympathize with me.*

When my name was called, I was confronted by a large woman perched at a desk in a small corner of the office. She wore a shapeless dress printed with big brown flowers, her bulging cheeks reminded me of a soft white rice bun, and her big bottom hardly fit on the little chair. She introduced herself as Ms. Jones.

As soon as I heard her say "Ms.," I said to myself, *Uh-oh, you're in trouble.* In Korea, when I used to work for GIs, it was a well-known fact that American women resented Asian women marrying American men.

"Why do you want to go to the States?" demanded Ms. Jones.

"My fiancée was wounded in the Vietnam War," I replied. My mouth felt as dry as if I had swallowed a handful of sand. "He's in a hospital in Washington DC, and I want to visit him."

Her grayish eyes behind her thick glasses reminded me of the eyes of dead fish I used to watch my mother clean.

"I worked in the consulate in Seoul after the Korean War," Ms. Jones said icily. "There were lots of GIs there who wanted to take their girls back home, but we didn't allow it. If they were really serious, those guys had to spend money, which they often didn't have, to come back and marry the girls first."

I sat there listening to her lecture me, as if I were the one who had done something wrong. I knew what her answer was going to be.

"If I give you a visa, you'll go to the States. Maybe you'll marry your boyfriend. Maybe you won't. But whatever happens, you'll never go back to Korea." She put my application away in a file. "Tell your fiancée to marry you first before he takes you back."

I left the consulate, not knowing where to go or what to do. Now I believed I might never see Ron again. The city that had seemed to be paradise only a month earlier with Ron now appeared as dark and gloomy as my own soul. I returned to the guesthouse and lay on my bed feeling the long, long ache of desperation.

I stayed up all night, every night. And every morning at dawn, I began waiting, waiting, waiting for Mr. Wang, the guesthouse owner, to slip a letter from Ron under the door. He wrote how crushed he was to learn about the rejection of my visa. Kenneth told him that a mistake had been made in putting down the reason for my coming to the United States, and they were working very hard to straighten things out through the U.S. State Department and the White House. He told me that the old maid at the consulate was not being mean or deliberately keeping me out of the United States; she was simply following the law, and we had to convince her that I wasn't coming to the States to settle down permanently. Ron sent a long cable via Kenneth to tell the consulate that I had many attachments in Korea that I did not intend to abandon. I was supporting my mother and brothers there and my singing career that I planned to continue. Ron advised me to stick with Kenneth and do exactly as he said. I shouldn't have been so depressed, because in all of the great love stories, the lovers are separated for a while so that they can realize how much they love each other. If the visa took too long, Ron promised to fly to Hong Kong, but for the time being, his doctor would not let him.

Although I lived for his letters, they did little to help me fight the depression that had overtaken me. *Did all true love suffer? Was this the only way to know how much I loved him?*

Even during that time when I thought I was dying of tuberculosis, I hadn't felt this much pain and hopelessness. This time, the pain seemed to paralyze me, and I couldn't perform anymore. I sang with tears rolling down my face, and I lost so much weight that all my costumes hung loosely on my body.

Then Mr. Tung booked Mimi and me in Taipei. I didn't care about Taipei or anywhere else. I didn't want to leave Hong Kong even for one day, thinking that I couldn't get Ron's letters while I was gone. But when Ron heard that I was going to Taipei for two weeks, he called NBC to track me down and tell me that I should apply for a visa again when I got there.

When I received his message, I was skeptical. *What miracle would change my fate?* I had already been rejected once, but I went ahead and applied at the American Consulate in Taipei. During the next two weeks, my life continued in the same dreary pattern. Every night I managed somehow to get through my performance, and every morning I woke up and tried to remember if I'd had any good dreams.

At the very end of our two-week engagement, the consulate called me in, and I went with Mimi.

"So you're the one who knows the big shot in the States, eh?" the consul said, taking my passport and waving it in the air as he walked out of the room. I wondered what he meant. A few moments later, he was back.

"Your passport," he said. "And your visa for the United States."

I thought I had heard incorrectly. "You are saying . . . I can go . . . to the States?"

"Yes."

"When?" I managed to say.

"Anytime. Right now, if you have a ticket." I had been standing, but now I had to sit. Mimi was wiping away tears. I didn't know if she was crying because she was happy for me or sad about her own uncertain future.

Back in Hong Kong, I gave most of my music (but I saved a few and it came handy later when I worked at the dinner theater) and costumes to the other Korean performers I knew. Assuming that my new life would be one long string of parties at nightclubs, as I had seen in so many old American movies, I had evening dresses and a satin coat made. I even bought a fur wrap on the advice of another Korean singer who convinced me that furs were very expensive in the United States, though I later learned that she received a commission from the store for handing out such advice. I even had a long white Chinese dress with French lace and a matching jacket made for my wedding ensemble. We hadn't made any real wedding plans, but why else would Ron bring me to the States when he knew I had to work for a living?

On September 25, 1966, I left Hong Kong on Northwest Airlines. The plane was literally empty. As we took off, I realized that I was more nervous than excited. A few years earlier, I would have been thrilled simply to be en route to the United States, a destination dear to the hearts of most Asians. Now I didn't care where I was going, just as long as Ron was there. But I also wondered if I was pursuing the right dream. *Would this plane crash for my defying the Jealousy God?* I looked out the window and saw the cotton-ball clouds covering the ocean below me. They reminded me of the winter comforter my mother had made when I was a little girl. I had tiptoed around the edge, pretending I was floating in the air. My mother's voice still rang in my ear: *Young-Hee yah, get off the cotton. You'll flatten the cotton.* In spite of all my struggles, I was still at heart the same good little Young-Hee who had warmed her toes under her mother's comforter so many years ago. I prayed softly, "Please, God, don't let this plane crash."

When the plane landed in Seattle, Washington, I found myself in a different world. Everyone seemed tall and had yellow hair and white faces. I stood in the baggage area, waiting and waiting. All the baggage had been claimed, but mine was nowhere to be seen. *Was this a sign of God's jealousy?*

"Your baggage probably will arrive on the next flight. You can wait for it until then," a customs official suggested. He gave me a six-month visa. But I couldn't wait to see Ron and left the agent a forwarding address, the only one I had, which was Ron's mother's apartment in Washington DC. Ron had moved to New York to work on an NBC special on Vietnam, but I didn't know that yet.

At the John F. Kennedy Airport, the first thing I saw was Ron and Jill waiting for me. I suddenly felt shy and nervous. I had lost so much weight over the past two months that I was embarrassed to face him, so instead of running to meet him, I walked off the plane behind a tall American. When I popped out from behind my human shield, Ron jumped in surprise. Then he hugged me and held me close to him for a long time without speaking. Jill stood next to us, wiping away her tears. As for me, I was absolutely numb. Why? I don't know. I wasn't sure I was actually in Ron's arms.

In the taxi from the airport, I expected to see the same sights I had seen in all the movies about New York—tall skyscrapers, sleek limousines, glamorous women entering and exiting their canopied apartment buildings with doormen in tall black hats and long tailcoats. Instead, I saw crowded, dirty streets, seedy buildings, and scowling pedestrians bundled up against the cloudy, raw weather. Then Ron took me up to his run-down, walk-up apartment on First Avenue on the East Side. It was not the apartment with shiny marble floors that I thought every American lived in. In fact, it made my humble house in Seoul seem like a castle. In the bedroom, there was a high brass bed with the mattress sunk so low that I thought it would touch the floor if anyone lay on it. In the living room, there was a dirty old mushy couch that a Korean wouldn't consider sitting on. Later I discovered that Ron had to find a place in a hurry for my arrival and sublet someone else's apartment.

It was cold in New York, and I had no clothes except for the summer suit I had worn on the plane. My only solution, for the time being, was to change into one of Ron's T-shirts until I got my suitcase back, which wouldn't be long, I thought. For the next few days, Ron called the airport repeatedly but was unable to find out anything about the luggage. One morning I overheard him in an angry conversation; his mother had the suitcase all along but had not bothered to tell us. He left the apartment, saying he was going down to Washington to pick it up, but he neglected to tell me how long the trip would take. When he hadn't returned by two that afternoon, I started to worry again. I wanted to call his office, but when I looked at all those letters next to the numbers on the telephone, I wasn't sure how to make the call. All I could do was sit on the couch in Ron's T-shirt, looking out the window at an iron fire escape. At six o'clock that evening, he got back, carrying my one small cloth suitcase. Ron asked, "Is this bag all you brought?" Not knowing exactly how much the airline would allow me to bring and conditioned by Madame Chang's nagging about how she didn't want to pay for excess baggage, I had discarded all the dresses I had accumulated in Asia—all the beautiful sequined dresses that would have come in handy later for White House events. Now we both realized that I didn't have any proper clothes for the New York winter.

The next morning Ron took me to Bloomingdale's on his way to work and shopped with me for half an hour before leaving me to my own devices. I rode the escalator up and down, buying dresses, sweaters, miniskirts, fishnet stockings, and a beautiful plaid pantsuit, all with the cash Ron had given me. At the end of the day, with several shopping bags filled with clothes, I ended up on the lower level, where the shoe department was located. I put my bags next to a chair, thinking I would never do this in Korea, but what a wonderful feeling to be able to trust people here. I was busy trying on all the beautiful shoes. Finally, I picked a pair and looked for my bags before paying. They were gone. The salesman suggested that I go up to the lost-and-found, but I knew it was hopeless.

I left the store empty-handed. The street was dark, and there was a huge rush of cars and people going in every direction. I don't remember how I got back to Ron's apartment. I wondered how I could tell him what had happened. When he came home, I was crying. At first I couldn't answer, but with encouragement from Ron, I eventually blurted out the story.

"You'll just have to go back tomorrow and buy them all over again," he said.

Soon after, there was a fire in the apartment next to ours. I grabbed my new pantsuits, and Ron took his briefcase with our passports in it. The firemen stopped the fire from spreading to our apartment, but when Ron told his friends about the incident, he jokingly said, "There was a fire, and Cindy only worried about her new pantsuits from Bloomingdale's." I knew he was kidding, but I wondered what else I was supposed to worry about.

Ron took me with him for one of his weekly checkups at Walter Reed Hospital in Washington DC and dropped me off at his mother's apartment. I had seen photographs of her, so I knew what she looked like. But I was unprepared for her attitude toward me. She sat me in a corner of her kitchen at the breakfast table and put some cookies in front of me. What his mother didn't know was that Koreans aren't very fond of sweets. However, she had far more important subjects to discuss before Ron got back.

"Ron's sister, Sheila, married a young man we were against," she began. "On their wedding day, it snowed so hard that we couldn't open the front door. It was God's way of saying that this wasn't a good wedding." Then the phone rang and she answered. "Yeah, she's here. I'll talk to you later." I assumed it was Ron's sister calling to check on what was going on. Then she turned back to me. "Of course, children never listen to their parents. Sheila got married anyway, and soon after that they were divorced."

Going back and forth to the kitchen counter, she continued, "When Ron was wounded and sent home, it was another message from God. Ron is not the marrying kind."

People had told me that Jewish mothers could be very possessive and disapproving of their sons marrying women from other faiths. But it's the same way with Korean woman. I wondered if she was trying to prevent me from getting hurt, or if she just did not want a Korean daughter-in-law. When she never asked me a single thing about me and I didn't say much more than yes and no the whole time, I became convinced that the second was Mrs. Nessen's attitude.

After that, whenever Ron and I went to Washington, we avoided visiting or calling his mother. Eventually, she called me one afternoon when I was alone.

"You mean to say that you were here and did not tell Ron that he should see his mother?" I didn't want to lie, but also I didn't want to make her angry. "Mrs. Nessen, please," I said. "We Korean girls are not in the habit of telling our men what to do."

She hung up without saying another word.

Food proved to be another of the biggest hurdles to my adjustment. Shortly after my arrival in New York, Ron took me to a small neighborhood grocery store. He grabbed a cart and led me up one aisle and down another. "You have to do this systematically," he said.

What use was a system, I wondered, when all these strange jars and cans meant nothing to me? I was looking for Korean "fat rice" and *kimchi*, Korean spicy pickled cabbage, which is essential for every Korean meal. Neither was available, so I reluctantly settled on a small bag of long-grain rice, which brought back unpleasant memories of having to eat this type of rice after World War II, when we Koreans were the starving recipients of American CARE packages. Ron, in the meantime, had loaded our cart with strange heavy doughnuts he called bagels, a sickly-looking yellow fish he called smoked whiting, and white paste called cream cheese.

When Ron was in town, we went out every night to Italian, Chinese, and French restaurants. Nothing ever tasted right to me, not even Chinese food. On top of every dish, I poured Tabasco sauce and even put Tabasco sauce on custard. When we went to restaurants with friends, I studied the menu forever, since I had no idea what the food was like. Embarrassed, Ron would say, "If you don't like what you choose, I will eat it."

"When Koreans can't have *kimchi*," Ron used to tell his friends jokingly, "they go into withdrawal symptoms after a few days." I think there is more truth to his statement than Ron knew. Our brains don't seem to function well without *kimchi*. (Much later, when Ron and I were in Japan, Ron acted just as badly about not having sweets.) When I first arrived, however, I became obsessed with my desire for it and walked around in a kind of daze, thinking about it all time.

I also had trouble adjusting to customs regarding food. Ron and I were invited to dinner at a lawyer's house, and I literally starved all day. In Korea, we don't entertain at home a lot, but when we do, so many different dishes are served that the legs of the table strain under their weight. These lavish offerings reflect the host family's utmost sincerity and respect for their guests, but at my first U.S. dinner party, I was stunned. The food they served was so tasteless and bland that I hardly touched it, and when I came home, I ate my own.

Soon after I arrived in New York, Ron returned to Asia to cover President Johnson's trip there. He was gone for four long weeks. Day and night, I sat in front of the TV watching *I Love Lucy* or thinking about food. I wasn't sure which was worse: being by myself in the big city or not having *kimchi*.

So I looked in the yellow pages and found a Japanese grocery store on the West Side that carried Japanese rice. I ran down the three flights of stairs and jumped into a taxi. When I arrived at the shop, I discovered that the rice came in only one-pound or fifty-pound bags. Since I ate three times a day and didn't want to run out, I bought the fifty-pound bag without considering how I would take it home. The cab driver left the bag in front of our apartment building and reality hit. No one offered to help, so I, who weighed less than ninety pounds, dragged the bag into the building. One stair at a time I kept dragging with all my might. When I landed on the first landing, I looked up to see how far up to go. When I finally got that bag into our apartment, I sat on the couch, totally exhausted. With that fifty-pound bag of rice, I finally felt at home.

When I arrived in New York, the first thing I did was call my pen pal Sharon. When I was working at the optical shop, a GI introduced me to one of his girlfriends who he was writing to. I was terrible with English, but Sharon and I kept writing to each other. When I came to New York, she was married and living in Connecticut. One weekend, we decided to meet. Ron was away for one of the assignments, and she was to stay with me that weekend. Her husband drove her down and he took us to a restaurant. When we came out from dinner, her overnight bag was stolen from their car. I was stunned. What kind of place is New York? Does everyone steal everything here? That night, Sharon slept in a pair of Ron's old pajamas.

On the last Sunday before Ron was due back from Cambodia, Jill came over to the apartment early in the morning. She seemed jittery but wouldn't say why. She wanted us to go to a movie together. I thought it was odd and thought she might having a problem with her boyfriend, Dean. I had hardly ever seen her or talked to her all the while I was in New York, and it was odd for her to suddenly show up without warning and ask me to go to a movie. Not only was I shy and insecure, but her strong personality intimidated me. So without asking a question, I went with her. It was only eleven in the morning, and we went to one bad movie after another. Afterward, we went to a small sandwich place. She ordered a big ice cream sundae, and I had a Coke.

"Look, Cindy," she said, "why would a person buy the cow if he can have a milk for free?"

I didn't understand what she was talking about.

"What I mean is why should Ron marry you if you stay with him, cook for him, take care of him, and sleep with him?"

Ron told me that back in Saigon, Jill used to needle him about leading me on even though he had no intention of being serious. I assumed she felt sorry for me, a naïve women who seemed head over heels in love with a wolf, not knowing what she was getting into.

The waitress brought our orders. It was true Ron never mentioned marriage. I stared at the Coke, thinking that perhaps it was time for me to go back to Hong Kong. If marriage wasn't in my future here, I couldn't afford to hang around New York.

"If you promise me that you will not see him for two weeks, I'll let you stay with me," Jill said and bit a cherry from its stem that she'd picked up from her sundae. "The best time is when he misses you."

I was horrified by her suggestion. It has been almost four weeks since Ron had left, and I missed him so much that I felt almost physically ill. How could I do what she said? But again I couldn't say no.

Ron was due back in a day, and the phone kept ringing all night. Because of the time difference, I knew he was calling from every stop he was making. It was all I could do to keep from answering it, but I'd made Jill a promise. I kept wondering if I was doing the right thing. He loved me. Why did I have to do such a stupid thing that would pain us both? I didn't have any answers to my questions, but I thought I had to do what Jill told me to do. She was an American woman who understood American men.

The next day, I left a letter and the vest I'd been knitting for him on the dining room table. I left the apartment around the same time that Ron's plane was supposed to land and took a cab to Jill's apartment. When I saw Dean there, I missed Ron even more. I sat down on the couch in her living room and began to sob. I was picturing how Ron would run upstairs to his apartment, open the door, and look for me. How would he feel when he discovered I was gone? I wanted to run back to him. I didn't care if he married me or not. But instead, I stayed and cried my way through the night.

The following evening, Jill told me that Ron had been frantically calling everyone who knew me. She and Dean had been discussing us, and Dean was against what Jill was doing. He told her that Ron was going to Israel the next day to interview Prime Minister Moshe Dayan and warned her about the freewheeling reputation of Israeli girls. I was entirely confused and desperate.

The next day, Jill told me that I should meet her at a cocktail party that she was invited to at one of the posh hotels near Lexington Avenue. She had no idea how my every thought was with Ron. I literally felt that I would be paralyzed if I didn't see him. She gave me the address and told me to meet her there. I didn't care about going to any party or anything else, but again I thought I had to do what I was told. I dressed in a pink mini cocktail dress with silver stockings and shoes and carried a rhinestone evening bag. When I got there, the room was packed with strangers, but I felt I was all alone. My thoughts were consumed with Ron, and when

I saw Jill and Dean among the crowd, I couldn't take it anymore. I ran down the stairs, went into a phone booth, and called Ron.

"Hello?" he said. His voice was the sweetest sound on this earth, but I couldn't utter a word.

"Hello?" he said again.

"Hi," I finally managed to say.

"Hi . . . where are you?"

"I don't know. I . . ."

"Cindy, listen to me. Come home. We'll talk about whatever you want to talk about, okay?"

I ran outside, caught a taxi, and went to Jill's apartment, thinking I would change my party clothes and take a cab to Ron's place before Jill got home. But to my astonishment, when I arrived and peeked into Jill's bedroom, Jill and Dean were already home, having left the party while I was in the phone booth. They were sitting on the bed, and both had concerned expressions on their faces. Jill said, "Ron left a message for me to call."

Afraid that Ron would tell Jill about me coming to his apartment, I ran down two flights of stairs and dashed to a pay phone to call Ron. The line was busy. I was frantic. I caught a taxi to his apartment, ran up the stairs and put my ear to the door. I could hear him talking and laughing, never bringing up anything about me. Softly, I knocked on the door. I thought he might open the door without hanging up, and then I would tell him not to say anything about me being there. Instead, I heard him saying to Jill, "Gotta hang up. Cindy is at the door." Now I was in trouble, I thought. Between my fear of Jill's anger and not knowing how Ron felt, I just wanted to run away. Ron opened the door, and when I stepped inside he slapped me across the face. I tried to run out the door, but he held me back. The slap didn't hurt. I just felt guilty for putting him in such agony. He led me into the living room. I saw that he had a can of soup on the stove. Warming the soup in a can. *Poor baby*, I thought.

"Cindy, do you know how much I have been worrying about you? I thought I was going to find your dead body in the bathtub." The Boston strangler had been on everybody's mind. "Where have you been staying?"

"I don't know . . . somewhere . . . an apartment, a walk-up apartment."

He told me that he had even called our friends Barbara and Grant in Hong Kong when he read the note that I left on the dining room table. He opened my evening bag and found the address of the hotel.

"You'd better tell me where you're staying," he said. "I'm responsible for you while you're in this country. If you don't tell me, I'll have to report you to immigration. What person has planted vicious and poisonous thoughts in your mind? Was it my mother? It must have been a sudden decision because your hairbrush was still on the sink."

"Ron, I didn't come to this country to sightsee!" I spilled out my heart for the first time, "If we're not getting married, please tell me, so I can start to plan my life without you!"

"Do you know what it's like to lose your baby in your arms?" he asked and started to cry. I remember seeing him crying once in Vietnam when he was talking about his son.

"Ron," I pleaded, "are you going to stop living your life just because you had one bad experience? No one can guarantee what is on the other side of the bridge except God," I told him. "Should I be afraid every second because our futures are not guaranteed? I don't know what kind of life I will have if I marry you, an American man. All I know is that I love you, and nothing else matters to me. I would live in hell to be with you."

He showed me the letter he had written to me in case I returned to the apartment while he was at work. We both were incapable of expressing our inner feelings verbally but could say so much more in writing. When I was in Vietnam, I used to write my innermost feelings in my diary, knowing Ron would read it. The letter said that he was shocked into numbness and that he thought he would have been better off if he had died that day when he was shot in Vietnam. He wanted to know why there had been a sudden change from all the love letters I had been writing, letters asking him to bring me this and that from Hong Kong. How could I suddenly just leave him without a word? He asked what kind of person was filled with so much hate that she could not stand to see two people so supremely happy. He also wrote about how my love brought out the very best in him. He said that I was wrong when I said that he didn't want to marry me; he just wanted to make sure that he was good enough for me and wanted to make sure that he would not go back to his old ways instead of settling down. I should also admit, he wrote, that our love was not an ordinary love but the greatest one any two people could have. He said he would kill those people who poisoned my mind. How each time the sound of footsteps coming up the stairs made him stop breathing, hoping it was me. He begged me to come back. It was a long, pleading love letter, which no one could write without real love. I felt awful, and I wasn't sure I had done the right thing. I knew he loved me just as much as I loved him. Why, then, was I playing this terrible, painful game?

We continued to talk throughout the night without resolution until Ron finally fell asleep. At about three o'clock in the morning, I left and sneaked back into Jill's apartment. I stayed up all night. Ron was leaving the next morning for Philadelphia. Knowing he would be up early for his trip, at six o'clock I called him. He asked me to meet him in front of Rockefeller Plaza where NBC is located.

In Philadelphia, Ron was to give a speech at a convention at one of the hotels, and I sat in the audience.

"When I was in Vietnam, I learned to love Asia so much that I decided to bring back some of it with me." Then he called my name and introduced me to the audience. Everyone clapped and smiled at me. I was taken aback but was able to bow to the audience with my face as red as a hot pepper.

When we retuned to New York, it was early in the afternoon. Ron was to leave for Israel that night. We went to see the movie *Alfie,* a story about an aimless, amoral young Englishman who exploited the women with whom he became intimately involved. At the end of the story, he is alone, standing on a bridge next to a stray dog. When we left the theater, I was sad, confused, and worried. Ron was leaving, and I had to face Jill again. I didn't want to go back to her apartment. The streetlights looked like diamonds in the night air, but my heart was black as the ink that I used when I did calligraphy. Ron kept looking at me as we walked together, silently.

"I know what you're thinking," he said finally. "You're comparing me to that man in the movie."

I didn't answer him. *How sad it is that we seem to be in two different worlds,* I thought. We went to a small nearby restaurant, but I wasn't hungry. He ordered lasagna and a salad while I just had a Coke. I just sat there, not saying anything. Finally, at the end of the dinner, Ron looked at me.

"I want you to move back while I'm gone," he said. "We'll set the date for our marriage when I get back."

That night, I went to Ron's apartment and slept like a baby on his terrible old mattress. I went to Jill's the next day to pick up my things. She was very cold to me.

"Cindy, if you keep seeing Ron, I'm afraid you cannot stay here anymore."

I was so relieved to know that I had some place to go.

"Oh, I'm moving back into his apartment," I said. "We're getting married when he gets back from Israel."

Jill was stunned. "Boy, that didn't take long."

Upon leaving, I was so anxious that I even failed to thank her.

Ron came back from his trip, but as before, there was no further mention of any wedding. Thanksgiving Day came, and we went to the John F. Kennedy Airport pick up Caron, Ron's daughter. On the same plane was Caron's stepbrother, the son of Ron's ex-wife's new husband. Also, meeting the plane was the stepbrother's mother who lived in New York. It reminded me how once in Hong Kong, Ron had taken me to see an American movie called *Divorce American Style*, a comedy about the chaotic life of divorced people with different sets of children. I didn't know how real that movie was until I was at the John F. Kennedy Airport with that blended family arriving. A few days later, when we brought Caron back to the airport, we ran into the mother and son once again. She and Ron decided to have a bite to eat together after the children had been put on board.

I was bored and didn't care about what they were saying. They seemed to have a lot in common, especially marriage and divorce. They were so into their discussions that they acted as though I was just a sack of rice. I paid no attention to their conversation until Ron said, "I'm very gun-shy about marriage."

That was it. That night I slept on the beat-up couch and considered whether the next day I should go to Los Angeles to see a friend, visit my friend Sharon in Boston or go straight back to Hong Kong. What about my costumes and music? I literally felt like killing myself. Once again, I looked to the movies for some sort of clue. I remembered the film *South Pacific* in which an officer falls in love with a Polynesian girl during World War II. He is tormented because he loves her but can't bring himself to marry a woman from such a different culture. Perhaps Ron faced the same dilemma. He had loved me while we were still in Asia, but here in America, I no longer seemed so desirable, I thought.

Having made the decision to leave, I felt a weight lift from my body. At least in my own mind, there was no more confusion. And there were no more awful games to play. Ron was anchoring the morning news at the time, and the next morning, as usual, he got up at four to take a shower. As usual, I got up from my couch, went to the kitchen, poured a tall glass of orange juice, and left it on the night table in his bedroom for him to drink after his shower. Then I went back to my couch.

After he left for work, I went into the bedroom and crawled into the saggy bed. I would leave, I thought, as soon as the sun came up. I was thinking about my day when the phone rang around five thirty in the morning.

"Would you like to come and have lunch with me today?" It was Ron.

"No," I said.

"Why not?"

"Because I won't be here then."

"Where are you going?"

"I don't know yet, but why do you care?"

"Look, Cindy, you've waited for two years. Do you think you could wait one more week?"

"Yes, I guess I could."

For a whole week, we went about things as if nothing had happened. I just didn't care one way or the other. If he said he wasn't going to marry me, I was prepared for it. The last morning of the seventh day, Ron woke up and went to take a shower. I put on cotton kimono, which I'd brought for Ron from Hong Kong. There was no belt, so I put it on backward to hide my skinny front. I went to the kitchen and poured a tall glass of orange juice and put it on the night table. Then I sneaked into the bathroom, I peeked behind the shower curtain. Ron was busy shampooing under the shower. I put my hand between his legs and pulled it up the crack of his butt and ran out. Once in a while when I was in a playful mood, I did that to Ron. Usually he screamed but would keep on doing whatever he was doing. But that morning, he jumped out of the shower, dripping wet and chased me into the bedroom. He grabbed me from behind while I was falling forward, desperately trying to hang on to the kimono, which was falling off my back. I couldn't stop laughing while Ron tried to pull the kimono away from me. I was laughing so hard that tears were rolling down my face. To hide my naked back, I rolled onto my back and looked up at Ron, still laughing, who was looking down at me. He stopped pulling and just stood there looking at me. It was a look that I cannot express with words, a look of love and affection that I had never seen in his eyes before. Finally, he stood up and went into the bathroom. While he was getting dressed, I lay on the bed and watched him. As he was putting on his tie, his said, "You know we are getting married, don't you?" he asked.

"No, I don't know," I said. By that point I didn't care any longer. I had made up my mind, and it didn't matter to me one way or the other.

"Today, I want you to go this doctor's office and have a blood test done." He gave me the phone number, but my mind was doing funny things. I reasoned that God probably didn't want me to get married, and that was why He was making it so impossible.

A couple of days later, Ron took me downtown and left me at an upstairs restaurant with all of his secretaries from NBC News. Since I didn't know them too well, I asked Ron to stay with me. Ron said, "No, this is a girl thing," and he left. I didn't know why I was there with those strangers without Ron. The girls took out little packages and told me to open them. There was one ashtray, some old earnings, a blue garter belt, and a handkerchief. I sat there, wondering about the odd things the girls were giving to me. No one told me there was such thing as "bridal shower."

On January 6, 1967, Ron and I were married in a ceremony that Ron liked to say was the Carlyle Hotel's first Buddhist-Jewish wedding. Jill was my maid of honor, and Ron's boss walked me down the aisle. The guests were the girls at my wedding shower and a few men from NBC. I bought a small inexpensive veil at Bloomingdale's and wore my white lace Chinese *cheongsam*. Ron didn't invite any of his family, but I was sad that mine could not be there, especially my mother who had always dreamed that I would marry a good man who would take care of me for the rest of my life.

I said "I do" softly so that the Jealousy God would not hear.

Mexico and Hong Kong

I will not give my love to anyone else.
Do not be envious of someone else's love;
Our love will last a lifetime,
And we will live happily ever after.

—Anonymous

Keep your eyes wide open before marriage, half shut afterwards.

—Benjamin Franklin (1706-1790)

After our wedding, Ron sublet a beautiful apartment near NBC at Rockefeller Center. It had a canopy at the entrance and a doorman with a big hat. I was free from fears and worries for the first time since we'd met, and I felt safe and looked forward to raising a wonderful family and to the joy of being a wife.

Soon after, Ron made what he thought was an exciting announcement. "We have to move to Mexico," he said with great pleasure in his voice. "I'm going to be in charge of covering all of Latin America from Mexico City."

Mexico City? Who wanted to be in Mexico? I thought. I hadn't even adjusted to the United States, and now he wanted to move to an even stranger place? Still I was his wife, and so Mexico it would be.

On the plane that would take us to our new home, I carried my survival kit—a small bag of rice, a bottle of soy sauce, and a bag of red peppers—in a big straw bag. I felt bad about leaving my fifty-pound bag of rice behind, though Ron had filled two steamer trunks with almost everything else we owned. In Korea, rice was as precious as gold, and as a little girl, I remembered my mother picking up every single grain of rice that had spilled and putting it back in our rice chest.

"This comes from the blood and sweat of farmers, and if you waste it, God will punish you," she would say.

Ron was obviously excited about going to Mexico, but I was still bothered by the prospect of being "rice-less" and living in a place where I couldn't speak the language.

Suddenly it occurred to me that I hadn't actually seen the large bag of rice when we'd left the apartment for the last time. I stared at him thumbing through *Time* magazine. He lifted his head and looked back, puzzled.

"I didn't see the bag of rice in the kitchen when I left. You didn't throw it out, did you?" "Yeah, I threw it out," he said, as casually as if he were talking about a day-old newspaper.

I was stunned. "How could you do that?" I demanded, and didn't say another word all the way to Mexico.

My life in Mexico started out as the following poem:

Last night I slept alone,
curled up like a shrimp;
and the night before I slept alone,
curled up like a shrimp.
What sort of life is this?
Every night without a break.
But today the man I love has come:
I wonder whether I'll stretch my legs and sleep tonight.

As soon as we arrived, Ron went on an assignment to Brazil for four weeks. Then he chased the revolutionary Che Guevara through the Bolivian jungle and covered the fighting in the Congo. Again, his letters were the only connection I had with him, but sometimes even the letters took weeks to arrive. In one, which arrived from Bolivia where he stayed in a little jungle village seven hundred miles from La Paz, he wrote about how the hotel was like a horse stable, without bathrooms, sinks, or windows in the rooms. There were two stinking *baños* in the back, which didn't flush and made him want to vomit just to smell them, and two showers also in back, but they didn't work, so guests had to bathe in the dirty river nearby. With only two outdoor sinks for the whole place and the weather being quite cold, he had to stand shivering to wash up, and at the only decent restaurant in town, he tried to sit where he couldn't see the filthy kitchen. The streets were unpaved, just dust and mud, and the sewage from people's houses ran in the gutters. He said that that trip was the worst trip he had made for NBC.

He wrote that he often thought about Grant Wolfkill's book because he felt very much as if his room was a prison cell, and he was struggling through one day at a time until he could come home to me. He remembered how excited he used to get about those trips, but now he realized how much I meant to him, and how much I had changed him into a better person who cared about someone else instead of just himself. How happy he was that he loved me! How happy he could be, with any amount of money, in any place, as long as he was with me. Whenever I was unhappy with the reality of our marriage, reading his letters always made me love him all over again. I felt helpless and sad over the harsh locales, the lack of sleep, and his frustration trying to get permission to cover a story that he felt mattered. Sometimes he couldn't even get into the country where he was supposed to work and had to stay someplace else, waiting. In every letter, he assured me of his love and need for me and promised me that the current trip was the last he would ever take without me. With each letter, I renewed my vow to be understanding and uncomplaining about my needs and my loneliness because his hardships were suffered for our happiness.

I anticipated that whenever he returned, he would hug and kiss me and tell me how much he missed me. But instead, he acted as though he had never left. Not even a hug. He spent most of his time with Jim, the cameraman who lived in Mexico City, plotting what kind of story he should cover. Although his love letters expressed his innermost feelings, he never demonstrated those feelings when he returned. I'm a passionate person and was starving for his affection, to hear how much he missed me, for him to hug me and kiss me and ask me how much did I miss him. I knew he was eager to cover the right story, but what about me? He talked about his work and world affairs to others but never everyday, ordinary subjects to me. I felt so alone and lonely even he was in town.

But if this was where I was going to live for three years, I needed to adjust. I registered at the Spanish Language Institute and took an intensive course. In the afternoon, I watched television dubbed in Spanish, and I didn't understand a word. Again, food was constantly on my mind, and I knew that I had to find rice and cabbage for *kimchi*. I called the Korean Embassy and asked them where I could get the ingredients I needed. That call led to a party hosted by the ambassador, and the buffet, where I saw and ate real Korean food for the first time in years, was heaven.

The next day, carrying my straw bag on the bus, I started off to the market. A three-piece mariachi band was playing at the entrance, but otherwise, it was much like a market in Korea, with all kinds of fresh fish, vegetables, dried foods, and so forth. First thing I saw was a Japanese man standing in middle of the market selling cabbage. I was so happy that I bought as much as I could carry. I also learned that the man would bring whatever I needed directly to my apartment. Of course with black market price, all imported things were taxed 100 percent. Once I asked Ron, who was in Argentina, to get me something from the PX. In his next letter, he said how funny I was because there were no GIs in Argentina. My request reminded him of when we first met and how he had tried to impress me by telling me how much money he made and the things he could get from the PX. He said now how much money he made wasn't important to him anymore because he had me.

Back at the motel, I tried to make my own *kimchi*. I cut each cabbage into four sections, lengthwise, and sprinkled the pieces with salt. Then I waited about two hours for the cabbage to wilt. I chopped garlic and several green onions and mixed them with the dried red pepper that I had brought with me. I knew I should have also add either fish or shrimp sauce, but since I had neither, I put the mixture in a big plastic container and waited for it to ferment.

I examined the cabbage every day, but soon it was clear that something was wrong. It had rotted and smelled awful. Sadly I threw it away and wrote to my mother for help. She wrote back, telling me that I should use much more salt to make the cabbage completely soft. On the second try, the process worked, and my spirits rose.

I went back to the market and bought pork to make *kimchi-chige*, a stew made of *kimchi* and pork. Every day, I came back from my language class and sat in front of the television eating my rice and *kimchi-chige*, my only source of comfort. For the first time in my life, I was putting on weight. (Looking back, it might have been the doughnuts I had every morning at one the the cafes before I went to Spanish Language Institute.) I remembered my mother used to say, "A skinny girl will get fat when she gets married," and so I had to laugh as I took out all of my Chinese *cheongsams* at the waist.

Tired of living in a motel for three months, we moved into a big flat with three bedrooms, overlooking Chapultepec Park. It was a huge flat, with an elevator that stopped right inside our apartment, but I might as well have been living in an empty warehouse. Ron was gone most of the time, and all I did was to go out onto our balcony and stare at the lovers who came to the park to be together.

On one rare occasion when Ron was in town, we went to a bullfight. Although I had seen them in movies, I found them barbarous in reality. Outside the bullring, taco stands were lined up, and we ordered a few. Later I overheard Ron telling people how worried he was when he saw the man with his dirty hands and dirty fingernails slapping the tacos together and how he thought he was surely going to have diarrhea. On the other hand, Ron once took me to someone's house for lunch, and the hostess served us grilled cheese sandwiches. I had never had such smelly stuff in my life and didn't touch it; Koreans never serve such meager, bad-smelling sandwiches to any guest, and I couldn't believe that she had.

If those small cultural differences between us were dismissible, Ron's invitation to a soundman to stay with us wasn't. Ron brought him back from a long assignment in Guatemala. The man, a stringer who didn't speak a word of English, was supposed to stay in Mexico City until NBC gave permission for Ron and Jim to return to Guatemala. Since the man wasn't to be paid while he wasn't working, Jim told Ron that they should help the man by reporting phony hotel bills to NBC and then giving the stringer the expense reimbursement. Jim's wife didn't want the man at their house, so Jim asked Ron if we would put him up since we had extra bedrooms and no children. Ron, who always wanted to please other people, thought it was a great idea and never bothered to ask me what I thought. I had only been married a few months with hardly any time to be alone with my husband. Now I had to spend every waking hour with a man with whom I couldn't even communicate. I cooked his breakfast and fixed his lunch; he even went to restaurants with us, never offering to contribute anything when the bill arrived. He and Ron ate and talked while I sat. After dinner, the two of them sat in the living room, talking more, smoking cigars, and drinking while I lay in bed waiting for Ron. Remembering how Ron had mentioned his first wife's nagging, I tried to be a good, patient wife, but my insides were boiling. Since Ron had no idea what was bothering me, he told me to snap out of it. One thing led to another until we fought. Crying nonstop, I told him how lonely I was and that I wanted to go back home. I felt as if I was nothing but a maid who was supposed to cook and clean the house. The next day, Ron put the man in a motel, rented a car, and took me to Acapulco for the weekend.

Acapulco was heaven, with blue sky, beautiful sea, and freshly broiled lobster served to us next to the beach. I wished I could live there forever.

When we came back, Ron took me with him to Guatemala. The cabin attendant from the economy section came up to our seats in first class. Ron was reading a magazine, but she stood at the opening and grinning at him with her hand on her hip until he noticed her.

"What are you doing here again?"

Ron looked at her and then me with strange, guilty look. "Oh, I like it so much that I decided to bring my wife with me this time."

Her expression stiffened. Without looking at me, she spit out, "We are happy to have her with us," and walked away. In Guatemala, even when he wasn't working, he was always out with his staff, drinking and talking the night away.

Shortly after our return to Mexico, he had to go to the Congo on a long trip. Ron decided I should stay in New York while he was away, but when he tried to get a visa, it was rejected because I had a Korean passport. After Ron made several phone calls, the consul met him at the embassy with my visa, and Ron instructed me to study for my citizenship exam while I was in New York. Four weeks later, when he returned from the Congo, he attended my swearing-in ceremony in Washington DC. He jokingly said, "Funny, you don't look like an American."

Back in Mexico, Ron was restless and frustrated. The world didn't seem to care what went on in Latin America, and no matter what story he had covered, it wasn't put on the air. I was lonely and wanted to visit my family in Korea and to have Ron finally meet them. So on September 15, 1967, we arrived at Kimpo Airport in Seoul. My family was surprised to see how chubby I had become, and my mother laughingly reminded me of what she had said about wives gaining weight.

We stayed at the house that I'd bought before I left on tour in 1964. The only thing that concerned me was that we didn't have a Western-style toilet—or sink, shower, or bathtub—in the house. I told Ron what to expect and thought that since he had experienced worse places covering his stories, he could handle the situation and go to the bathhouse with the rest of us. The only running water was in the kitchen, so in the morning, I brought a washbasin into the bedroom for Ron to shave and wash his face. I hung a small mirror on the wall for him and held a towel while I waited for him to finish.

Every morning after breakfast, Ron asked me to take him to Bando Arcade near the Chosun Hotel, where I had taken him the first time we had come to Seoul.

"I really like shopping at that arcade," he told me.

So the whole family took him there every morning. Little did I know that the real reason he wanted to go there was so that he could use the hotel bathroom.

But while we were in Seoul, Ron was restless. He kept going to the
Eighth Army Military Information office to call NBC. He still had to
be where the action was.

A week after we arrived, Ron told me that we should leave Korea
and go to Hong Kong. We were supposed to take my mother and my
brother Tong-Kun to Hong Kong with us, but their passports weren't
ready. So, Hong Kong it was. A reporter from the local newspaper
interviewed me and wrote an article about Cindy Song , who used to
sing in Hong Kong and who had married an American journalist. Ron
and I stayed at the Grand Hotel on the Hong Kong side, and when my
mother and brother Tong-Kun arrived later, they stayed at a guesthouse
on the Kowloon side. Linda, who had encouraged me to buy the fur
wrap before I left for the States, said I should buy a jade ring because it
was good deal in Hong Kong. She took me to a store, and I picked out a
nice-sized oval jade designed with forty-eight diamond chips around it.
(Ron was always good at bringing me many interesting rings everywhere
he went. But ironically, right before our divorce, a burglar came in our
home and stole every ring I had, including the jade ring.)

Ron traveled to Cambodia and Indonesia while I stayed in Hong
Kong with my family. In Indonesia, he chased President Sukarno for
an interview. Again, he kept writing me about every incident. One story
was about his cameraman, who lived in Hong Kong with his Korean wife
who wanted to chase around every prostitute. Once, he wanted Ron and
their driver to wait while he visited the red light district on the way to
their hotel. The place was like a garbage dump, built alongside a smelly
canal where the whores lived in the filthy shacks in tiny little rooms.
The driver wanted Ron to walk around with him instead of sitting in the
car while the cameraman went to ten different whorehouses, looking
for a girl he liked and making a lot of noise and commotion, which
made Ron and the driver embarrassed. The girls were the ugliest and
dirtiest Ron had ever seen. After the cameraman couldn't find anyone
there, he made them stop at a big open market where prostitutes sat
in pedicels and waited for men to come along. Even the driver tried to
discourage the cameraman, but he was crazy when he wanted a girl. He
saw two girls sitting in a pedicel and told them to get in the car. They
were very young, dirty, and didn't speak a word of English. But the man
kept saying, "Oh, look how cute they are. Aren't they adorable?" Ron
finally insisted that he wanted to go back to the hotel. So the driver
dropped him off, and the cameraman and the driver disappeared with
the two girls. Ron said he didn't see how the man could go home and
face his wife and children.

While I was in Hong Kong, I met Ms. Lee Kyung-Hee, a very pretty Korean woman married to a Chinese man who worked for a shipping company. Just as Ron did, her husband traveled extensively; sometimes he was away for six months at a time. Previously, she'd been a mistress of the chairman of Samsung, and while still in Korea, the chairman bought her a house for lunch-hour trysts. Eventually, she either became tired of her life as a mistress, or the chairman wanted to end the relationship. In order to get her out of Korea, he arranged for her to chaperone Miss Korea to the Miss Universe pageant in Paris. After that, Ms. Lee (a Korean woman who'd kept her maiden name even after her marriage) came to Hong Kong, met and married her Chinese husband, and they had a little girl.

When I met her, her husband was away as usual, and she came to visit me at my hotel daily. Everything she owned was expensive designer stuff, and when she was around men, she acted as if she was on stage. At NBC in Hong Kong, a tall, handsome Canadian cameraman named Jimmy worked as a stringer, and Ms. Lee started to go out with him. Jimmy was married, but the man never told her. As I was loyal to my fellow Korean woman, I felt that it was my duty to tell her, but Ron said that I shouldn't. Also, she was trying to get Jimmy to buy her a diamond ring, which was previously hers. Jimmy didn't know that it was hers.

One day, Ms. Lee came to my hotel with a black eye. She told me that her husband had come back from his trip and she still came home late. They fought all night, and he threw her all over the place. Soon after, she found out that Jimmy was married and asked why I had never told her. I lied and said that I didn't know, but she didn't believe me, and that was the end of our "friendship." I had been brought up in the Korean tradition where it is our unspoken duty to alert friends to betrayal. But I also felt that I should follow what my husband said.

The reason I wanted my brother to come to Hong Kong was so that he could get passport to travel to US. With his studies for the bar exam derailed by his hospitalization, he was slowly despairing that he would never achieve his goal even though his desire was burning like a coal stove with the lid closed. Most of his rich and well-connected friends were in America, studying for master's or doctoral degrees, but who could help him? The reality in Korea was brutal: without money or influential friends, it was almost impossible to succeed, and thinking that his future was doomed, he tried to kill himself.

My mother's maid had found him in a pool of blood. He had cut both of his wrists after taking Seconal. He survived, but it was obvious that he needed help. At the time, it was impossible for him to get a visa to go to the United States while living in Korea. When I told my mother I would take her to Hong Kong, her words were "Never mind about me. You have to help Tong Kun." In Hong Kong, Ron sponsored him in order to obtain a tourist visa to America.

In December, we all went to Japan to finish our "vacation." Although the Korean people have reasons, both political and historical, to hate the Japanese, I couldn't deny the nostalgic feelings toward their culture that were embedded in my soul as a child. Since I'd always loved Japanese movies, especially samurai movies, I took Ron to see them almost every night, even though he didn't understand one word of Japanese. We saw the famous Takarazuka performance, and I felt as if I was in a dream. Kabuki was an all-day project, beginning at eleven in the morning and lasting until four or five o'clock in the afternoon. A huge restaurant sold *obento* lunch boxes, and during the long intermissions, the crowd poured out to eat their *obento* boxes. In the evenings, on the way to our hotel after seeing a show or movie, we stopped at steaming *odeng* stands and had a few sticks of ground fish served with hot broth. Just as I craved *kimchi* in New York, Ron bought cookies every night on the way to the hotel.

When it was time for us to part, Tong-Kun, full of hope, flew to New York while my mother returned to Busan. After sending them off to their destinations, Ron and I were relieved to be alone. Although I loved my mother dearly, she had to be constantly entertained, and I was exhausted being sandwiched between her and Ron. He and I went to Kyoto by train and stayed at a big hotel called the Miyako. Our room had a Japanese bath with a sunken wooden tub; I'd missed those baths so much that I loved just looking at it. We ate Japanese *chiri*, a seafood soup, for dinner, walked back in the cold night, and got into the hot bath, soaping and rinsing and soaking our bodies in the deep wooden tub. Then, sitting on a little wooden seat, I scrubbed Ron's back and soaped his body and mine. It was a scene right out of *Sayonara*. The next day, we saw magnificent Buddhist temples, Shinto shrines, Zen monasteries, and Amida temples—palaces, gardens, and pleasure pavilions. After spending New Year's Day in Tokyo, Ron told me that he had to go back to Saigon. We had been away from Mexico since September, nearly four months.

"Look," he said, "when you get back to Mexico, pack up as much clothing as you can and fly back to New York. When I get back to New York from Vietnam, I'll talk to the president of NBC News and ask him to assign me somewhere else. I want you to wait for me in New York. You can stay at the Warwick Hotel, which is right next to NBC. It's elegant there."

Though the original assignment had been for three years, we were moving again after less than a year. But I had no regrets about leaving Mexico. Anywhere else would be better. With the thirteen pieces of luggage that we had accumulated in four months, I flew back to Mexico, repacked every suitcase we had, dutifully flew back to New York, and checked into the Warwick as I'd been instructed.

With little or nothing to do in this transitional state, I stayed in my room except to go out for lunch and dinner. I didn't know anyone or where else to go. After three days of this routine, I came back to the room and found that some of my makeup, which I'd bought in Japan, and jewelry, which I had bought in Hong Kong, were missing. My beige suede jacket, which Ron had bought me in Hong Kong, was also gone as was his portable typewriter. I always carried lots of cash with me, but fortunately the thief had been in a hurry and hadn't seen the several thousand dollars I'd hidden in the clothes drawer under my clothes. I was shaking when I went downstairs to report the theft.

"You're supposed to check your valuables with security," the hotel clerk said. *Was I supposed to check my old jacket and Ron's typewriter too?* I wondered. I wasn't sure how to handle the situation and decided to move across the street to the Hilton the next day.

I called my brother to help me, but on the morning of the move, he walked into my hotel room with his face looking like something out of a horror movie. He was covered with a terrible rash and told me he had to go to a hospital for a shot to counteract his food allergy.

Mother told me that when we all were in Hong Kong, he'd thrown up all over the bathroom floor in the middle of the night after eating spaghetti one evening and had a rash all over his body then. The only place I could think to take him was a small clinic at the NBC building that handed out aspirin and Band-Aids. He lay down on a bed while the doctor, an old man, kept poking him and asking him questions.

"Just tell him that it's some food poisoning. All I need is a shot," Tong-Kun kept telling me. Then he told me he had to go to the bathroom.

"I'll give him a bed pan," the doctor said, but my brother insisted. I helped him walk to the bathroom, but as he reached the toilet, his eyes rolled back in his head and he passed out. I screamed and started crying. The doctor called for an ambulance. I called Ron's office and asked the secretary if they could move my suitcases to the Hilton hotel.

My brother lay in the emergency room all that day while I sat by his side, convinced that he was dying. No one from the staff came to check on him, and finally at night, he got up on his own and announced that "we should go now."

The street was lit by the store displays, and we didn't say a word. We passed several restaurants, but neither of us was hungry. The next day my brother was to take the entrance exam to New York University, but I wasn't sure he would make it. My room at the Hilton had two double beds. He went right to sleep, and I watched over him. Several times in the middle of the night, I put my ear close to his mouth to make sure that he was still breathing.

We awoke early the next morning because he had to be at NYU by eight. Instead of going to the hotel restaurant, we walked around the street looking for an Asian restaurant. I desperately wished that I could find some hot noodles or Korean soup for my brother. When I realized we would have no such luck, we went a small diner. Neither of us was fond of American breakfasts, especially not that early in the morning. We stared at the menu for a while and decided on the pancakes. When two huge mountains of them arrived, we just stared, left, and walked to the subway.

"Call me when your exam's finished," I said, watching him disappear down into the subway station. I waited all day, sitting next to the phone.

Finally around six thirty, it rang.

"*Noonim*," said one of my brother's friends. "Tong-Kun just finished his exam but had to go back for another one." The friend spoke so excitedly that he didn't give me time to ask any questions. "He had the best score among all those taking the test, and he went back to retake something."

"Is he okay, though?" I asked, in tears.

"Oh yes, do not worry. He is fine. I will call you again as soon as he is through."

He'd passed with a very high score, which would allow him to waive the English course requirements, and was called back for another interview.

At about nine that night, I met my brother and his friends at a Korean restaurant, Sam Bok, on Forty-Second Street and Broadway. Tong-Kun was beaming with joy, but he still hadn't eaten anything. Such was my second welcome to New York City.

As for Tong-Kun, our efforts were worthwhile, as he eventually graduated with a master's and a Ph.D. in public administration with highest honors. My duty to him was fulfilled. He went back to Korea and took a position as a professor at the prestigious Hanyang University.

In New York, every evening, I was glued to the television, watching the news. People had told me that they had seen Ron on television when he'd been wounded in 1966. Would such a thing happen again, and would I see him? He had been sending letters through reporters who came to New York from Vietnam. He was anxious when my letters to him were delayed because of the war. He seemed torn between the guilt of leaving me behind and wanting to get ahead at NBC. In his every letter, he told me about his anxiety about his job. He couldn't relax; he had to fight to get the best story he could. Since I didn't understand his work, I could only read his letters and feel saddened by his frustration. Every time he didn't get the story he wanted, he wrote me long, depressing letters about how he wished I was there to comfort him. When he finally got my letter describing my problems with the robbery and Tong-Kun, he told Ron Steinman, his old boss, that he wanted to leave right away. But they wanted him to stay two more weeks until they got a replacement. He also told me how bad the office in Vietnam had become since he was there last. A young soundman, who acted crazy and carried a gun, had accidentally shot the secretary in the head while he was fooling around. Her head was shaved from the operation, and after the accident, she walked with a cane and only had partial use of one of her arms. I had known her in Vietnam and was frightened that this had happened to a friend.

From Ron's letters, I could tell that he'd finally gotten out of his system his ambition to cover the best story regardless of the danger to his life, and for the first time he sounded afraid. Vietnam was on the news every single night, and that was all he wanted to cover—that is, until the Tet Offensive. Then he said that he didn't care who won the war or how the United States got out; the important thing was to stop killing people. I was convinced that he would be killed this time and wondered what I would do alone in New York.

When Ron finally came home in one piece, he talked to the president of NBC News and negotiated an assignment in London for six months, since he had to be out of the country for that long in order to receive a tax benefit. I had thought that getting married would finally give me some roots, but it was no different than when I had lived the life of a gypsy, singing wherever I could. However, when the path of one's life is arranged by God, how can one question it? There was nothing else to do but obey.

Washington

If my tears were pearls,
I would save every drop.
In ten years, when he returns
I would build a castle for him and me.
But my tears are not pearls;
How would I build a castle
When he returns?

—Anonymous

Fear not for the future; weep not for the past.

—Percy Bysshe Shelley (1792-1822)

When we arrived in London in March, it was raw and raining and cold. Ron sublet a simple but elegant apartment near Kensington Palace, where Princess Margaret resided. The city was clean, and there was a nice park in the middle of city. I especially loved when Ron took me to see Hampton Court, the Tower of London, and other historic places. I felt as if I were reliving history since I just finished reading about Henry the Eighth. When I walked through Hampton Court, I felt as though I was actually witnessing all the scenes that happened. At the Tower of London, I felt sad and eerie as though I was actually seeing Anne Boleyn being beheaded.

In March, when we moved to London, we assumed the weather would be warm and sent all our belongings to America to be stored until we arrived in August. How wrong we were. Most of those six months, mostly without Ron, I was frozen half to death even inside the flat. Not only was the weather raw and gloomy, but also the heat in the apartment building was automatically turned off on the first of May, no matter the temperature outside. I didn't know that England had a different electric voltage, so when I used my American-made portable hair dryer, it blew up. I didn't have an electric space heater, and I never thought of going out and buying some warm clothing for myself. I would fill up the tub with hot water and try to sink my body in as low as I could, but the top part of my body was always exposed to the cold. How I wished I could soak my whole body to the neck in a deep tub as I had done all my life. When I got out of the tub, I'd run into the bedroom with my teeth chattering, take the blanket from the bed, and wrap it tightly around my body all the way down to my legs like a mummy. Then one little step at a time, I'd go back to the bathroom, where I would put my hands around the hot water pipe to warm them before holding them over my nose, which felt as though it would fall off from the cold.

When Ron was in South Africa for four weeks to interview the heart surgeon Christian Barnard, who'd performed the first artificial heart transplant, I threw my back out in the kitchenette. When I reached down to the tiny, two-foot-tall refrigerator under the counter, my back cracked, and I was frozen in a doubled-over position. I stood like that for what seemed an eternity. Finally, carefully and slowly, I lowered to my knees, crawled to the wall, and sat against it. I couldn't reach the phone, which was in the bedroom, and I didn't know who to call anyway. What if I couldn't move until Ron came back? I just sat there like a mummy for a couple of hours until I could crawl into the bed for the rest of the day.

Ron returned in time to celebrate his birthday on May 25. It seemed that I only lived for the days when Ron came back from one of his trips. This time I bought a birthday card and wrote a poem:

> *My life started when I met you.*
> *I never felt the warmth of the sun before I knew you.*
> *I didn't know the moon up in the sky was for lovers*
> *like you and I before you came along.*
> *I didn't know the breeze*
> *could whisper the sweet songs in my ear*
> *when it caressed my face before I walked with you.*

I didn't know the raindrops on my tongue
would taste like sweet wine before you kissed me.
I never thought my heart could sing
until you held me in your arms.
So my dearest, there will be nothing on this earth for me
if you are not with me.

Ron slowly looked up to me with his glistening eyes.

While I only saw the sun once during our six months in London, Ron took me to Greece for a week in April 1968, and the sky was clear and the city was beautiful. Ron was there to cover the first anniversary of George Papadopoulos's military dictatorship. On the first day, after Ron went to work early and I was left alone in the hotel, I dressed in my miniskirt and knee-high boots and went out to explore. But as I started down the street, the men sitting at the outdoor cafés all followed me with their eyes. I didn't know what to do, so I rushed back to the hotel and sat on a sofa in the big reception room, wondering if I should go outside again. Ten minutes later, I walked out and kept on walking, feeling the men's looks following me. In the next block, a mob of people were gathered at a storefront where a young blonde woman inside the shop wearing a miniskirt. It was the end of the 1960s—the era of mod in London, but I didn't know that the Greek military government didn't allow women to wear such revealing dresses. There weren't any Asians either, and I suddenly understood why the men at the cafés were so intrigued by the strange sight of me coming down the street.

Finally, our foggy London assignment was over. On our way home to Washington, we stopped in Miami so that Ron could cover the Democratic convention, and the hot sun never felt so good. While Ron kept busy covering the event, I did not know who was running or even interested. The hotel was built near the water, and I could see little fish from my balcony. To pass the time alone, I tied a hook on a string, caught a couple, and cooked them in my hotel room.

In Washington, we moved into a nice apartment in Chevy Chase, and I was relieved that we wouldn't be moving around like gypsies anymore. Before the furniture was delivered from storage, Ron gave me instructions and went out of the country on assignment. When the men brought our furniture, it was a nightmare. Every box, every piece of furniture and the Oriental rugs were soaking wet. I had no idea how to reach Ron. I did not know who to call or what I was supposed to do. My only thought was to clean up the mess before Ron returned, and I called my brother in New York and asked him to help me. He flew down, and we unpacked continuously for three days. I didn't even know where to take him out to eat in the new neighborhood. After he left, I continued my mission—climbing up and down the small steps, unpacking box after box, and replacing the covers of Ron's books with paper. After two weeks of this labor, I developed hemorrhoids and couldn't stand or sit. I didn't know where to find a doctor or what medicine to get. Ron's family lived in the area, but he'd never attempted to put me in touch with them, and I didn't drive or even have car. I just suffered.

The following September, Ron took me to the West Coast for his annual three-week vacation. In San Francisco, Ron made sure our hotel was in Chinatown so I could find the food I liked. Chinatown reminded me so much of my days in Hong Kong, and I wished I could live in San Francisco with its deep Japanese influence. After a week in San Francisco, Ron rented a car and drove through Big Sur on the way to LA. Ron might have thought that it was a great treat, but to me, hour after hour with nothing to see but the water was too much. I was raised around the rocky beaches of Busan. I love the beach, but not for hours and hours. I didn't have the heart to tell him that I'd rather drive through some of those honky-tonk towns where stores lined the highway. That was another sign of cultural differences.

When we arrived in Los Angeles, the first place Ron took me was to the University of California, Berkeley, which Ron seemed to admire, and I didn't understand. It was 1968, the hippie movement had swept the whole United States, and Berkeley was the saddest sight I'd ever witnessed in my life. Young people on drugs were sleeping out on the streets, their clothes dirty and their feet bare. It reminded me of old Korea where people suffering from the devastation of the war had nothing, not even shelter. What was happening in this rich country? These people were not beggars. Asians had always looked up to the United States as a paradise, filled with beautiful and fortunate people who had the freedom to speak their minds, the country where everyone had the opportunity to better himself. How could these kids not know or appreciate that? I wondered how they could be so ungrateful while Ron reveled in their rebelliousness.

We went into a small diner for lunch and were the only older ones there. A young waitress took our order. She wore no bra, and I could see her nipples. To lift up my spirits, I tried a small joke.

"Did you see her nipples?"

I thought he would laugh. Instead, he frowned and accused me of making fun of her. Now I was even more upset and didn't feel like eating. Sometimes, I felt lonelier around my husband than I did being by myself. I like to make wisecracks, tease, and laugh. But since Ron never talked to me about anything, I didn't know who I was supposed to be. We sat in a little plaza where a man was playing the guitar and was singing. Even the music didn't help my state of mind; I sat away from Ron and started to sob.

Ron seemed perplexed and asked what was wrong. I kept sobbing. Then I told him how upset I was to be there. He stood up and rushed to our rental car. We seemed to be on two different planets.

When we arrived in Los Angeles and went to Koreatown, I had to pinch myself to see if I was awake. After years of suffering from not being able to get my kind of food, or even seeing any Koreans, this seemed like a dream. Korean signs were everywhere, and an old woman in a *hanbok* carried a baby on her back. I wanted to buy everything, especially the big fat cabbage. Ron suggested that we buy some, but we had a week more to go on our vacation. I told him we couldn't, but he insisted and bought a box. The next day we resumed our trip by car to Las Vegas with the desert sun baking down. My mind and my thoughts were with the cabbage, which sat in the trunk of our car. In the hotel room, I put the box in our closet. As if I was paying homage at a shrine, the first thing I did when I got up and the last thing I did before going to bed was check the box of cabbage. Every day I had to peel off the rotten outer layers. Five days later, when we were ready to leave, I had hardly any cabbage left.

Back in Washington, money, not cabbage, became the next cultural difference I had to struggle with. In Korea after the war, no one trusted anything but cash; and when people did use a bank, it was mostly for business transactions. Ron and I had used cash only in Vietnam, Mexico, and London, and in Washington, he gave me pocket money before he left for work. Since I didn't go anyplace without Ron, I didn't miss having money. His mother told me that I should get an allowance, like the $200 she had was gotten weekly from Ron's father, who owned a store in downtown DC. A Korean friend married to a U.S. Army officer explained their joint bank account and how she managed all the household accounts and gave her husband a weekly allowance. Like me in Korea, she'd been the sole breadwinner in her family and had taken care of her younger brother and her mother. "My husband and I even drew up a will," she said. "Now I know exactly how much will go to my family if anything happens to me."

When I told Ron about our conversations, he added my name to his bank account and agreed to give me an allowance of $200 per month.

I had no idea how much Ron was making, but I thought that I was supposed to buy everything, including my clothing and other necessities, from that amount. I didn't even know there was such thing like credit card. When he was away, I took the bills to one of his secretaries as he instructed me. I was embarrassed but did as I was told.

One day, out of blue, Ron took me downtown and bought me a Hammond organ. I guess he wanted to surprise me, remembering me talking about how sad I was to lose my organ. I really wanted a piano, but he never asked what I wanted, and I never expressed my wishes. Whenever he went away, I took lessons, and when I got tired of practicing, I looked out the window and watched people pass. A year later and after much discussion, we bought a small rambler in Bethesda. Ron didn't want to buy it, but I insisted. In Korea, a house is the best investment, like the ones I'd bought for my family in Busan and Seoul. Finally Ron gave in. I decorated the house in an Asian style and planted flowers in the yard. We put a thirty-six-foot swimming pool in our backyard so Ron could do his breath therapy, and after watching the first part of eleven o'clock news, Ron swam forty or fifty laps.

Otherwise, when he was home, all he wanted to do was to be left alone to read. How could I talk to a person whose face was blocked with either a paper or book all the time? But I tried to be patient and uncomplaining, telling myself that this was what he needed. Still, I felt like a little puppy sitting around for my master's command. Ron never liked anyone who talked too much, but he always wanted me to be there with him.

About this time, the Manson Family murders were in every paper and on every newscast. I didn't know where it took place and was scared to death, especially after a person was killed in our neighborhood and the police came. They went door to door, questioning everyone and searching for the killer. I couldn't sleep, thinking that someone would come into the house and kill me the way Sharon Tate had been murdered. I locked the bedroom door and jumped each time the air-conditioning came on.

Although Ron didn't seem to be close to his mother or any other member of his family, I liked his mother. She seemed very sweet and considerate. Even years later, when Ron and I took vacation to Grand Cayman, we stopped at his mother's apartment in Florida. She lived there all alone after her husband passed away not too long before. She wanted to come with us, saying she would pay for her trip, but Ron told her that he couldn't get her a ticket, and we didn't bring her along. On the beautiful beach, all Ron did was read and sleep, while I walked up and down on the beautiful sand. How I wished his mother was with us so I could have someone to talk to.

Ron seemed to be intent on making up for all the fun he'd missed during the three years he was out of the country. The hippie movement was in full swing, with pictures of a nude John Lennon and his wife and news of arrests for smoking pot in the paper. While my Korean friends were married to American military men and got support from the other military wives, Ron got together with singles who smoked pot and then went swimming naked, things common at the time but completely alien to me. Once when this group was at our house, everyone but me was drinking and talking, and Ron sat alone with another woman. When I told him that hurt me, he said I had a dirty mind. I thought about going back to Korea, but remembering the article about how Song Young-Hee was married to an American NBC reporter made me shiver. He talked about open marriage, and I told him to go on without me. I read that a person drove into the Potomac River and drowned and thought about doing the same thing. Would Ron know then what my pain was like?

I felt as if I had landed on a totally strange planet, and even small things that might've given me comfort were alien. Since I didn't know what movie was in town, I only went to whatever Ron wanted to see. He often took me to see Woody Allen movies, but they were neither funny nor sad. Besides Woody Allen being the ugliest movie star I've ever seen, I had no idea what the story was about. We saw other pictures about Jewish families, but Ron never explained to me about Jewish culture, and I thought all Americans were like that. On the other hand, when Ron wasn't around, I didn't know how to get to the theater, nor did I know what was playing.

I was shocked when he took to me see *Hair*. I couldn't believe how those people on stage could perform naked.

Since Ron was away so much, I wanted to go to school, but Ron didn't want me to, saying, "You speak good English. Why?"

After we arrived in Washington, Ron didn't have any particular assignment other than being sent to cover bits and pieces here and there out of the country. He was restless again, and I kept thinking if I could only give him a son, he would find an important focus. I remembered how he used to cry when he talked about his five-year-old son who had died in his arm from cancer. On the street, I saw all the women with big bellies. *Why did everything I wanted so badly seem so hard to get?* But I kept telling myself that there couldn't be any problem; I just had to be patient.

Immigrant

When the flowers bloom,
I think about the moon.
When I see the moon,
I think about wine.
When I see the flowers, the moon and the wine,
I think about you, my friend.
When will it be when I can share all these things with you?

—Lee Jung Bo

Happiness does not consist of what you want,
but wanting what you have.

—Confucius (551-479 BC)

In 1970, South Korea discovered several tunnels at the thirty-eighth parallel, and I was scared. What if there was another war? What if my family was killed? I felt compelled to hurry up and bring them to the United States. I would never forgive myself if I didn't and something terrible happened to them. Two years after they first applied and hundreds of documents later, my family finally got their passports. Tong-Kun was already at NYU at the time, and it would have been easier to bring the rest of them in one at a time. But I was afraid of an impending invasion by North Korea and arranged for them to immigrate in a group: my mother, my eighteen-year-old brother Young

Chang, my brother Tong-Ho, his wife, their three young children, and my Pomeranian dog.

In September of 1970, Ron and I went to Korea for our annual vacation in order to bring my family back to the States with us afterward. I sold of both of my houses and took the proceeds the only way I could—in Korean *won*, but at that time, it was still illegal to take hard currency out of the country. I had only one choice: spend it all. My mother and I shopped every day, buying Korean furniture, artifacts, and pictures that we could take with us.

My mother told me that we had to move my father's grave site before we left for America because the old one was to be destroyed in a road construction project. Ron, my mother, and I went to Busan where the grave was on top of a steep mountain called *hakobang*. Cardboard shacks were lined up all the way to the top. When the four men she'd hired dug up the grave, there was a huge sepulcher, the tomb of rock, as big as two large men put together. My mother told me that my grandfather, who was heartbroken over how young my father was when he died, wanted to make sure his ashes were well preserved after cremation. Thus, grandfather put the ashes in the rock and sealed it properly.

The only instruments the men had with which to move the rock were two long linen cloths, two four-by-four timbers, and two shovels. They made a sling of the cloth and timbers to carry the sepulcher on their shoulders. Walking down the steep mountain, they chanted in rhythm while Ron videotaped the whole process. When my uncle Min-Shik, Tong-Ho, Mother, and I arrived at the new burial site, people were everywhere. Most of the men wore special robes made of coarse hemp with a hemp rope around their waists and tall hats made out of the same material. As I served rice wine and bowed, Mother said, "Young-Hee and her husband are here to bid farewell. You stay in peace and look after their lives." Then she wiped her tears with a handkerchief.

Soon after Ron arrived in Seoul, his mother called to tell him that Ron's father had been diagnosed with intestinal cancer. She called every day. We shortened our vacation and came home.

On September 25, 1970, the new family began a new life.

Our house in Bethesda, Maryland, was an ordinary small rambler with three bedrooms on the ground floor and a finished full basement containing a fourth bedroom. Soon it became a refugee camp for my family. Everybody took turns cooking and eating in the kitchen. Since bananas were scarce in Korea and everyone loved them, I bought a big bag every day.

Waiting to enroll in American University, Young Chang took a job that I'd found him in the Kenwood Country Club dining room, where I would drive him every morning at 7:00 AM. No students work in Korea, and my mother was upset that I got Young Chang a job. "Who would have thought that he would have to work so hard?" she complained.

My family believed that they would have a comfortable life in America, just as I'd thought my life here was going to be one unbroken string of parties.

Two of my nephews enrolled in the public school near our house. The eldest boy, William (Korean name Woo-chul; Ron made up American names for the two boys), adjusted well and made friends quickly, but Mitchul (Minch-chul), the six-year-old, had a hard time. I kept running back and forth to the school because he was constantly in trouble fighting with other kids. Because he had problems communicating and was misbehaving in class, the school authorities suggested that we take him for a psychological evaluation, but he couldn't be evaluated without knowing the language. Besides, I was busy taking my brother Tong-Ho around town for job interviews. Ron kept teasing me, saying, "You should have several hats."

In Korea, people live in very close quarters, usually all in the same room. As a result, my mother, who'd shared a room with her children most of all her life, had no concept of privacy. She walked in and out of our bedroom without knocking while Ron and I were still asleep. After dinner, she wanted to sit at the table to talk all night long and reminisce about her life in Korea. I understood her loneliness and her longing for the familiar environment, but I was torn between my sympathy for my mother and my duties as Ron's wife.

Although I gave her her own room, she couldn't bear staying by herself and went to the basement to be with the others. My mother and sister-in-law, Young-Ja, were both strong-willed people and never stopped fighting. When not arguing, Young-Ja kept crying. Whenever she saw an Asian, and there weren't many in the States in the '70s, she begged me to buy her a one-way ticket back to Korea. To keep them busy, I had them to knit children's mittens and booties to sell door to door, which was a good distraction. They made money and kept busy.

In the beginning of December, we decided that we should make *kimjang*, or winter *kimchi*, if we were going to have an ample supply for the whole family. Nowadays, I know many Americans have eaten *kimchi*. Some love it, some hate it, and some have no idea what it is, including my editor. But let me explain what *kimchi* is. *Kimchi* is the most relished food in Korea. In Korean food culture, no other food has the importance of *kimchi*. *Kimchi* and rice is like what Americans say, "Love and marriage is like horse and carriage." For instance, a meal without *kimchi* is unthinkable, and even if such existed, the meal is not "complete"; it is considered to be lacking in style and grace. Rice and *kimchi* constitute the basic meal for Koreans. The two alone will suffice as a meal. No one really can say how many different *kimchi* there are. Also, the kind of *kimchi* vary according to the length of the fermentation period, with some being edible instantly, like mild summer *kimchi*, while others require a longer fermentation period. That is the category of *kimjang*. Mostly *kimjang* is created because Korean winters are cold and harsh. It was hard to find vegetables of any sort a long time ago, and *kimchi* provided Koreans with vitamin C that, otherwise, was hard to get. Besides, the freshness of vegetables and the refreshing intestinal regulation of the lactic acid all added *to kimchi's* nutritional value. *Kimjang* is eaten all during the winter and until the next spring, or even until summer. It was because Korea had such wonderfully glazed pots that fermented foods could be produced. Therefore long before the age of refrigerators, Koreans thought up ways to keep *kimchi* at relatively stable temperature in order to eat it for a long time, and they were buried in deep in a dark corner of the earth. But recently when I visited my brother in Seoul, I was stunned to see his new apartment came with a *kimchi* refrigerator along with the regular refrigerator and stoves. *Kimchi* now has its own entry in the *Encyclopedia Britannica*.

When I lived in Korea, all the cabbages, turnips, and red peppers were harvested before the ground froze and brought into the city so that every household could prepare their supply. *Kimjang* season was one of the biggest events to all of Koreans. Each house scheduled this big project so that the neighborhood women could help each other. In our house in Bethesda, to prepare *kimjang*, I went to several hardware stores to see if I could find pots for making the *kimjang* and putting it in the ground. But there was nothing like the Korean earthen pots that were especially made for the purpose. I had no choice but to buy a couple of tall pots. They were one and a half feet tall and fifteen inches in diameter. I didn't know what they were at the time, but looking back, I know they were for big plants.

Three of us went to the store and bought a big box of Chinese cabbage and turnips. Then the "*kimjang party*" started. First we spread the several pages of the *Washington Post* on the whole floor of the kitchen. Mother and Young-Ja sat down on the floor and went into production. Young-Ja cut cabbages into quarters lengthwise, washed them, and sprinkled enough salt on them so that they would wilt. Mother peeled tons of garlic. Next, she combined green onions, fish sauce, chopped garlic and ginger, lots of dried ground red pepper, and thinly cut strips of turnips. When the cabbages were wilted enough and ready, Mother covered her hands with vegetable oil to protect her skin from the hot spices and stuffed the mixture of spices in between layers of cabbage leaves. Each stuffed cabbage was rolled and packed into the pots. She pushed them well down so that the juice from the cabbage covered the top. All three of us carried the pots out to the backyard, dug up the ground, and buried them. If some American saw it, they might have thought that we were burying a corpse. Then we had to wait. When we finally ate the *kimchi* later, it didn't taste as good as when we made it in Korea. Looking back, I am sure it is because we didn't have proper earthen crockpots.

After six months, Ron bought a small house in Rockville, Maryland, and moved Tong-Ho's family there. Tong-Ho got a job as a bartender at a downtown restaurant called Blackie's. Although everyone else seemed to adjust to their new life, my mother was still having a difficult time. She was very sociable and had had many friends in Korea. After the Korean War ended and the American wind blew through the country, everyone started to learn ballroom dances, and she'd become very good. Singles or widows are not as lonesome in Korea as they are here, as all the women get together and socialize. Here in the States, she had no one but me. She would often cry and say, "I have a mouth, but I cannot talk to anybody. I have legs, but I have no place to go to."

When I was in Korea, I catered to her every need and took her with me wherever I was performing, so she thought I would do the same when she came to this country. In self-defense, I finally decided to find an apartment for her and Young Chang. I could hear her crying every night. "I came to this strange country, thinking my life in my old age was to live with you, not someplace else." After they moved out, I found her a job at a bowling alley as a babysitter to keep her mind off her loneliness. Then one day a man from the bowling alley called me and said I should come because Mother fell on the floor and couldn't move. When I rushed there, she told me that her head was spinning so badly that she couldn't lift her head up. She was admitted to a hospital for a week but was discharged when they couldn't find a problem.

Meanwhile, Ron was getting restless. He felt that NBC didn't seem to care about him after he almost got killed while working for them. When we lived in England, he was disappointed that he wasn't selected to go to Paris for the Vietnam peace conference, and he didn't think he had a future with NBC in the United States, covering only insignificant events. He began to explore opportunities with CBS and ABC. When he came home, he talked about buying a farm, which neither one of us knew anything about, or moving to Los Angeles. Of course, Los Angeles was the last place on the Earth I wanted to move. That definitely would be a disaster with all those flower children running around naked. I felt helpless not knowing what to say or how to help him.

On December 1971, a few days before Christmas, he was assigned to cover Bangladesh's independence from India. His first letter, written as a diary, arrived from Calcutta, where he was waiting to get into Bangladesh. He sounded happy to be with the other newsmen he'd been with in Vietnam. No matter how difficult the assignment and the hardship he had to endure, he always seemed to be in good spirits whenever he was chasing an important story.

Therefore, regardless of how unhappy I was about being alone, I thought I should endure it also and be grateful that he was happy. Besides, once we moved to Washington and I had roots, I wanted to have a family. I'd thought I would get pregnant soon after I stopped taking the pill, but it had been five years. "What was wrong with me?" I asked my mother.

"The fortune-teller told me you will have a son late in your age."

"Then where it is?" I kept asking her. I checked every day to see if my periods had stopped. I thought about all the wives of Henry the Eighth who were beheaded because they couldn't give him an heir. In Korea, if a woman can't give her husband a son, she has no right as a wife. One night I told Ron that if I couldn't have a baby, we would go to Korea and find a nice woman for him to have his own son with.

I prayed to every god, and every Sunday, Mother and I went to a Japanese lady who had a Shinto shrine in her apartment. Finally, I decided to seek a doctor who could help me. Ron and I both had tests, and we learned we were both fine. I was in and out of the hospital for different tests. I took my temperature every morning to check for ovulation, and Ron switched to baggy underwear instead of the tight bikinis he'd been wearing. Finally the doctor decided to try artificial insemination. I went to the doctor's office once a month, carrying a little bottle of Ron's semen under my arm to prevent it from freezing. One month went by, then a second, and a third. I was getting more depressed. But the fourth month, the doctor examined me and said, "We got it this time."

Now I had another worry. I'd heard that older mothers have a greater chance of miscarriage, and I hardly walked for fear of losing the baby. During the third month while Ron was out of town, I started to bleed and went into a panic. The doctor ordered bed rest. I stayed in bed for a week, praying and getting up only to go to the bathroom. Luckily, I didn't lose the baby. In Korea, when a good thing happens to you, you're not supposed to utter a word about it. My stomach was getting big, but I kept still about the pregnancy. I didn't prepare a nursery room. I didn't buy any baby outfits. When I was eight months along and Ron was back in Vietnam, his mother stopped by. I had a big brocade housecoat on and stood as far as I could from her, afraid she would touch my stomach. Of course, it was like "calling meow with your eyes closed," which means that something is obvious. She looked at me and asked me, "Are you pregnant?"

I stepped back uneasily. "No."

She came close and swept her hand over my stomach. "Yes, you are. How could you hide it from family?"

I knew no one would accept my explanation.

A month before Ed was due, Ron came back from Saigon. On March 13, 1973, at five in the morning, Ron drove me to the Washington Hospital Center in DC. We waited and waited. Ron kept taking pictures. The baby wouldn't budge. At two in the afternoon, the doctor finally decided to do C-section. As I was being rolled into the operating room, a nurse asked me what I would have, a boy or a girl. "Of course, it'll be a boy," I told her. When I started to wake up, the nurse asked if I wanted to know what I'd had, but I wanted Ron to tell me, "You have a son." Edward was born one day before my birthday, as if he couldn't wait that extra day.

Ron came every day, sitting next to me from ten in the morning to ten at night, not even eating lunch. He told me, "Boy, you should see the baby's nose. You think mine is big." While I was half drugged, I remember saying to him, "Ron, this is my second happiest day. First is the day I married you." He told me he couldn't feel the ground when he walked. He also told me about all the dishes that were piled up in the sink. I told him not to worry; I would take care of it. I was very weak and wanted to stay in the hospital more than three days, but Ron kept saying that I had to come home. When I got home, I saw a big color TV on the dresser, which I had been asking for a long time. But nothing mattered then, not money or fame, except Edward.

Finally, finally, finally, my real dream had come true. Edward was born, and my life seemed to be in perfect order. Mother was happy to spend most of her time with him, whom I would've given my life for. My family was close by, and they finally seemed to be happy too.

But not having an exciting story to cover, Ron was not happy. He was never home on Sundays, and I didn't know where he went. One Sunday when Edward was six month old, he fell off from a chair and had a big cut on his forehead. The blood ran out profusely. I ran to the neighbor and the man took us to the emergency room. I called NBC, but no one was there. Sometimes Ron called me from LA and told me to come and pick him up at Dulles Airport, about forty miles from our house. At two o'clock in the morning, I'd drive a completely isolated road with a baby in the bassinet, scared to death that my old Nova would have a flat tire and break down. When Edward was three months old, Ron and I took him for five days on a rented houseboat in Annapolis. Ron took the boat out to the middle of nowhere and read all day on deck. The boat was beautiful, the sun was warm, and blue water stretched out for miles and miles, but I felt all alone. In the middle of the night, it started to rain, and I got up to give milk to the baby. But there was no electricity, and the raindrops were dripping on the baby where he was sleeping, so I moved him to a dry spot and warmed the milk under my arm. Ron called someone somehow, and the next day they came and towed the boat to a nearby village. He didn't know the electricity had to recharge in the evening. Next evening Ron tried to hook up to the village electrical outlet and blew out the fuse, and the whole village went dark. The rain never stopped as Ron listened to the Watergate hearings on his portable radio. It poured the next day, too, so we decided to leave early. When he tried to dock the boat, he bumped into and damaged the boats on either side as I stood with Edward in my arms, swaying back and forth, afraid I would fall into the water. Ron never wanted to go anywhere on holidays, saying it's best to stay home since everyone left town.

That was the last vacation we took.

NBC offered to move us to Hong Kong, the place we both loved dearly. While I was looking forward to our assignment there, Ron covered Vice President Spiro Agnew and his indictment on corruption charges. Every day, from dawn to late at night, Ron camped out in front of the vice president's house in Kenwood, Maryland.

Soon afterward, Agnew resigned, and NBC assigned Ron to cover the new vice president, Gerald Ford. While the Watergate investigation was in full swing, the new VP traveled constantly, and I hardly ever saw Ron. But this time, I didn't mind. I was busy with my baby, my family was settled, and the anticipation of starting our new lives in Hong Kong kept me happy. Seeing Ron so happy and excited made me think that I could endure anything. Still, I kept waiting month after month for details about Hong Kong, but it seemed that Ron had forgotten all about the assignment. Finally, I asked him.

"Watergate is the most important event in history," he said, "and I just don't think we should move now. Who cares about Hong Kong or anything else right now?"

Of course, my disappointment was beyond description. But for Ron, it was the best decision he had ever made in his life.

Looking into White House and wondering who lived there
when I first arrived in Washington

When I first came to NY

The first Buddhist-Jewish wedding at NY Carlyle Hotel

Jill as a bride's maid.

Me in Korean outfit Mother made for me to wear at my
wedding reception.

Our arrival at Korea International Airport

Ron's first trip to Korea

Honeymoon at Palm Beach

Rare vacation at Grand Caymen

Caymen Island '68

First Home, 1992

Vacation in Japan and Hong Kong. At Abarddin restaurant
picking a lobster. Ron eating at the motel. Tong Kun,
Mother and me

Hong Kong,
Mother, me, Tong Kun

Accapulco

After a bull fight

Greece 1967

Hotel Las Vegas 1967

1966 My Birthday in Mexico

In HK. Me with orange juice

Keep off the grass

Assignment in London

Vacation in Hawaii

In Hawaii

With my friend Shim.

Posing as Marilyn Monroe

The puppy Ron bought me on Christmas day

Vacation in Hawaii

During the 60's hippie movement, Ron in Mao jacket

Cindy gives it all up

Do you remember Cindy and the Two Apple.

The song and dance team was quite a hit with Hongkong nightclub audiences a couple of years ago.

Now Cindy is back in the Colony. But there are no Apples this time—just her husband, NBC cameraman Ron Nessen.

Cindy, a 5ft 3in Korean beauty, decided on a singing career six years ago.

"Rather than "go it alone," she joined the Two Apples . . . the dancing side of the act.

While the three girls were entertaining troops in Saigon, Cindy met Ron.

But the couple had to separate, as Ron, recovering from mortar wounds, was sent to Washington.

In the capital, Ron realised "He couldn't live without me," said Cindy.

They married last February, and since then have lived in Mexico and the United States.

The Nessens are now in Hongkong for six weeks — on Ron's latest assignment.

Cindy will not be making any nightclub appearances . . . "I'm strictly a housewife now," she says.

Cindy before . . .
The bright lights

Cindy after . . .
Just a housewife

Hong Kong paper saying I gave it all up and became a house wife when I went back to the US with Ron after I got married

The White House

Do not envy fame;
The other side of fame is disgrace.
Do not envy wealth;
The other side of wealth is greed.
Envy simplicity and humility;
These are better than fame and wealth
For they'll bring richness to your soul.

—Kim Sam Hyun

Avoid shame, but do not seek glory,
nothing is so expensive as glory.

—Sydney Smith (1771-1845, English writer)

On Thursday evening, August 8, 1974, President Richard M. Nixon appeared on national television and announced his resignation. The next morning, Gerald Ford was sworn in as the new president of the United States. To add to the confusion, President Ford was informed that King Hussein of Jordan planned to visit the United States beginning August 15, and that a state dinner had been planned for Friday, August 16, long before Nixon's resignation. Instead of postponing the event, as some thought he should, President Ford decided to go ahead with it.

President Nixon seldom invited the media to such occasions and was known for holding reporters at arm's length. Now, the new president wanted a more open and friendly relationship with the media. With that in mind, President Ford added six White House correspondents to his guest list: John Herbers, of the *New York Times*; Carroll Kilpatrick, of the *Washington Post*; Helen Thomas, of UPI; Thomas DeFrank, of *Newsweek*; Eric Sevareid, the CBS television commentator; and Ron Nessen, representing NBC.

Ron brought home the White House invitation on Wednesday evening, just two days before the state dinner. Emblazoned with the gold presidential seal, it read, "The President and Mrs. Ford request the pleasure of Mr. and Mrs. Ron Nessen at dinner on Friday evening, August 16, 1974, at eight o'clock."

Although I thought my life in America would be one long string of visits to fancy nightclubs, the only time I had worn an evening gown was soon after I arrived in New York in 1966, when Ron had taken me to a huge banquet to receive an award for his work as a journalist in Vietnam. I wore a long pink satin skirt with a slit up the side that was beaded and a pink sequined top that I'd had made in Hong Kong. Since our marriage, however, there had been no opportunities for me to put on fancy clothes and go to parties, let alone to a black-tie affair, and now, we were invited to the White House state dinner.

I hurried to Georgetown and chose an inexpensive but elegant dress—royal blue with spaghetti straps, free-flowing pants, and a matching chiffon cape. The cape had designs that looked like floating bubbles to match my mood. I also bought a pair of silver sandals like the kind I used to wear in Hong Kong when I sang.

That evening, I had my hair up, put on simple pearl earrings with small teardrop pendants and slipped on the big turquoise ring that Ron had bought for me when we were in Florida. Ron had never looked as handsome as he did in his tuxedo and black tie, and he arranged to have a limo for us waiting at the curb. Mother came onto the front steps, holding little Edward, and I waved good-bye. Mother lifted Edward's arm to wave back. As we drove down Massachusetts Avenue past the foreign embassies, I kept thinking that I, Song Young-Hee from Korea, was about to go to the White House. The little girl who had once planted rice while leeches slithered up her legs and made her own straw slippers because she had no shoes to wear was now wearing silver sandals on her way to meet the most powerful man in the world.

I looked out the window of the limousine, not really seeing anything, and became absorbed in a question that had suddenly gripped me. It was a question that I would ask time and time again in the ensuing years, and one, in fact, that I still ask myself whenever life takes me in a new direction: *Who is it,* I wondered, *that draws the path of our lives beyond our ability to understand it?*

The only time I had seen the White House was when Ron brought me down from New York soon after I had arrived in September of 1965. I stood outside its iron fence, staring across the vast lawn at the grand structure and feeling like an outsider in many different ways. Now I was a guest of the powerful man who lived there.

The driver pulled up to the south gate, and a policeman stepped up to the car as Ron handed him our invitation. He examined it for a moment and then told the driver to drop us off in front of the south reception hall, already filled with people standing shoulder to shoulder and chatting. I had never seen so many gorgeous gowns and glittering jewels in one room and thought the scene I was witnessing was only possible in the movies.

The reception hall was small and round, with walls covered with historical murals. Soon people lined the stairway leading to the second floor of the White House. Ron and I followed and moved slowly up. The excitement of the unknown paralyzed me. What was up there? What was I to do when I arrived at the top? I heard the band playing.

When we stepped up from the last stair, I saw the United States Marine Band, wearing their white summer uniforms, playing in one corner. A good-looking young marine, dressed in the most handsome uniform I had ever laid eyes on, walked up and extended his arm. As he guided us to the entrance of the East Room, I felt as if I was in one of Chagall's paintings, floating over myself.

"Your dress is beautiful," the marine said, evidently trying to make me feel at home. I wanted to smile, but my face felt as if it was frozen.

As we paused for a moment before actually entering the East Room, I saw President Ford, standing next to King Hussein, Mrs. Ford, and Queen Alia, greeting the rest of the guests. The young marine escorted me to the chief protocol officer, who asked my name. He then announced, "Mr. and Mrs. Ron Nessen."

First I shook hands with President Ford, and then with King Hussein. As I passed by the president, I heard him call Ron's name as he was being introduced to the king. The king had a warm smile below his sexy little mustache. Next, I was introduced to the First Lady Betty Ford wearing a white crepe gown trimmed in ostrich feathers. Queen Alia looked young enough to be the king's daughter (she was only twenty-five) in a blue chiffon gown and large diamond earrings. After all of the guests had been received, we went into the dining room. Ron greeted several of his friends and acquaintances on the way, but I was still in a state of bedazzlement. When we entered the dining room, Ron and I were seated at different tables. Holding my table number, which was stuffed in a small envelope with the gold presidential seal, I found myself at a large round table with nine complete strangers. No one seemed to know each other, but the men stood behind the ladies' chairs until all the ladies were seated. I exchanged hellos with the two men on either side of me. They both seemed preoccupied and were looking around to see who else was in the room. The Fords and their guests of honor sat at a long head table, which was how President Nixon had entertained, but after that night, President Ford never again used a head table as he wanted all the guests to be equal.

I studied each face, trying to identify anyone I knew. Finally, at the opposite side of the table I recognized Warren Burger, Chief Justice of the Supreme Court, who kept looking at me. No other Asians were among the guests, and I am sure he was wondering why I'd been invited to a state dinner.

It had been a long time since the White House had hosted such an occasion. Everyone, including the chefs, had worked overtime producing an eleventh-hour state dinner, which usually was planned months in advance. The White House flower shop pulled together centerpieces of blue delphiniums, cornflowers, and yellow chrysanthemums, representing the colors of President Ford's alma mater, the University of Michigan. The White House calligraphers wrote the place cards even though they didn't have all the names until late in the week.

I kept examining all the details of the table to imprint them on my brain forever. Besides the gorgeous flower arrangements and candelabras, the table was dressed with yellow, and the china, which was used during President Nixon's era, had wildflowers surrounding a federal eagle. There were four glasses at each place setting and more silverware and crystal at the table than I'd ever seen before. An elegant menu was provided for each guest. The meal began with *poached salmon en belleve* and ended with a mousse *au chocolat.* In between were roast sirloin of beef with sauce *Bordelaise, mushrooms provencal,* and *artichokes St. Germain,* followed by Bibb lettuce served with Brie. I didn't know what anything was, except *mousse au chocolat,* which I had tasted when I went out to dinner with Ron and had hated. I kept watching others to make sure that I did not make mistakes.

I was still having a hard time getting used to Western food, but that night, I liked everything. Every time I was served a new dish, the waiter poured a different wine that I didn't touch. Before the dessert, they brought out little bowls of clear water with a piece of lemon floating in them, and I watched the other guests. Some didn't touch theirs. Others dipped their fingers and wiped them off on their napkins.

Koreans never like sweet, especially chocolate, and I asked only for a small dab. But when this mousse touched my tongue, it melted away immediately, and I decided to ask for a second helping. But I didn't know that there were no second helpings at formal dinners, and the man who'd served it never returned.

As the champagne was poured, strolling marine violinists scattered to the different tables, played a few bars at each, and moved on to the next and the next. I knew all the songs, and while I was mouthing each melody, Chief Justice Warren Burger, just across the table, watched me. I smiled and kept on. He never took his eyes off me. When the dinner was over, a lady who had been sitting on the other side of my dinner partner introduced herself, "We haven't had a chance to talk. My name is Estée Lauder. What's yours?"

I couldn't believe it. *The* Estée Lauder? To women in Korea, Estée Lauder products were considered pure gold. They were the only foreign cosmetics known in Korea at the time, and any Korean woman would pay anything to get her hands on them. No foreign goods were legally allowed into the country, and Estée Lauder products were often sold by the wives of GIs who had privileges at the post exchange. After this first meeting, I got to know her, her son Leonard, and Leonard's wife quite well, and she once told me that her makeup was the source of her smooth skin.

As I left the dining room, I noticed other familiar faces that I had seen on the news. Mr. and Mrs. Robert McNamara, Speaker of the House and Mrs. Carl Albert, Secretary of the Treasury and Mrs. William Simon, Secretary of Defense James Schlesinger, and many more. Near the entrance of the dining room, Henry Kissinger caught my eye. It struck me as funny to see him looking up at his wife, Nancy, who was six feet tall and towered over him, and lovingly patting her on her cheek. Before he was married, Kissinger took out a lot of young starlets, and his famous quote, "*Power is the ultimate aphrodisiac,*" said it perfectly.

After dinner, everyone headed toward the East Room. As I followed the others through the Blue, the Red, and the Green Room, I stared at gold-framed portraits all the way up the tall walls and at the elegant sofas, each one the same color as the room it was in, with gold frames and a gold pattern of eagles on the upholstery. I noticed the figurines and the ornate glass ashtrays placed on each of the coffee tables. As I passed a large mirror, I saw my reflection and paused for a fraction of a second to make sure I was really there.

By the time I got to the East Room, the band was in full swing, and people were dancing. Near the entrance, I saw a dozen or so women sitting at tables that struck me as odd, but I was too busy trying to take in everything to think too much about it. The band was playing old-time swing music like "*C'est Si Bon*," "*Mack the Knife*," and "*Tea for Two*." It was the kind of music that I loved and used to sing. I couldn't find Ron, who was busy catching up with famous people, and I stood by myself singing quietly and watching the dancers, but mostly my eyes were on the band. Finally, I couldn't stand it. I went over to the bandleader on the stage and beckoned him.

"May I sing a couple songs?" I asked. "I was a singer before."

"What do you want to sing?"

"Can you play 'Around the World' in the key of F?" It always had been my opening number.

They didn't play my usual swing tempo, so I swung my arm faster as a sign for them to keep up. It wasn't exactly the way I used to sing, but it was okay. When I finished, the bandleader asked me, "What else do you want to sing?"

"How about '*Blueberry Hill*,'" I said.

When I'm on stage, I fear nothing. A couple of hours earlier I could barely walk up the stairs because I was so numb, and now I was giving the White House band instructions. As they struck the first rolling notes and I broke into the song, the dancing stopped. Those on the dance floor turned and watched and listened and several started clapping to the music. I felt as if I was back in Seoul when I was singing at Moo Hawk Sung dance hall in 1960. I told the bandleader, "Thank you," and blew a kiss to him as everyone applauded.

When I stepped back onto the floor, I felt as though I was ten feet tall. By then President and Mrs. Ford were on the dance floor dancing nearly nonstop with the king and queen only a little less energetic. Everyone was in a festive mood, and dancing continued without a break for more than an hour. Around eleven thirty, the royal couple departed, and President Ford escorted them to the foyer. Then he returned to the East Room and the dancing. Ron and I bumped into the president dancing with his daughter, Susan. Ron and the president spoke, and then Ron turned me toward the president and said, "Time to change partners, Mr. President."

My mind was whirling at that moment. Tall and strong, the president acted as if he was on top of the world. Why shouldn't he? He was almost there, I thought. I don't remember what exactly we talked about except that he asked me how Ron liked covering the White House stories, and

I blurted out, "Mr. President, Ron is like a little boy sometimes. But he is a good man."

The president gave me a big chuckle and said, "You said it. I didn't."

Ron had been waiting anxiously for a response from the president regarding a party he had planned for his colleagues who had covered Ford when he was the vice president. So I looked up at the president and asked, "Are you coming to our party? We've been waiting patiently for your answer."

Looking back, I now know it was a bold question. But President Ford was so friendly and approachable and had such a great sense of humor that I felt as if I was dancing with an old friend, which is how he always treated me in the many days to come in our relationship.

Looking down at me, he asked, "When is it?"

"Sunday, the twenty-fifth," I said. "Ten days from now. Do you have any plans for that day? I mean, I have to prepare the food, so I need to know how many are coming. Will you be there?"

He looked at me and laughed again. "Okay, tell Ron I'll be there."

Then the slow dance number ended, and the band switched to Jim Croce's *"Bad, Bad Leroy Brown."* For an instant the president seemed unsure of himself, but this was my kind of music. I released his hand, smiled, moved back a couple of steps and started to move my whole body to the tempo. With my cape draped over my shoulders, I spread my arms as if they were the wings of an eagle and moved slowly, swaying my hips, just as I had done so many years ago on the stage, driving the GIs wild. The president seemed a bit embarrassed and kept giving his famous Charlie Brown chuckle while trying to keep up with me. It might as well have been just him and me in that big room.

I could see that shaking his behind was the last thing the president wanted to do in that hall with the 120 guests watching him, but he was a good sport, so cute and brave trying to do something he felt so uneasy about. But he was having too much of a good time to give it up. And I wouldn't let him, either.

By this time, others on the floor had stopped and circled around us, including the white-uniformed military aides, and everyone started clapping to the music and encouraging the president to dance. Ron stood at the edge of the dance floor with a big smile on his face and a glass of champagne in his hand. When the music stopped, the president, still chuckling, hugged my shoulder while the guests and I and even the band members applauded.

When I tried to leave the dance floor, I was surrounded by strangers, all women who'd been sitting by the door when I'd come in and now holding little notepads in their hands. For a moment, I was confused. Every one asked, all at the same time, "Who are you?"

"I'm Mrs. Ron Nessen," I replied.

"Where are you from?" one of them asked.

"Bethesda," I told her.

"No," she said. "I mean, originally."

"I'm Korean."

Then one lady asked me in Korean, "Are you Korean?"

Later, I found out her name was Ms. Moon, a reporter for Reuters News Service among the other women reporters who covered social events at the White House. She had been a strong opponent of the Korean dictator Park Chung-hee and had been banned from our country. I could not know it then, but she would be the one who would instigate my "confinement," which was soon to come.

A few minutes later, the Fords were ready to depart, and we followed them to the entrance hall. "I enjoyed it. I enjoyed it very much," said the president. And with a wave and another of his famous chuckles, he and Mrs. Ford left for their home in Alexandria, since he'd only been president for a week, and they hadn't had time to move to the White House yet.

Later, shortly after 1:00 AM, we left with all the other guests.

In the limo, Ron said, "Now, what can top that?"

I was still dreaming. I had sung at the White House. I had danced with the president of the United States. What would people in Korea say if they knew? For Korean people, the White House was a place they could only dream about. Had it been a dream? The Broadway song *"If You Could See Me Now"* went through my mind.

Finally, very casually, while I was still looking out the window, I said, "The president is coming to your party."

Life in a Fishbowl

When the day ends,
The sun goes down behind
The mountain.
On the fifteenth day
The moon starts to diminish.
Like the sun and the moon
Fame, and glory will disappear.
It's only a matter of time.

—Anonymous

No matter how far the sun shines,
Still it must set.

—Ferdinand Raimund (1790-1836 French poet)

In the following days, I became a celebrity. Pictures of me dancing with President Ford showed up on television and in magazines and newspapers.

On Sunday, August 25, 1974, the day that President and Mrs. Ford were to come to our house, the warm, dry weather could not have been more perfect. Since there were hardly any Korean grocery stores in Washington at the time, my sister-in-law and I made several hundred *mandoo* or Korean dumplings, skin and all, overnight for 150 guests. Besides, I had no idea that there was such a thing as catering. My mother-in-law and I went to Rockville to rent chairs and tables, and I never thought of hiring anyone to help. In Korea, you do your utmost for your guests to let them know how much you appreciate their coming to your house. We also cooked *bul-gogi* (barbecue beef) on our outdoor grill, along with many vegetable dishes, pan-fried fish, and, of course, *kimchi*. My brother Tong-Ho and his friend tended the bar, and Tong-Kun and Young-Chang greeted the guests at the front of the house. Ron kept saying, "You have to tell your family not to come outside."

That morning, I saw the neighbor's children standing around the front of our house.

"What are you doing here?" I asked them.

"We heard on the radio that the president is coming," one of them said. I realized then that when it came to the president of the United States, nothing is secret.

First, a half-dozen Secret Service men arrived and inspected every corner of the outside of our house. The police surrounded the outside of the house. Shortly thereafter, Mrs. Ford arrived, accompanied by more Secret Service men. She wore a long lime green flowered skirt and a yellow long-sleeved turtleneck shirt. She had just had a mastectomy and seemed to have lost a lot of weight and looked very fragile. Everyone talked to her and wanted to have their picture taken with her. Late in the afternoon, President Ford arrived after his morning golf game. What a wonderful, down-to-earth man he was to agree to come to our small and humble one-story house, just for the enjoyment.

All afternoon, people ate and drank. With his colleagues, Ron put on funny sketches. Sitting between the president and Tom Brokaw, holding Edward in my arms, I couldn't stop laughing. A pipe in his mouth, President Ford kept looking at me with a big grin on his face. While everybody was eating in our backyard, my mother and my sister-in-law were busy feeding all the police outside. Toward the end of the evening, my mother came out from the kitchen, bowed before the president, and asked him how he liked the Korean food, which she had prepared.

Standing up from the lounge chair, he said, "Oh, everything was delicious, although the *kimchi* was a little hot for me." Then he gave one of his famous Charlie Brown chuckles. This was the most rewarding day of my life. In Korea, for the president of the country to come to a house such as ours would have been unthinkable even if he were a friend.

When the party was over, Ron said, "We can't top what we had today." But in fact, it was just the beginning. In September, Jerald terHorst, President Ford's press secretary, resigned, and Ron was approached about the job. He became the White House press secretary on September 20, 1975. Even the night before, everyone knew, and they called Ron to congratulate him. He was lying on the bed answering the calls.

"It was that Korean reporter, Ms. Moon," Ron said, after hanging up the phone. "She warned me that the Korean government will now try to approach you for special favors. You better not see any Koreans other than your family and close relatives." Naïvely, I was angry with Ron. I thought no Korean would do anything to harm me. But much later I realized he was right.

The next day, his picture was splashed all over the world. Ron left the house at 6:30 AM in a limousine instead of our old Nova. He didn't return home until nearly midnight. The first time I called him at work, I almost hung up when the operator answered, "The White House." When he came home at night, he would go into Edward's room and wake him up. Eighteen-month-old Edward would get excited and stay up past midnight, and I would be in and out of his room for the rest of the night trying to get him to go back to sleep.

One Sunday, about twenty-nine minutes after Ron took Edward out for a ride on his motorcycle, Ron called from the police station and told me that I should come and pick up Edward. The police had detained Ron because Edward wasn't wearing a helmet. I then realized that in America, it doesn't matter who you are under the law. In Korea, the police would have bowed and apologized for causing Ron the inconvenience.

A month later, at eleven thirty one morning, while I was taking my shower, Ron's secretary called and said that I should pick up his mother and come to the White House in one hour for Ron's swearing-in ceremony in the Oval Office. My hair was still wet, so I threw on a wig, grabbed Edward, my brother, and my mother-in-law and rushed off to the White House. The staff from the press office was invited, as was the Chief of Staff Donald Rumsfeld. After the ceremony, the president said to me, "I'm sorry your husband is working such long hours and coming home so late."

"Yes, I know," looking up at him, I replied with Edward in my arms. "When do you think you can send him home early?"

Everyone in the Oval Office burst out laughing, including the president. Ron looked uneasy and said, "Oh, it's not all that bad."

On the way home, Ron's mother asked me, "How can you think of saying something like that at such a time?"

My brother agreed. "Yeah, *Noonah*, you are something else."

"Why?" I asked. "The president's a person just like you and me. What's the big deal?"

Ron always seemed nervous when I was with the president and could never understand how I could be so relaxed around important dignitaries. I could never understand why Ron acted so uneasy when he was with others, especially with important people. President Ford was so comfortable to be around, and I loved his warm and genuine laughter. I always joked with him, and his sense of humor was one of his many exceptional qualities. Few other people in the Washington power circles were as approachable, and most didn't bother to carry on a long conversation with someone like me, a housewife. President Ford was the only one who never looked over my shoulder to see if there was someone else more important behind me.

On a Christmas trip to Vail, Colorado, we rode in Air Force One to Denver. The President and Ron, of course, were flown out to Vail on a helicopter. But the White House staffers, their families, and I had to ride an Air Force bus that climbed hills at five miles an hour while the traffic passed us. The little children with us cried and cried no matter how their mothers tried to calm them, and I wanted to get off and push, just as I had wanted to do on the day we moved to Yangsan on that beat-up truck. Finally, I asked, "Who is responsible for this Air Force bus?"

Ed Weidenfeld, the husband of Sheila Weidenfeld, the press secretary to Mrs. Ford, said, "It's President Ford, Cindy. You should give him hell."

That evening, when we were in line for the buffet dinner, I said to the president, "Someone told me that you are in charge of the Air Force?"

Puzzled, he said, "Yeah?"

"In that case, I think you had better straighten out the Air Force in Denver so they will make sure their buses are in shape. Do you know how long it took us to get here? Five hours!"

He gave another of his famous laughs and said, "You know what? You're lucky I didn't know you when you were in Korea."

Mrs. Lynne Cheney, whose husband, Dick, had become the White House chief of staff when Donald Rumsfeld was appointed secretary of defense, was helping herself to food and just kept grinning.

Shaika, a dinner club in Vail, belonged to President Ford's ski instructor, and it was named after his wife. Usually, all the reporters and their families spent their evenings there. A famous old singing group, the Ink Spots, was performing. Could I stop myself from singing? No. I sang "Around the World" and "Blueberry Hill." Afterward, the president hugged me and his wife. In the picture, along with his signature, he wrote "Two arms full."

As soon as Ron began working in the White House, we began receiving gifts, even from people I didn't know. Ron warned me that I should not accept anything, even though it was perfectly legal if the item cost less than $15. Ron even sent back a box of Kikkoman soy sauce, and I felt sorry for the sender, whoever it was. Once, a Korean family who knew my family sent me a small package that I was dying to open. But after keeping it for several days, I sent it back. Old friends and strangers wrote to me through the White House and asked me for all kinds of favors. I helped one man, who asked me to extend his visa. All letters were opened before they were sent on to me. The press staff even answered some and signed my name to them.

Korean friends thought I had influence, like the wives of powerful men in Korea. Others thought that I had become too good for anyone because of my husband's new position. Once my friend Linda (the one who had advised me to buy the fur wrap) wrote me a letter and enclosed a $500 check. She said that a couple of very important prosecutors were arriving in Washington from Korea, and I should introduce them to Ron and dine with them. She had no idea how my hands were tied. Not only did I hardly ever see Ron, but there was no way I could influence him in any way, shape or form. I sent back her check and tried to explain the situation here in Washington. But she didn't understand and was offended, accusing me of being paranoid and giving her a ridiculous excuse.

I agree the Ron was right not to let me keep any gifts or see any Koreans. Otherwise, unknowingly, I could have become involved in an unpleasant scandal like Koreagate, which revolved around Tongsun Park, a once-well-known Korean deal-maker in Washington. As was a customary practice in Asia, Mr. Park "contributed" a lot of cash to decision-makers in Washington. Eventually, an investigation forced many powerful men, including congressmen, to either resign or go to jail. In the middle of the investigation, the FBI came to our house to inquire about whether Ron and I were involved. Ron told me that my name was among a dozen prominent Korean businessmen and others who lived in the Washington area and were listed as agents for the Korean government. Soon after he became the press secretary, Ron was called into the National Security office and warned that they had intercepted a wire from the Korean government to the Korean Embassy to find out who was the closest to the Nessens. He reminded me, "You got mad at me when I told you to be careful with dealing with any Koreans other than your family."

Before Ron became press secretary, Tongsun Park invited us to one of his well-known power parties at his mansion off Massachusetts

Avenue. Every famous decision maker was there, including Elizabeth Dole, who had not yet married Bob Dole. After Ron became press secretary, Mr. Park invited us repeatedly, but Ron didn't respond, and that was the end of it. Ron and I were nicknamed *"bamboo"* or *"not a drop of blood,"* the Koreans would say, *"even if they were poked with a needle."* Meaning that no one could corrupt us.

But Koreagate ended up a serious scandal. The IRS confiscated Park's mansion, and he was banned from Washington for a long time. Koreans were embarrassed. Even before Koreagate broke, Tongsun Park had invited Betty Ford's personal secretary, Nancy Howe, to a resort island with all expenses paid. When it was reported in the paper, her husband, a West Point graduate and a retired general, put a gun in his mouth and killed himself.

While Ron worked at the White House, our lives were very glamorous. A limo picked us up and dropped us off for such events as the Kennedy Center Gala. Established to honor five well-known artists a year, the evening started with an invitation-only dinner at the State Department, followed by the reception and actual award-giving ceremony at the White House, and then the Kennedy Center Gala performance, shown on TV every year. I'd never seen so many movie stars and powerful people in one place, and for us it was free. When I met Kirk Douglas, I told him that he was my mother's favorite star. With his famous grin, he said, "Yeah, your mother's, huh?"

The greatest thing about the White House for me was that I could see all the wonderful shows from the presidential boxes at the Kennedy Center. Eight seats in the Opera House, twelve in the Concert Hall, six in the Eisenhower Theater. There was a small room in the back where guests could sit and visit during intermissions, and in the next room was a refrigerator filled with drinks, including champagne. The only time we couldn't use the box was when the president was there for an official function, like the gala. Since Ron was too busy to go, I'd book the whole eight-seat box at the Opera House or the twelve seats at the Concert Hall for every show I could and took my family and friends. During the bicentennial year, 1976, ballet companies and orchestras came from all over to perform, and I must have seen every ballet in the world during that time. Once, I took my mother, my brother, and his friends to see a ballet from Denmark. In one number, all the ballerinas danced stark naked. My mother, absolutely flabbergasted, kept saying, "What is going on? What is the matter with them? My God, I have never seen anything that crazy."

Every time we traveled with the president, I was fascinated by how well orchestrated everything was. As soon as Air Force One landed at

Andrews Air Force Base, a line of limousines waiting by the side would pull up to the plane one by one to take everyone home, and by the time we arrived, our luggage would have already been delivered to our front door.

We went to every elegant party in town. For formal occasions Ron often got dressed at his office and went directly to the party from the White House; his secretary would call and tell me where to go, or Ron would leave the invitation so I could meet him at the event. I was invited to other affairs on my own, as when Mrs. Kissinger hosted a party for Mrs. Rabin, the wife of the Israeli Prime Minister, on *Dandy*, a sightseeing boat that sailed the Potomac River, and invited all the wives of the cabinet members to attend while the men were at the White House having a meeting.

We also attended two prestigious white-tie events that took place while Ron was working in the White House—one for French president Valéry Giscard d'Estaing and the other for Emperor Hirohito of Japan. While dressing for the first, I ran up and down from the basement to the bedroom trying to finish the laundry before I left. Finally, I grabbed Edward, put him in our old Nova, drove him to my mother's house, and then sped to the White House since I wasn't allowed to ride in the limo without Ron. It was pouring rain, and I could hardly see the street. I parked my car in the lot and ran to the entrance of the press office. Rain soaked the bottom half of my gown, and while I took off my rain boots, I suddenly thought, *What a life!* I was at a white-tie party for the French president, but I was alone; I never saw Ron on those occasions, and everyone else was looking around to see whom they could talk to.

The parties were endless. Sometimes, rich Republicans gave big formal parties at their homes. At the beginning, I only went where Ron went and stayed home when Ron couldn't go because of his schedule. Later, though, instead of sitting home by myself, I went on my own and had fun. I met Christina Ford, the wife of automobile tycoon, Henry Ford. She was fun, and we hit it off. After one state dinner, she invited us to a luncheon at the residence of the French ambassador, where she and her husband were staying. I don't know why, but Ron didn't want to go. I wouldn't miss the party for no reason, so I went by myself. In contrast to all the white-tie parties and other fancy events we attended, Ron still cut our lawn in his old clothes. Mother often looked out our window and murmured in dismay, *"What a strange country this is. If this were in Korea, there would be a guard in his uniform and hat standing in front of the house. How odd . . . how odd."*

It was true. Much later, when I went to Korea for a business trip, I visited a friend of ours who had become the second most powerful man in Korea. When I went to his house, sure enough, there was a guardhouse at the gate with a guard.

During those years, I always had to beware of whom I talked to or what I said. One day, Nancy Howe told me that Mrs. Ford wanted to buy a fur jacket for her daughter, Susan, as a graduation gift, and she had arranged for a famous fur company called Christie Brothers from New York to come down and put on a fashion show that I was invited to attend. Buying a full-length fur coat was the last thing I had on my mind, but I thought it would be fun to see the show. Although I had the fur wrap that I had bought in Hong Kong, I'd had no occasion to wear it until I started to go to the White House functions. No matter how my life had changed from the time when I couldn't afford any decent clothes, no matter how often in my new life I associated with some of the wealthiest women on the face of the Earth, deep inside I was still the young woman who was afraid to, or thought she shouldn't, waste money on anything that was extravagant.

Since Christie had brought only a tall model from New York, the man from the fur company asked me to try on two coats in small sizes. One was a full-length coat made of baby mink pelts that were soft and light as a feather. I didn't know much about furs, but they glistened and were beautiful. But I still wasn't interested, and when I tried to slip out of the room, the man followed me to the door. He asked me how much I was willing to pay, and I gave him a low figure to get rid of him, but he accepted. I called Ron, who was away with the president, and he said I should buy the coat. I hardly ever asked Ron to buy me anything that was beyond our means, but on the rare occasion when I did, he never told me I couldn't. The next day, when a reporter, Maxine Cheshire, from the *Washington Post*, wrote about the great deal I'd gotten on my coat, Ron was angry and called her up.

Another time, a White House social reporter, whom I often saw at functions, called and invited me to lunch. I should have been more wary of an invitation from a reporter, but Ron said that she was a nice old lady, and I should go. In a posh restaurant near the White House, I found myself sitting with the reporter and two strangers, a woman and a man. I felt uneasy. The woman casually asked me all kinds of questions about Ron. That night, Ron found out that the woman was doing a story about him. Late at night, I heard him yelling at the reporter on the phone for tricking his wife, who had nothing to do with his business.

It was not only small people like me who had to be careful with whom they talked to or associated with. Once, in Los Angeles, Frank Sinatra invited President Ford to his house. The President wanted to go, but the staff was against it because of Sinatra's infamous reputation and connection with the mob, not to mention a rumor that Mr. Sinatra dreamed of becoming the ambassador to Italy. So even President Ford had to decline his invitation.

Occasionally, Ron worked at Camp David on the weekend. The wives accompanied their husbands, but we never saw them. We were in the middle of nowhere, and I didn't hear anything or see anything. Each guest had their own small quarters with everything that was needed. The pool was heated, and the wives spent their time just lounging around. In the evening, we all ate at the small dining room, where dinner was served by a navy cook. One evening when Ed was three, we brought him along, and he was so good through the whole dinner, playing with the small umbrella that came with my beverage. The other wives commented on his good behavior, but I never got to really know the other White House wives personally; I mostly just mingled with them at functions, and it seemed they were uneasy with each other.

Once, Mrs. Rumsfeld invited all the White House wives to her house near ours for coffee and sweets, but everyone seemed to be on their guard, never discussing anything significant, either about their husbands or the White House. Of all the wives, I felt the most comfortable with Betty Ford, perhaps because there were many opportunities for us to be together in more casual settings. I often had trouble understanding when she spoke because she slurred her words, and although people whispered about her addiction to painkillers and alcohol, I didn't know the extent of her problem. Once, at a state dinner, she sat with her eyes closed while the guest of honor was making the toast. I'm sure she developed her problem trying to cope with the difficult life being a political wife, raising all four of the Fords' children practically by herself while her husband traveled constantly, the way I often thought about starting to drink or smoke pot to ease my mental pain. On another occasion, after dinner at someone's house in Vail, Colorado, we were sitting next to each other on the sofa. I don't recall what we were talking about but suddenly she asked, "How do you say 'number one' in Japanese?" I was startled because I am Korean, not Japanese, but I told her, "*Ichiban.*"

"I want to be *ichiban*," she said with a smile. I asked her, "How can you be more *ichiban* than you are now?"

In Palm Springs, we were together again, and she said, "Once, when I was very young, I went to have my fortune read. The fortune-teller said that someday I would be in a palace. At that time, I thought I was going to dance in a palace. Little did know I was going to live in

one." She'd been a member of "Martha Graham," a contemporary
dance company before she met her husband, and she was sweet, open,
and down-to-earth, just like him. Because of her straightforwardness
and honesty, she was a very popular first lady. I wish I had had more
opportunity to get to know her better, and I am sure we could have
been good friends.

Once I got very angry at Ron because he said that Mrs. Ford was
very insecure. He mentioned now and then that President Ford liked to
be around starlets, and that once a former Miss Texas, who'd become a
sports reporter, asked Ron for an appointment with the President, and
Ron turned her down. Later, she went straight to the president and got to
see him. Ron wasn't too happy about that. Ron also mentioned President
Ford's wandering eye. Ron had written an article in *Playboy* magazine (July
1977) where he recounted this story: "Once, the attractive entertainer
Vicki Carr was invited to sing at a White House state dinner. As Ford
escorted her to the door at the end of the evening, she asked, 'What's
your favorite Mexican dish?' 'You are,' he quipped. Mrs. Ford overheard
and directed, 'That woman is never coming into this house again.'" I
remember that evening. President Ford was with Ms. Carr throughout
the evening, and I didn't know where Mrs. Ford was.

If I was having a difficult time with public life, my mother was having
a worse time adjusting to life in America. When her doctor told me that
the best thing for her illness was to send her back to Korea, I made the
reservations for September 24, 1974, four days after Ron became press
secretary. It was her first return visit since she'd come to the United
States three years prior, and she was looking forward to it.

Before she left for Korea, I warned her not to talk to anyone, especially
reporters. Still, we both had no idea of the scope of the problem.

"Oh, don't worry," she said. "I will just tell them that I don't know
anything . . . which is true."

Mother knew vaguely that Ron had started to work at the White
House, but she didn't care what he did, especially when returning to
Korea consumed her every thought. Even then, I had no idea of the
scope of Ron's position; I was never interested in politics, and it was
just another job for my husband.

When my mother's plane landed at Kimpo Airport in Seoul, she
heard her name called over the loudspeaker on the plane.

"Madame Choi Soon-Ok, please come forward."

The announcement was repeated several times, but my mother was
distracted by her thoughts about her upcoming family reunion and was
not aware that they were paging her. She thought that there must have
been someone else with the same name on board.

Finally, there was another announcement: "Madame Choi Soon-Ok, mother-in-law of White House Press Secretary Ron Nessen, please come forward."

When she went to the front of the plane, two men in black suits whisked her down the ramp and into the terminal. She was shocked to see her brother and his wife from Busan standing there because she hadn't told them that she was coming.

"I guess you still don't know about your son-in-law," my uncle said.

Several men were trying to move her along beyond a yellow protective cord, but she insisted that she had to pick up her baggage. But the man told her that it was all taken care of.

She was rushed into a VIP room full of reporters.

"I had never seen so many men in black suits in one room," she recalled. "I was so ashamed because of my appearance. I'd been crying and wasn't wearing anything decent, and here I was in front of all these men. I had my old ragged-looking handbag and my old suitcase tied together with a rope, and here I was the mother-in-law of the press secretary to the American president. What an embarrassing experience."

Instead of her usual sad face that I had been seeing for three years in Washington, now her smile beamed from the pages of every Korean newspaper. The reporters asked her about the party, and the papers that came out later said,

> "Madame Choi Soon-Ok, the mother-in-law of the White House Press Secretary, Ron Nessen, said that President Ford came to a pool party one Sunday afternoon at the Nessens' residence. According to Madame Choi, the president was a kind and gentle person. When she asked the president how he enjoyed her Korean cuisine, he replied, "Oh, I enjoyed everything, especially the *bul-gogi*, but the *kimchi* was too hot."

In the 1970s, with not many Koreans in Washington, it was unthinkable for any Korean to be associated with the White House. Under President Park Chung-hee's regime, the Korean government was not well accepted by the United States because of human rights issues. The news that I, a Korean woman, was able to associate with the president was not only a pleasant surprise, but also a historical event in Korea. Every newspaper and magazine interviewed everyone with whom I had ever worked and wrote about my life in detail and sometimes in exaggeration, describing my schools, my grades, my skill at dancing and singing, my relatives, and my singing career. Meanwhile, my mother was having a grand time. Reporters followed her everywhere, and she was even invited to be a judge on television game shows.

But I was very nervous about her visit to Korea, remembering what Ron told me about the Korean government trying to reach me some way. Suddenly, I felt guilty about being Korean and being Ron's wife. I wished that I had yellow hair and blue eyes and wasn't in this kind of public jail without bars. Many other women wished that they could be me, but, ironically, all I wanted was a simple life with a husband who was content and could enjoy being a husband and a father.

Then the president's trip to Russia came up, and President Ford was scheduled to stop in Japan on the way. But the White House did not know what to do about Korea because of the human rights issues with the Korean government. The White House did not want to show any eagerness to visit Seoul. On the other hand, it would be a slap in the face if the president did not stop in Korea while he was visiting Japan. There was no denying that South Korea was an important ally of the United States, so it was a difficult situation for both countries. Finally, as a goodwill gesture, President Park freed a number of political dissidents from jail, and in response, President Ford agreed to visit Korea.

I decided not to accompany the presidential party to Korea. For weeks, entertainment people tried to contact me. They anticipated my arrival with Ron and were planning to hold grand receptions for me. As it was, Ron was already angry that my mother was in the limelight.

On November 22, 1974, when President Ford arrived in Korea, Korean Congressman Row Jin-Hwan took my mother to the Seoul airport, where she was seated in the VIP section. Ron came down from the plane and talked briefly with her. He was trying to stay low-key so that the Korean reporters would not focus on him, but Secretary of State Kissinger needled Ron about how my mother was being escorted by the Korean CIA.

At the airport, the president made his remarks in Korean:

> "Twenty-one years have elapsed since I was last here in Korea. I was then a congressman, a member of our House of Representatives. Now I return as the third American president to visit you while in office. President Eisenhower came here in 1952, and again in 1960. President Johnson came in 1966. Those visits as well as mine demonstrate the close involvement of different American administrations over a quarter of a century.'

President Ford's visit was the biggest event in Korean diplomatic history. A sea of people holding both Korean and American flags lined the road from Kimpo Airport to Seoul City, about thirty miles away. When the motorcade arrived in the downtown area, confetti fluttered down from all the buildings like snow. In the middle of City Hall Plaza, there were huge Korean and American flags, and the message "Welcome, President Ford" was made up of chrysanthemums.

My mother was invited to the reception President Park held for President Ford. She trembled with fear, standing next to Congressman Row, and she said later, "I was trying to hide from Ron." She didn't want to face him because I had told her how upset he'd been over her visit to Korea. At first, she refused to go through the receiving line, but with others' encouragement, she finally agreed to accompany the other dignitaries.

When President Ford realized that my mother was there, he ignored all protocol and laughed out loud, exclaiming, "Oh, Cindy's mother." Then he hugged her around the waist in front of everybody. Dr. Kissinger, standing next to the president, shook hands with her, and she bowed to him. The whole time, she hardly lifted her head.

People brought all sorts of gifts to my mother so that she could give them to Ron. One special gift was a pair of fur boots for him to wear in Russia.

A month later, I went down to Andrews Air Force Base to greet Ron on the night the president returned from Russia. The first thing Ron said when he saw me was, "Your mother is so bad."

My excitement at seeing him crumbled. I felt like a little girl being punished by her stern father. Without really wanting to know, I asked him, "What did she do?"

"I'll tell you later," he said. On the way home in the limo, neither of us spoke a word.

"Kissinger kept telling me that Korean CIA agents were accompanying your mother everywhere," he said after we'd arrived home. "He kept teasing me about your mother. Things like, 'Your mother-in-law was the only woman who kissed my hand.'

"Tell her to come back as soon as possible."

I called my mother every day and told her to stop fooling around in Korea and to come back to the States. Mother, however, wanted to know what was she was doing that was damaging the American government or her son-in-law. She was not a spy or a secret agent. She was an elderly woman being treated with respect and having a good time.

"What do you mean Korean CIA?" she asked me. "Your friend Congressman Row helps me out sometimes, that's all."

"Maybe he works for the Korean CIA," I said.

"I never heard anything so ridiculous," she scoffed.

"Why did you kiss Dr. Kissinger's hand?" I asked her.

"Are you crazy or something?" she said, furious at my question. "How can I tell Ron I am innocent of wrongdoing when I can't talk to him?"

We ended up shouting at each other.

I told her finally that Ron didn't like her being in Korea, and he wanted her to come back. I didn't like what I was suggesting. After all of these years of waiting to go back to her homeland, she was now being forced to go back to the United States.

In Korea, people catered to anyone connected to the Blue House and to the members of their families, especially parents and older people. Others sometimes tried to curry favor through the families of those who worked in the Blue House, but no one took it seriously. No one was allowed to talk back to his elders. Here, Ron spoke against her. My mother concluded that in the United States, it is heaven for children, but hell for the elderly.

Reluctantly, Mother shortened her visit and came back to the United States. She was still angry when I picked her up at the airport. My mother had her own life—she was a strong, independent woman who did not take criticism lightly. She did not say a word, and I didn't know what to say to her. I was confused with guilt and frustration because of my mixed loyalties. While I was putting away her luggage, she poured herself a glass of cold water and sat down at the breakfast table with one leg propped up on a chair. She still had a hard time adjusting to sitting on a chair.

She was looking outside toward the patio. It was the end of autumn, and golden and red leaves were on the trees in our backyard. But I could see that she wasn't really looking at them.

"Just because your husband is Mr. Press Secretary, am I supposed to stop being a human? I am Korean. My friends are Korean. I might as well be dead if I cannot see my friends. If people want to be kind to me, to be with me, what harm is done to the White House?"

I could not give her an answer. To this day, I still regret making her come back against her wishes.

"I'll tell you one thing," she continued. "Your husband's job won't last. I went to see the fortune-teller, and he told me that your husband's high and mighty position will be short-lived. And what happened to the sweet old Ron who came to visit us in Korea? I tell you this. He has two faces."

I wanted to dismiss her prediction. I used to scorn her for wasting money on fortune-tellers, but so far everything they had told her had come to pass.

In September 1975, my brother Tong-Ho checked into the Washington Hospital Center, complaining of a pain in his abdomen. While he was going through tests, Mother was with him every day. Finally, she told me a doctor drew something on a piece of paper and explained it to my brother.

"I didn't know what the doctor was saying, but all the blood from Tong-Ho's face drained," my mother said. The doctor left, my brother put on his hospital slippers, and walked out of the hospital building. Mother followed, asking what the doctor had said. Tong-Ho didn't answer. He lay down on the grass and looked up to the sky, saying, "The men don't have a long life in the Song family. Our grandfather died when my father was a baby. My father died at such a young age. Now it's me." The doctor had told my brother that he had liver cancer. "When he was a small boy, he told me he would take care of me when he grew up," Mother said, crying. "My sweet boy, when he made money shining the GIs' shoes, he brought the money to me and said we should buy rice cakes with that money."

I didn't understand how a doctor could be so thoughtless as to talk to a patient without consulting his family first. I was angry, but I never thought of confronting him. That is how Koreans are, seldom questioning authority, especially in a foreign land.

Soon after, the chief of surgery at the hospital wanted to meet with me. One day, I went to his office. He explained, "The tumor in your brother's liver is very big, more than half the size of his liver," he said. "But the biopsy shows no sign that it has spread anywhere else." He stopped, leaned against his swivel chair, and stared at me. "I have done many liver operations. Sometimes in car accidents, the livers were crushed, and there was hardly any left. But if even one-tenth of the liver is left, it will regenerate and grow to its full size. Your brother is a young man. It's like he is in a river, and someone is shooting from behind. Either you try to swim and reach the other side, or you get shot."

I sat in front of his desk. My tears blurred my vision.

"I want you to let me know if we should operate on him," the doctor said.

That night I came home and cried all alone. How should I bring this up to my brother? I went to see him the next day. His children were in his hospital room. They were still too young to know—ten, eight, and six years old. Finally, I told him what the doctor told me. He looked out the window silently. "What do you think?" he asked without looking at me.

"What other choice is there? Your children are young. You have your whole life ahead of you. The doctor said that it has not spread, and your liver will grow back in no time."

He agreed. On the morning of his operation, my mother, my sister-in-law, and I were at his side. I held his hand while in the elevator on the way to the operating room. The doctor told me that a nurse would come and tell us if they were going to go ahead with the operation or not. I didn't know what that meant. We stood at the door of the waiting room, looking toward the operating room, waiting, waiting for what seemed an eternity. About eleven in the morning, a nurse came.

"The doctor thinks, uh, we will go ahead with the operation."

At the time, I didn't know why she was being so vague. I learned later that several doctors were against the operation. But the chief of surgery, whom I had contacted earlier, decided to take a chance.

After the operation, my brother started to hemorrhage. We were told he needed blood, and I called every Korean I knew to donate. Two days later he was moved to another room, out of intensive care. He was exuberant, thinking that his life had been renewed. He asked me to bring him some classical tapes to listen to. He was walking up and down the corridor with his wife and friends, who came to visit him in the hospital. I thought the worst was over, and I didn't go visit him often since I was exhausted by the whole ordeal. One morning, my brother, calling from his hospital room, woke me up.

"*Noon-im*, please let me borrow your mouth one more time," he was begging me. "Please call the doctor and tell him that I need for him to come to my room and help me."

"What's the matter?"

"My stomach is blown up like a balloon."

They rushed him back to the operating room but couldn't understand why fluid from his stomach was not being absorbed into his body. He was back in the ICU.

My mother, my sister-in-law, and I stayed at the hospital every day from morning to night, waiting for the doctor to tell us something, anything. Since the other two women didn't speak English, I had to communicate with the doctors and the hospital staff. But the doctor wouldn't or couldn't give us any answers. As a matter of fact, he seemed to be uncomfortable whenever he saw me in the corridor, and even seemed to be avoiding me.

One gorgeous Sunday morning in November, my brother's wife brought his children to the hospital.

"Don't you want to see your children?" she asked him.

"No, it's too painful. I want them to remember me as a healthy man," he said and looked out the window, tears rolling down his face. I saw falling leaves drifting down from the trees, like beautiful, colorful butterflies.

"*Noon-im,* I was busy working so hard, I didn't have a chance to take my children to Disney World," my brother said, letting his tears fall. "Next year, when I had saved enough money, I was going to go to Korea and visit friends and relatives. Now, I know I won't have that chance." Then as if he was whispering to himself, he said, "We never know if tomorrow will come."

I wanted to hug and kiss him and tell him how much I loved him. I wanted to reassure him that he wasn't going to die, not after all we had been through. He even tried to kill himself at sixteen knowing he couldn't afford to go to school. I took him to a doctor to pump him out. I had brought him to America to have a better life. Instead, swallowing my tears, I watched the nurse turn him to relieve the pain from his bedsores. I kept telling myself not to fall apart in front of his wife, my mother, and the children. They thought that I could fix anything and everything. I was dying inside, but I couldn't let them see it. I was the pillar of our family. If I let myself crumble, whom would they hang on to? At night, I cried in bed, covering my face so that I would not disturb Ron.

Ron told me that the White House doctor said there was a fifty-fifty chance of recovery, but in the end, the doctor told me that there was nothing else they could do for my brother.

"You have to think about letting him go with dignity."

All my family—Tong-Kun, Young Chang, and the three women—sat on the floor in one small room next to the corridor, crying and trying to figure out what else we could do. Tong-Kun showed me an article in the paper about Dr. Michael C. Gelfand and his dialysis method. I didn't know what it was, but I didn't want to give up. Against the doctor's advice, I moved my brother to Georgetown Hospital, where Dr. Gelfand practiced. Again, Tong-Ho was subjected to many painful tests. He was too weak and fragile for exploratory surgery to see if the cancer had spread. At night, I went down and watched him from outside the hospital room attempt to disconnect the tube that was connected to his vein. Soon after he was moved to that hospital, I heard him telling a nurse that he had a beautiful house, and that is where he wanted to be when he died.

One day, the hospital called and told me that Tong-Ho had gone into a coma. We all rushed to the hospital, and Mother sat next to his bed, talking to him, "Tong-Ho yah, forgive me for not being a good mother. But you know you will be at a better place when you leave this world." As if he wanted to respond, he made a strange groaning noise.

He died that night, a few days before Thanksgiving Day, at the age of thirty-nine, still holding on to his American dream that someday he would see his children grow up and have a better education than he did. When Ron wasn't working at the White House any more, we took the three children, Michele, William and Mijee, to Disney World.

By the second year he served as press secretary, 1975, Ron seldom spoke to me or to the other members of the family, including his mother. We stopped making love. He was tired every night, he said. On Sundays, I would patiently play with Edward, waiting for Ron to wake up, hoping we might be able to do something as a family. But by the time he got up, it would be three or four in the afternoon. Or he would go to the White House to play tennis. Looking back, why didn't I do things on my own instead of waiting and being frustrated and getting angrier by the minute? (I was so upset I took tennis lesson. When I kept beating him, he didn't want to play with me anymore.)

When his mother came over, Ron didn't even say hello to her. She would ask me, "What is wrong with Ronnie?" It seemed as though I was watching a stranger walk around our house. On the rare occasions when I complained about something, he would say, "Everyone thinks I am great except you." I looked at him and said, "I suppose President Ford would say to Betty, 'I am the president of the United States. Everyone follows my orders and you should do the same.'"

I am not sure Ron was happy at all. The White House reporters, who were known as lions, were constantly criticizing him. At home, the man I once thought was an angel had become someone I couldn't relate to. I knew our situation was bad and getting worse, but I did not know how to make it better. Then NBC invited Ron to be a guest host on *Saturday Night Live*. He was delighted and agreed even though Chevy Chase, the star of the program, often ridiculed the president for his clumsiness. When I first saw it on television, I was furious. How could they make fun of the president? The thought of Ron agreeing to participate in one of those shows was beyond my comprehension. Ron didn't want me to go with him for the show, but I insisted, and NBC provided us with a suite as big as a house overlooking Central Park.

The first day, someone called on behalf of Andy Warhol, the famous artist, and said that Andy would like to invite me to his studio. I asked Ron and he said it was okay. Someone picked me up, though I still had no idea why I was invited. His studio was a huge warehouse with big paintings hung everywhere. He had white hair, white skin, and small eyes. He hardly talked. He was eating lunch, which looked like thin, white threads that he picked up with chopsticks. Alfalfa sprouts, I learned later. He acted as though he was a skeleton without a soul. Then someone took some pictures of me and him that appeared in *Newsweek*, which said that Andy was thinking about making a movie with me. *That was pretty odd*, I thought. He never made such a comment. After that first meeting, whenever he came down to Washington, I was always invited to the parties he went to.

While Ron was busy rehearsing for *Saturday Night Live*, NBC provided me with a limo and tickets to a Broadway show. Ron had already arranged to go out with some people that evening, so I gave the tickets to my brother Tong-Kun, who was working at the New York University library during the day and was writing his doctoral dissertation at night. In the limo after dinner, Ron interrogated me as to why I'd given the tickets to my brother instead of returning them to NBC. I didn't want a scene in front of the others and just sat there.

At 12:30 AM, after *Saturday Night Live* was over, NBC gave a big party. I sat at a table with Tong-Kun, my friend, and her husband. The cast and others surrounded Ron on the other side of the room. Ron danced with Louise Lasser, the actress who played Mary Hartman on the TV show *Mary Hartman, Mary Hartman*. She had her head on Ron's shoulder, and I was embarrassed, but I pretended I didn't care. One of Ron's friends, Steve, a courtroom artist for NBC who used to work with Ron, asked me to dance. He and Ron used to hang out together in Washington, but I had never liked him because I thought he was a bad influence on Ron. That night, Ron had completely ignored Steve at the party. "I see Ron is still bad," he said while we danced. Since I had no idea what he meant, I made a joke about his comment. He led me over to Ron. "Hi, Ron," Steve said. Louise gave us an angry look as if to say, "Who are you, and why are you bothering us?" She put her head back on Ron's shoulder. Ron said, "This is my wife." After that dance, she stayed away from Ron for the rest of the evening.

Before we left New York, Ron called our friend Jill, the photographer friend of ours, who invited us to stop by and have a bite to eat before we left. By then she was married to Kurt Vonnegut, and I invited my brother, so I could see him before I left New York and have him meet Mr. Vonnegut, who was his idol. Mr. Vonnegut was tall with unkempt, bushy hair. We went to a small neighborhood restaurant for dinner, but Mr. Vonnegut was a quiet man and didn't say much. He asked my brother about a Korean poet, Kim Ji-Ha, who was jailed under President Park's regime for speaking out against his dictatorship. In a taxi, all the way to the airport, Ron angrily asked me why I had invited my brother to the dinner. What was my crime? That I'd wanted to see my brother before I left? My brother was enduring every hardship to achieve his lifetime goal of getting a PhD from NYU: living in a cheap cockroach-infested apartment, cooking his own rice from the pot he invented that went on as he walked in his apartment; eating hotdogs from street vendors everyday, almost getting killed by young mugger in Greenwich Village. In the old days, there was nothing I wouldn't have done for him. Was it a sin for me to want to help my brother? In the old days, when Ron was sweet to me, he wouldn't have minded a bit. He even helped pay for first the two years of school for Tong-Kun. There was nothing he wouldn't do for me and my family, and he never scorned me. That night, though, I knew he was angry with me for disobeying his wishes and ruining his adventure in New York by joining him. I could only ignore him and stare out the window.

In the spring of 1975, the whole White House staff and their families went to Palm Springs for a work-vacation with President Ford. Ron gave me all kinds of excuses why I shouldn't come. I didn't care what he said. Why should Edward and I stay home when all other people were going? Of course, Ron wasn't happy. When we got there, he told me that I was on my own and not to look for him.

I walked out of the room with Edward. When I came down to the middle of the courtyard, children were in the pool, and the grown-ups were either lying around on lounge chairs or in the pool playing with their children. They were mostly family of the White House staff but I didn't know any of them. The scene was idyllic, but I was in despair. *Where am I? What am I doing here? Who cares about me? Who cares about Edward?*

Soon the news of the fall of Saigon reached us at the resort. The people in Saigon were desperately trying to evacuate, and a cargo plane evacuating the Vietnamese orphanages crashed. I felt numb. Was the timing a coincidence or fate? Was the fall of South Vietnam a warning sign that my marriage was also over? Reports kept trickling in. We learned that the half of the passengers on the cargo plane had been killed. I thought how ironic it was that when I was last in Vietnam a decade earlier I'd thought I had found the love of my life.

I saw no sense in staying, not with my state of mind. I wanted to be as far away as I could from Ron. I called my friend Ms. Son, who used to sing at Walker Hill and now lived in Los Angeles, and asked her to pick me up. Anywhere else would be better than where I was. In Los Angeles, she took me to the nightclubs where my old colleagues were singing. Not knowing how unhappy I was, everyone enviously asked about my life in the White House, saying, "One never knows what destiny a person possesses."

Many times, I thought about leaving Ron, but the idea of seeing a big article in the Style section of the *Washington Post* about our breakup always stopped me. Besides, where could I go with our four-year-old son and no money? My insides felt all hollowed out.

In 1975, Ron traveled constantly with President Ford, who was running against Jimmy Carter. In the 1976 election, I was probably the only one in my circle of friends who hoped that President Ford would not be reelected. I admired Ford, but I wanted my husband back. After the election, they had a last-good-bye get-together trip in Vail. Ron wanted us to accompany him, but I didn't go. By this time, the White House years were over, and I was indifferent to what he did.

When Jimmy Carter was inaugurated, I was glued to the television. Because I was so wrapped up watching the swearing-in ceremony, I was late to arrive at Andrews Air Force Base to see President Ford and Mrs. Ford off. The plane was just taking off when I arrived. The crowd was already starting to leave, and I looked everywhere for Ron. He found me and threw his arms around me and began to sob. His face was buried in my knit cap like a child, right there on the tarmac.

However unhappy I was in our marriage, the White House experience was a privilege and a gift to me. I'd met Egyptian president Anwar Sadat who had big smile, and when I saw the news report about his assassination, I couldn't help but feel a sense of personal loss. I'd met Luciano Pavarotti, Barbra Streisand, Debbie Reynolds, Anthony Quinn, Gregory Peck, James Steward, Fred Astaire, Zsa-Zsa Gabor, Ethel Kennedy, Andy Williams, Elizabeth Taylor, Cliff Ronerson and many more. I'd stood in front of Emperor Hirohito of Japan and wondered that this small wooden man had tortured the Korean people and taken everything from us.

I often wished that I would have another chance to visit the White House. Then, not long ago, President Kim Young Sam was invited to a White House state dinner, the first and only president of Korea to be invited for such an event thus far, and I was invited to attend as well. It had been more than two decades since I'd last stepped through those hallowed doors. Nothing had changed, but what was so wonderful was that it no longer seemed like a dream, and I knew I would never miss it again. In those days, I was merely a young woman from a foreign country, an adjunct and attachment to my famous husband. I had been happy once in my marriage, but it had not been made as bamboo is, bending in the strong wind of circumstances but never breaking.

As I entered the White House that last time, I walked in as a woman alone, a woman who had earned the right to call herself a person, separate and inviolable. Our marriage was a case of *il-chim eemong*—two dreams on one bed, our priorities were like heaven and earth. Ron's were in heaven; mine here on earth. No matter how wonderful it was, to me it was only *"Il jang, Il mong, choong mong."* One part of the spring dream.

on the cover
Ron Nessen With His Wife and
President Ford's Press
Secretary Promises:
'I Will Never Knowingly Li[
by Lloyd Shearer

1973 Cover of Parade magazine

Ford introducing Ron to the White House press

Ron's swearing-in at the White House

First dance with President Ford

The first dance with President Ford
and Ron looking on with a smile.

Another dance with Ford

1974 Pool party for President Ford, Tom Brokaw, and my
mother-in-law in the back with glasses

Our pool party, on August 25, 1974

My brother and my mother-in-law standing and laughing
in the back when I asked him when can I get my husband
back

Singing with the Ink Spots at Vail, Colorado

Big hug from Ford after my singing with the Ink Spots.
Mrs. Ford on right.

Ed on Ron's White House desk

Sharon looks on while President Ford hugs me.

Ann Margaret approached us when she saw Mother with her *hanbok* on. She had gone to Korea previously and was happy to see someone in a *hanbok*.

Pavarotti

Ron shaking hand with Mrs. Valery Giscard Estang

Cindy with French President, Valery Giscard Estang

Mrs. Ford and me
at Palm Spring

Mrs. Rabin, Mrs. Kissinger and
me on Dandy

Me with Mrs. Kissinger at Palm Springs

Anthony Quinn

Japanese Empress Michiko

HE KREMLIN CARTEROLOGISTS

he Kremlin's experts on America are roing in on Presidential hopeful Jimmy arter. They are studying not only his rmal foreign-affairs statements but mi-official documents such as a letter nt to U.S. Jewish leaders by his campaign treasurer. They are also trying to fix here he stands in the Democratic Party. heir first question to a Carter acquaintance visiting Moscow last week was, Who's behind his candidacy?"

RIDDLE FOR A MIDDLEMAN

S. officials are investigating the American investment activities of Adnan Khaioggi, the Saudi Arabian businessman ho got more than $150 million from ockheed and Northrop in connection ith aircraft sales to his country. After rning down his offer to testify voluntarily, the Securities and Exchange ommission subpoenaed documents nnected with some of his U.S. investents. When marshals were unable to rve process on him, the Justice Deartment was asked to help. The SEC is robing possible non-criminal stock regularities; Justice is alert for possie criminal violations.

STAR IS BORN

rtist-impresario Andy Warhol is woong Cindy Nessen, Korean-born wife of residential press secretary Ron Nesen, to appear in a full-length movie he lans to shoot in New York City. The ast will include Carroll ("Baby Doll") Baker and Perry ("Mandingo") King in what one Warhol aide calls "a drama of sorts." Warhol met Cindy at a Georgetown dinner party in Washington, D.C., a week ago.

STAY OF EXECUTION

First beneficiaries of the $135 million program to inoculate the U.S. population against a possible flu outbreak will be hundreds of thousands of roosters. The male birds are needed to fertilize eggs used as incubators in the production of flu vaccines. Normally, most male chicks (which are not profitable as meat sources) are destroyed soon after birth. Because of

Flight: Adnan Khashoggi

Film: Warhol with Cindy Nessen

Flu: Roosters for vaccine

the huge increase in vaccine production needed this year—200 million doses instead of the usual 20 million—the roosters will be allowed to live on for their fertilizing role.

CHINESE PUZZLE

China experts are trying to figure out why a number of high-ranking militants in Peking have dropped out of sight and out of print since the downfall of Vice Premier Teng Hsiao-ping. The missing include Mao Tse-tung's wife, Chiang Ching; the Chinese Communist Party's second vice-chairman, Wang Hung-wen of Shanghai; Politburo member Yao Wenyuan, a leading ideologist; Second Vice-Premier Chang Chun-chiao, once thought a strong contender for the premiership; and Mao's 34-year-old nephew, Mao Yuan-hsin, a confidante and courier for C¹ ⁻ᵃⁿ Mao himself. One theory amo.. ..g-based diplomats is that the military commander of the capital, Chen Hsi-lien, has jailed the last three for having provoked a moderate backlash that resulted in riots in the city two weeks ago.

KEEPING FIRE FRIENDLY

Russian engineers have added a new touch to the Soviet shoulder-fired SA-7 "Strela" antiaircraft missile. It is an IFF (for "identification friend or foe") radio, built into an infantryman's helmet. During the 1973 Mideast war, Egyptians armed with the Strela reportedly shot down a number of their own planes. The IFF device will enable gunners to identify incoming planes and minimize such errors.

SADAT THE PEACEMAKER

Egypt's President Anwar Sadat told some visiting Americans last week that he planned to extend the mandate for the United Nations Sinai peace-keeping force for a year. He also used the occasion to spell out what he called his "defensive" needs from the U.S.: TOW anti-tank wire-guided missiles, electronic equipment and jammers, aircraft such as the F-5E but not the sophisticated F-15 or F-16 which Israel wants.

—JOHN A. CONWAY with bureau reports

Newsweek, picture of me with Andy Warhol

Every magazine and paper reported that singer Song
married Ford's press secretary

After the Fishbowl

Do not envy the freedom of the fish that play in the water:
The egrets soon come.
They dive up and down, the fish have no rest.

—Yi Chongbo 1693-1766

Who has never tasted what is bitter
Does not know what is sweet

—German proverb

When our White House years were over, Ron returned to his downstairs office and began working from nine to six every day on his memoir. I was overjoyed for the first time in our marriage, for I finally could be with my husband every day and know exactly where he was. During the first year of working at home, he sometimes traveled to give speeches and look for jobs, and I met many other former White House wives who told me I was lucky, since they disliked having their husbands underfoot. I thought it odd that they felt that way, but soon enough I realized what they meant. We began to constantly bicker about everything, especially about how to raise our son. When I tried to discipline Edward, Ron stepped in. When Edward cried because he didn't want to shampoo his hair, Ron rushed into the bathroom and asked why I was making him cry. I never saw anyone who couldn't stand to see crying as much as Ron.

One weekend, Ron had invited some of his friends over, and I was up at six o'clock to prepare Korean food. While I worked, Ron played with Edward in the basement. Edward came upstairs, went outside, and returned with a box of sand. I told him that he shouldn't bring sand inside the house and sent him back out. But he knew that Ron always rescued him when I tried to discipline him, so he started to cry and went outside. Ron ran upstairs, went outside, and brought Edward back into the house with his box of sand. As they walked in the kitchen, Ron snapped at me, "Anyone who gets a kick out of making a child cry should have her head examined."

Blood rushed to my head, and I felt like throwing my cutting board on the floor and walking out. But Ron felt he hadn't been a good father to his first son and wanted to make sure that he didn't make the same mistake again. The result was that there seemed no limit to what Ron would give Edward or allow him to do. Our son was changing into a spoiled crybaby. I'd never had patience for a pampered child and needed to do whatever I could to prevent it from happening to Edward. There's an old Korean saying: "*A child might be a flower in your eyes, but he may be a thorn in someone else's.*"

Ron had never cared or had time to tell me what to do, but now, he wanted complete control over our lives. Having him at home every day and night was as if I had a horn growing on my head. We argued without resolution, and I didn't know how to get to the source of our emotional turmoil. I believed my marriage was over and confided to a friend, who admitted that she was also having problems and was getting help from a marriage counselor, whom she recommended. I asked Ron, and he was willing. One of the things the counselor said was that I never forgave how he degraded me when he was working at the White House, and he never forgave me for not holding his hand while he was writing. During our sessions, I talked about how frustrated I felt, as though I was a piece of cloth caught between my four-year-old son and my forty-four-year-old husband. I talked about how Ron treated me as if I was an unwanted stepmother every time I tried to discipline Edward, and how I was given no voice in raising my son.

Then Ron went on his book tour, and I saw a good opportunity for me to work on Edward. I structured his schedule. We read or worked on books every evening after dinner. By the time Ron came home a month later, Edward had become a completely different child. Seeing how Edward had changed, Ron told our counselor that he felt his son might not need him. The counselor said that rearing a child should be with one voice and that disagreements should remain behind closed doors.

I felt I was suffocating, and I wanted to sing. But where? I hadn't sung for more than a decade. I told Ron that I would sing at community functions without fee. "Why sing for free when you're a professional?" he said. "Look in the paper for a dinner theater job." I went to several places for auditions and took one of my scores, "*I Enjoy Being a Girl*," from *Flower Drum Song*. I loved to sing that song, imitating the performance of Eurasian actress Nancy Kwon in the movie version. I was hired at Melody Fair Dinner Theatre in Arlington to play the main character Linda Low, a Chinese nightclub performer.

When I danced and sang every night for an audience, I renewed my self-confidence. I invited my friends, and the local Korean paper wrote an article saying that a famous Korean singer from the 1960s, Song Young-Hee, was getting attention in Washington playing the lead role in a show at a local dinner theater. They used one of my old publicity photos, and the article was even reprinted in Korea. I realized how much singing was a part of my heart and soul and how I had suppressed my desire to sing for so long. The only thing I hated was that Edward cried every night when I left the house. He was only five years old.

The show lasted three months. All the other dinner theaters were located far away, and there weren't many good roles for Asians. If I could have turned the clock back to when I first came to the United States, I wouldn't have given up so much of my own career. But like many other women, I'd thought I had to give everything to my husband.

By the third post-White House year, Ron had finished his memoir and started on a novel. Money seemed to be running out, and he had no choice but to get a regular job. Though he couldn't find any media jobs, two public relations firms wanted to hire him. Gray and Company was well connected to the Republicans and well known; the other was a small company from New York with a one-man operation in Washington. Mr. Gray was classy and I liked him, but I didn't like the man from the other company. Something told me that he wasn't to be trusted, but Ron chose the smaller company. I don't recall what it was called. Again, as an old Korea proverb says, "*Its better to be a fish in the pond than a fish in the sea.*" Still, his spirits went up, and mine went up as well. My joy at seeing Ron happy swept away the previous pain and loneliness. Slowly, things began to smooth out between us, and Ron's attitude changed. Edward became calmer and more obedient, and I began to have hope that our marriage was going to make it.

We decided to have a major renovation done on our house since we hadn't done a thing since we bought it in 1969. We had plans drawn up by an architect, an old friend of Ron's. The architect told us that people often divorced or separated while or after they renovated their houses. It was a strange and ominous thing to say, but I was too excited and busy to pay any attention.

I read many different magazines on renovating houses, and every day I carried the blueprints with me as I went from place to place to pick out all the necessary materials. One day, my mother came down from New York, where she was living with my brother. Seven-year-old Edward was not home from school yet, and while I made seaweed soup, I sang along to one of my favorite songs, *"Que Sera, Sera (Whatever Will Be, Will Be)"* sung by Doris Day, which was playing on the radio in the kitchen. As she always did, my mother sat cross-legged on her dining chair, with one knee propped up. She had a piece of paper in her hand.

"I had your fortune read for this year," she said while looking at the paper. "I think you should be very careful. It was a very bad fortune."

"Why, what did it say?" I asked absently while I was sautéing the little pieces of beef in the pot.

"He said that your husband has two rice cakes in his hands and cannot make up his mind which one to choose."

I added a little bit of dried beef stock, a couple drops of soy sauce, and soft seaweed. Then I poured water in and covered the pot.

"He must have meant Ron's indecision over which job to take," I said, remembering that Ron had trouble deciding between the offers from the two P.R. companies. Neither my mother nor I spoke.

The chime from the electric rice cooker signaled that the rice was ready, and I waited a few more minutes before I scooped out cooked rice into two bowls. Studying the paper in her hand, my mother finally responded, "I don't think so." She said, "It is more serious than that. Listen to this." She started to read from the paper. "'Disaster will befall your marriage. You will be in an empty room with a broken heart, thinking about your husband.'"

The soup started to boil. I turned down the stove and put the cover on, leaving the pot half opened. I stood next to the stove and listened.

Mother went on, "'Everything will disappear in one night. You have fame, but what good is it? You have important contacts, but they will not help you. In the beginning, everything seemed happy and well, but it won't last. You are fine when you are singing, but when you are silent, you are lonely. Your marriage is in turmoil because every place your husband goes, he calls his home. Do not see, do not speak, and do not hear. Pray day and night.'" My mother put down the paper and asked me to give her a glass of water. As I handed her a glass of water from the water cooler, I quickly dismissed her prediction. "That's all nonsense. If anything was going to happen to my marriage, it would have happened during the past two years. All our troubles are behind us. We are going to renovate our house." I took a spoonful of the soup, blew a little to cool it off, and sipped to see if the soup was ready. "I bet you that that fortune is wrong."

Soon after he started his new job, Ron used to come home and tell me about the troubled marriage of a man he worked with, who was also named Ron. He would say, "You know what, Ron told me that he had an affair with a married woman." On other nights he would say, "One time, Ron left his wife [his second wife] Sue and moved into an apartment with the woman whom he was having the affair with. The day he moved out with some of his furniture, his wife lay down in front of the moving truck to stop him." I thought it was odd he was so interested in talking about someone else's problems. He never before seemed to pay any attention to people's private affairs.

Another day, Ron came home unusually early and announced that we were going out to a Chinese restaurant in Bethesda. While we waited for the food, he told me again about his colleague and his problems. He said, "You know, Ron left his wife for the other woman, and three months later he moved back to his wife. He missed his three-year-old son so much that he couldn't take it anymore." I wondered why he kept telling me over and over all these things about this terrible man. "He said that it was so painful that he wouldn't wish that on his worst enemy."

Since I had known Ron, I had never heard him gossip, or even respond to mine. I thought that's what marriage was. Previously, we'd visited Sharon, an old friend, and her husband, Winston, in Florida. After every dinner, I sat on their sofa in the family room and watched them side by side doing the dishes. They laughed and talked about the neighbors or everyday events. They seemed so happy and so much in love. When I told Sharon how envious I was of their marriage, she said, "You know what, I never thought about those things until you just mentioned them. We have always been able to talk about anything. It's just our everyday life."

That evening, at the Chinese restaurant, I didn't want to hear about Ron's friend anymore. "You know, if that kind of experience could cure your ambiguity about our marriage, one foot in and the other one out, I wish you could experience it, too, so that I would know for sure where I stood," I said.

I saw his face suddenly light up. "That's what I want to talk to you about."

"What do you mean? You want to try it, too?" I asked.

"Well, if I tried what he did . . . I mean, something like that . . . I would never think about anything else. I mean, I will not think about anything else other than my life with my family."

"I don't care. If you want to try it, go ahead and do it," I said as an empty threat. I was too confident about how much Edward meant to him.

One weekend when Ron was finally ready to pick a contractor for the renovation, he wanted to drive around the neighborhood to see what the houses were going for. We went night after night and week after week looking at seedy houses. He acted as though we were looking for a house to buy instead of renovating ours. I became agitated and wished he would tell me what was on his mind. I am a yes-or-no person, and I have no patience for in-between. A few weeks later, Ron told me he wanted to see our marriage counselor again, by himself. I was relieved, but when Ron came home, he told me that I, too, should go to see her alone. We didn't have any money. In order to renovate the house, he had to borrow the money, a lot of it. He had lost everything to his former wife in the divorce.

As soon as I sat with the counselor, my anxieties poured out. "I don't know what the problem is. Three weeks ago, he told me that he was ready to sign with a contractor to renovate our house. But for the past three weeks, we have only looked at other houses. What is going on? Can you tell me?"

The counselor looked at me for a few moments. Then she said, "Your husband wants to leave you."

At first my mind went blank. Then I began to cry and kept on.

"Mrs. Nessen, I can't sit here listening to you cry all day."

I stood up. "Yes, that's right. You don't care and no one cares." I left her office and drove around aimlessly for several hours. When I finally returned home, the phone was ringing and ringing, and I knew Ron was trying to reach me.

I felt the world crashing down around me. Is there any way to describe my state of mind?. I called my brother in Korea and screamed into the phone. I told him that Ron was leaving, and he should go and see the fortune-teller to find out if this was really happening. That was the first and only time anyone in my family heard me cry. I would have called God if I could have reached him. Ron wanted to stay until he found the right place to move into, but I couldn't be in the same house with him. I told him to move out, and he moved into a hotel.

A year later, I filed for divorce, and it was finalized three years after that.

Looking back, I survived by hanging on to all the beautiful letters he had written to me.

By the time he wanted to come back, it was too late.

No use trying to put together a broken rice bowl.

Joy of Rebirth

Back to My Homeland

Many years have slipped by since
I left the path I used to tread.
For awhile I went elsewhere,
But at last I have returned.
And now that I have come back,
My heart shall never roam again.

—Hwang 1501-1570

The journey of a thousand miles starts with a single step.

—Lao-Tzu

In November of 1981, the year Ron left me, the chairwoman of the Korean Women's Association, Ms. Park Kumsoon, contacted me from Korea. She wanted me to arrange for a prominent woman from Washington to be the keynote speaker for an upcoming event that her organization was planning in Seoul. With three million members, the Korean Women's Association was very powerful. I contacted Mrs. Anna Chennault, General Claire Chennault's widow, who was a friend of mine. She was delighted, and the association agreed to pay for all of our travel expenses for a five-day trip. My spirits rose. I hadn't been to Korea since 1967. Korea was being called one of the "seven dragons of Asia" because of the rapid growth of its economy, and I thought this was a good chance for me to look into possible business opportunities there.

Ron had put a clause in our separation agreement that said that I couldn't leave the area with Edward, since Ron was afraid that I might move out of Washington, just as his ex-wife had moved and taken their children when she and Ron had gotten divorced. No way would I leave Edward behind. My lawyer talked to Ron's lawyer, and I was allowed to take him along for two weeks; I also took my mother so that she could look after Edward while I was busy. We took a long, tiresome Korean Air flight out of New York on a Saturday afternoon and landed at Kimpo Airport in Seoul early Monday morning. When we disembarked and went into the airport building, I was stunned. In 1964, and even in 1967, when I went with Ron, the airport had been only a run-down, shack-like building. But now, the airport was huge clean, modern, and better than the ones in America. Ms. Park, a couple of women, and my brother came to the airport to meet us. We drove through Seoul with high-rise buildings at every corner and streets filled bumper-to-bumper with black sedans driven by chauffeurs. Although I knew how prosperous Korea had become, actually witnessing it in person made me overwhelmingly proud.

They dropped us at the Lotte Hotel, one of the best in Seoul at that time. A Korean man who lived in Japan built the Lotte Hotel and had many other business interests, including a department store, food products, and the famous Lotte gum in Japan. Near the lobby was a large recessed lounge, with a ceiling two stories high, and outside of the glass wall was a waterfall. At the hotel, Anna had a suite, and I had a small room with two beds. The schedule for each day started with breakfast and ended many hours later with a reception and banquet.

One day, Mr. and Mrs. Chang, longtime friends of mine, took Mother, Edward, and me to a buffet restaurant in the Hotel Lotte. Each person was charged the equivalent of $50, and I know that you will never see a spread like that anywhere in the United States, with the best of every international food: American smoked salmon, raw oysters, raw clams, filet mignon, cold cuts, and pasta; Japanese sushi, soba noodles, tempura; and Chinese, Korean, and Italian choices too. For dessert, there was every international sweet and delicious fresh fruits and cheese. The funny thing was that Edward went wild over the cold cuts and would eat nothing else; I realized that he is a real all-American boy.

Anna and I met all the power players, from congressmen to the owners of the big companies. At the visit's conclusion, Anna and I met with President Chun Doo-hwan at the Blue House. For a second, I fantasized about staying in Korea.

Everyone was busy trying to set up businesses, and though I didn't have a specific idea of what to do, I could see that I could play a role by arranging for famous officials to come to Korea for events and TV interviews. My biggest concern was how long I could hide the fact that I was no longer Mrs. Nessen. I wasn't officially divorced yet, but it was pending; and in Korea, a divorced woman was considered a nonperson, especially if she had been the wife of a famous man. The newspaper reported my trip, saying that a former press secretary's wife was in Korea as a businesswoman. One day, in the hotel lobby, a young woman and a man rushed toward me and started to take pictures and ask questions. I was totally startled, and tried to hide behind a man who was standing next to me. Radio, TV, and magazine reporters wanted to interview me; but my brother Tong-Kun, who was a professor, and Chairwoman Park were both against it, for obvious reasons. If it were now, I would have been proud to reveal my new status, but then, I was too insecure.

I only had the child support money Ron gave me every month, and I couldn't afford the huge hotel bills, so I only used one room for the three of us. It would have been perfectly all right except Edward couldn't sleep at night because of my mother's snoring. Cranky and upset, Edward either tried to make his bed in the bathtub or take his blanket out in the hallway. During the day while I was busy, Edward went downstairs where all the shops were and made friends with young sales girls. They thought that he was the sweetest and cutest child they had ever seen. A week or so later, he was speaking Korean as if he had been born there.

After the five-day official trip ended, I went to Busan, where I was born, and visited my favorite uncle—Min-Sick, my mother's only brother—and his family. In spite of the time and the distance between us, he was always on my mind, and I was saddened that we could never see each other. I also decided to see if I could develop some contact with various businessmen. I went to see Mr. Yoon, whom I had met in Washington. After a nice lunch, I asked him if he could take me to the famous fortune-teller Master Park.

After we got out of the taxi, we walked up a little dirt hill and arrived at an old-fashioned Korean wooden gate. A small woman in a *hanbok* let us in, and we walked across the wide yard. I followed Mr. Yoon, and we took off our shoes, stepped up on wide wooden veranda, and went into the *ondol* room. An old man with a white *hanbok* and gray hair was sitting at the left side of the room and talking to a woman who was sitting across from him. A small makeshift dining table was in between them with notebooks and pens. Master Park peered at Mr. Yoon over his reading glasses and said, "Please come in and sit down." There were several women and a man already there. I wished I could be alone with him when my turn came.

"If you didn't lose your money this year, your health might have been in danger. So think in terms that the money wasn't yours to keep anyhow." Master Park was concluding a woman's reading, and he wrote down a long explanation and gave it to her. She folded the paper, put it in her purse, and took out a stack of ten thousand won bills. She held the bundle of notes, wet her fingers, counted out the equivalent of $40, and gave it to Master Park. He put the money under a square cushion he was sitting on. Mr. Yoon got up and went outside. In a little while, he came back, and the woman who had opened the gate for us followed him in. She went over to Master Park and whispered something in his ear. He nodded his head and glanced at me. The woman left the room. Master Park looked at me and said, "Can I help you? I understand you came all the way from America to see me." Mr. Yoon pointed his chin toward Master Park and said, "Go ahead." I slid toward the table. He took his notepad and held his brush in his hand while he wet it on the inkstone and asked me, "Year, the date, and the hour of your birthday in the lunar calendar?"

I told him 1935, February 10, and 6 AM, though my birthday is on March 14 according to the Western calendar.

"Your sign is the pig," he said and wrote down something. He kept writing.

"Please give her a good reading," Mr. Yoon said.

Master Park took out a piece of paper from another book with lots of Chinese characters. Then he started to fill in square boxes on the paper with writings. He was mumbling something under his breath as he wrote. The room was dead silent. He went on like that for about ten minutes. Then he put his pen down on the table and looked at me over his reading glasses. He started to explain my fortune, periodically glancing at the paper in his hand.

"Your body is earth in February," he said. "The earth is rich and immovable. Therefore the virtue of your character is truthfulness and sincerity. Because of this character, you are a man in a woman's body. You are affectionate and kindhearted and loyal."

I was thinking, *My god, he is something else. How does he know me so well?*

"Your marriage does not last, not because of lack of fortune with the man but because of your strong will. Your man is floating on the ocean. Therefore you met him, and marriage took place in a foreign country in your late age.

"Because you were born with such extreme fortune, if you were born as a man you could have been a great leader, but because you were born as a woman, you help your husband to become a famous politician.

"From the age of thirty-nine to forty-three, for five years, it was a splendid life under heaven. Your karma is with politics, fame, splendor. If you get married in America, your husband becomes high official in government and becomes famous. Because of the lack of metal in your element, you will earn your money through music. Earlier in life, you were talented in dance and music. That eventually led you to become an internationally known artist. But it stopped because of your marriage. You will never become rich but also you never have to worry about becoming poor. When you abandon nobility, the wealth will come. From the age of forty-four to forty-eight, your fame is diminished, your husband goes into the private sector, and your heart is full of discontent. From forty-nine to fifty-eight, for nine years, great fortune is in store. You will go into business. It is a fortune of wealth. You will make money but will also lose some and will spend it." He put down his paper and looked at me carefully. "Your mole under your eye is a sign of tears," he said. "Sometimes the tears in your eyes heal the pain in your heart. Your problem is your sagacity and your pride. You can't tolerate people who are dishonest and disloyal."

I was stunned. I could forgive anything but disloyalty. *How did this man know me so well?*

A person's fortune is called *Sujo,* or four pillars. When the four pillars are not well balanced, like a house, one's fortune will be in trouble. Those four pillars are the year, the month, the day, and the hour of one's birth, which influence one's fortune. If those four pillars are perfect, there is no need to read the fortune. Then there are five elements, *O-Heng,* which compose the human body—wood, fire, water, metal, and earth. All those elements should be harmoniously balanced. Because metal was missing in my elements, my marriage would not work. Also, it is believed that woman is superior to man as water is superior to fire.

There were so many things I wanted to ask, but I already took up others' turn and I felt guilty taking up more of his time. I asked him if he could write those things down in a language I could understand instead of in Chinese characters. "Of course," he said. And as he wrote in *hangul,* the Korean alphabet, he added, "No memory is the equal of even a dull pencil." Mr. Yoon gave him the money since another practice of Koreans is to always pick up a guest's expenses. They might not give gifts as Americans do, but they pay for all of their guest's expenses, restaurants, taxis, and so on. When I was in Seoul, Ms. Park took me to a beauty parlor where I got a perm. Before I was done, she had already paid for it. That is what Koreans call hospitality.

A year before, when Ron left me, Tong-Kun sent me the fortune that he obtained for me. "Because of your husband's childish behavior, you will experience terrible pain. The trouble began a couple of years ago. Do not try to stop him from doing what he wants to do. The more you interfere, the worse it will get. Ignore him and focus on your own life. Go into business and try to better yourself. Next spring, your husband will want to come back to you, but even if he does not, be patient. In five years, your life will come together, and you will find happiness and wealth. You are wearing a beautiful evening dress, but it is torn. Where could you go wearing a torn gown?"

In Busan, the evening before I left, I sat with Uncle on the floor after the dinner table was taken away. I told him about my separation and that I was in the process of filing for divorce. Uncle sat on a square silk cushion in his baggy gray *hanbok* pants and light blue *hanbok* top. Inhaling his cigarette slowly, he was deep in thought, looking at the tip of the burning cigarette, rolling its ashes this way and that in the ashtray.

"Why do you have to divorce him?" he asked. "Why don't you just live separately instead of getting a divorce?"

I sat on the floor leaning against the wall. "Why, Uncle? If your arm or leg is rotting little by little from an unknown disease, in the beginning, you try everything to get it cured. But when you finally come to the conclusion that there is nothing more you can do, wouldn't you cut that arm or leg off? Uncle, when marriage is dead, it's dead. I'd never run from anything and always believe in trying your best first. But when you realize there is nothing there to salvage, then it's better to walk away without looking back."

For once, I was thinking more like an American. I realized I finally found myself by losing Ron.

Business Tycoon

Don't be hasty when the things seem easy,
Don't be lazy when it gets hard
Only the constancy and hard work leads to success.

—Kim Chun Taek

An optimist sees an opportunity in every calamity;
a pessimist sees a calamity in every opportunity.

—Sir Winston Churchill

"After five years, your life will come together," the fortune-teller had predicted. I didn't believe I could survive another day after Ron left me. I was literally in bed every day. I only got out of the bed to feed Edward. I never answered the phone. It seemed that my life was over. Everyone seemed know of me as Mrs. Nessen. Everyone envied me. How would I survive? What would I do after the child support ended? How would I go into business? I didn't know a single thing. The humiliation and fear literally paralyzed me. I even developed severe sciatica, and could neither walk, sit, nor lie down.

But when I came back from Korea, I decided to live. I took action and looked up everyone I knew. Among many people, I called Director Lee of KBS, the Korean Broadcasting System. Because Korea was still under a military regime, the Korean government was constantly trying to promote the image of the country by interviewing important officials from

America. Not long after, Mr. Lee called and asked me if I could arrange an interview with Henry Kissinger. "MBC [Busan Munhwa Bangsong] is also trying to get him. And I want to make sure we get him."

I asked him how much KBS was willing to pay. I knew roughly how much it would cost to get a VIP like Dr. Kissinger, but I wanted to make sure they were willing to meet his fee. He asked me how much I thought they should pay, and I gave the top amount. Dr. Kissinger was so much in demand that without a special incentive, what would he care about KBS? Besides, not knowing what MBC was offering, I couldn't take any chances. He said he first had to get the okay from KBS in Korea. Because I was afraid of not being able to deliver their request, I secretly wished that the answer would be no. He called a couple of days later. "I got a green signal from Seoul. Go ahead." I was nervous. I knew KBS had interviewed Dr. Kissinger previously, and I thought that there was a strong possibility that he would accept the KBS's offer rather than MBC's. But I still couldn't relax. Anything could go wrong.

I called Dr. Kissinger's office in New York. The secretary said he was in Europe. That was another problem; he was always away. I told her who I was and why I was calling. I asked when he was due back. The secretary wasn't sure but said she would relay the message. I bit my fingernails. I couldn't sleep. I tossed and turned. This was my first big opportunity to prove that I was capable. For the first time since I was in Taipei waiting for my visa to come to the States, I started to pray for a good dream that night. What if MBC had already contacted Dr. Kissinger and he had accepted their offer? What if he couldn't spare any time? To nail down anything with Dr. Kissinger was to try to catch a star. I sat next to the phone and waited and waited. I could hardly keep myself from picking up the phone and calling his office. I waited one full day and couldn't wait another, so I called the following morning. Yes, he was back in New York, but out of his office. "I will tell him you called." I waited another day. Mr. Lee kept calling me. "Don't lose him now. I am depending on you," he said. There weren't too many days left until the third of October, National Foundation Day in Korea, which was when broadcasters wanted to set up something important.

I finally decided that I couldn't sit in Washington and wait. I told Mr. Lee to pay for my fare to New York to find Dr. Kissinger. He said he had to get the okay from Seoul, and that evening he called back and said to go ahead. First thing next morning, I got on a shuttle and arrived at Dr. Kissinger's office on Park Avenue a little after nine. The elevator stopped inside his office. A short, heavy receptionist behind the desk looked puzzled. I told her where I came from and that I needed to see Dr. Kissinger or his secretary. About ten minutes later, she told me to go in.

One of the assistants said that Dr. Kissinger was completely booked. I told
him that President Chun Doo-hwan was fond of him, and that it would be
a great pleasure for the president to hear Dr. Kissinger's opinion on South
Korea's problems with North Korea and other international issues. I told
him the amount of the fee. He said he'd let me know. I went straight to
LaGuardia Airport after the meeting. Not only did I not have money to
stay and shop, but I didn't want to get distracted from my goal.

That night I dreamt about three little pink pigs. The pig dream
is considered to be a good omen, but I couldn't talk about it for fear
of jinxing my luck. Mr. Lee called that evening, but I still didn't have
an answer for him. The next morning, I called New York again. The
receptionist put me through to Dr. Kissinger's secretary, Diana, whom
I had spoken with several times previously. She told me the date and
the time when Dr. Kissinger could be interviewed and directed me to
send the check as soon as possible. I thought I would jump out of my
skin and fly away.

I called Mr. Lee with the good news and met him for lunch the
following day. As he handed me the check, he said, "Boy, you are a very
good businesswoman." He didn't know this was my first deal. I deposited
the check and made out a check to Kissinger and Associates minus my
commission. On the day of the interview, I went to New York with my
mother, since she had already met him. Dr. Kissinger said hello to her,
and we had our picture taken.

The year after that, KBS had a new director, Mr. Lee Chang Soo, who
wanted to interview President Ford. After several calls to the president's
office in Palm Springs, President Ford's assistant told me that he could
fly in to New York on a red-eye the night before, tape the interview in
the morning at the Waldorf-Astoria Hotel, and leave for a convention
in Florida right after. I felt honored and extremely grateful.

Then a friend of mine, Tom, who was working for Pro Serve,
a company that promotes sports events, contacted me to see if I
could arrange sport exhibitions, like tennis games or golf matches,
with world-famous sports celebrities, in Korea. I wasn't sure. Unlike
Japan, where any company is free to invite any entertainers or sport
figures for events, in Korea, a company has to have permission from
the Korean government because of the hard currency law, and
oftentimes, the government discouraged big-money events. That is
why many foreign companies wanted to have someone who was well
connected with the Korean government. Also, business in Korea had
to be done face-to-face. I tried at the beginning to negotiate through
letters and phone calls, but they usually said, "Why don't you come
and we'll talk."

I flew to Korea and checked into the Lotte Hotel. My brother's apartment was far from downtown, and besides, he told me that even if my pocketbook was empty, I had to appear to be a prosperous businesswoman. Soon after I arrived on a Sunday, I learned who the minister of sports was and made plans to call him the next morning.

Later that afternoon, I made a courtesy call to Ms. Park, the chairwoman of the Korean Women's Association, and she invited me to a big banquet scheduled for that evening that would include many politicians and businessmen. Luck was with me, and at that dinner, I was introduced to the minister of sports, a handsome gentleman in his forties with great sense of humor. He invited me to his office the next morning, and we became very good friends. That's how I arranged for the famous tennis coach, Mr. Nick Bollettieri, who has a tennis training school in Florida, to come to Korea to give special lessons to players who were training for an international tennis tournament. There is an old saying, *"If your luck isn't with you, you break your nose even if you fall backwards. But if luck is with you, nothing could go wrong."* That night was the beginning of my carpet ride.

As my trips to Korea became frequent, I started to make more contacts with different business sectors. In early '80s, there were still restrictions on what foreign products the Korean government would allow into the country. One of the most popular banned products in Korea was Estée Lauder makeup. One of the big cosmetics companies in Korea showed interest in forming a joint venture with Estée Lauder, who used to send me special cream during Ron's White House years. So I went to see my "old friend" and her son Leonard in New York. I was never into makeup, and to me, Estée Lauder makeup was just another brand. But the magnitude of her company was indescribable. Of course, she was going to one meeting after another, but I appreciated whatever time she shared. Leonard Lauder put me in touch with one of their executives, and later I arranged for him to meet with a Korean company.

Once my confidence grew, I realized that Korea was my best asset. I traveled to Korea four or five times a year, meeting with politicians and executives. I didn't have to be invisible in Korea but could be myself and have a ball. I met many executives, including the chairmen from conglomerate companies like Samsung, Daewoo, Goldstar, Hyundai, and many others. I met CEOs and politicians at receptions, and those people would invite me to dinner and introduce me to their circle of friends. Big receptions were often a great opportunity for me to meet them all at once in a casual setting. They took me to the finest restaurants and then to karaoke or to the clubs to dance, never asking any favor from me. On the contrary, when I went to visit them in their offices, they would give me a fat envelope of cash, the typical way of giving a gift for Koreans, and there is no limit to their generosity.

Putting together events was glamorous and fun, but I couldn't make a living out of it and had to figure out a more stable moneymaking project. Then my friend Pete Teeley, who was once the press secretary to Vice President George H. W. Bush, set up a consulting company after he left the White House. He introduced me to a French company that was starting to develop into something similar to Amway, and the company wanted its products made somewhere in Asia. The president of the company sent me a round-trip ticket to Paris for a meeting, and I stayed there for three days. One of his assistants took me to their warehouse outside Paris, where they stored their merchandise, and asked me to find an Asian company that could provide those items at good price. When I came back from Paris, I told Pete about my trip and the meeting. I asked him how I should charge for my services, and he told me to charge my daily traveling fees and expenses. I asked, "Is that all?" It didn't sound right. Instead, I wrote the company saying that I need to be paid 3% of everything they bought including all my expenses. The agreement came.

I contacted a Korean businessman I knew in Hong Kong and asked him to find companies that made silk neckties, silk scarves, and leather goods. The French man and woman who'd taken care of me when I was in Paris joined me in Washington, and we went on to Hong Kong. It was my first trip there since 1967. I didn't think it had changed much except that it didn't seem like the paradise I had perceived long ago. We stayed three days and then went to Korea. Of course, we checked into the Lotte.

When I first started to look into different projects, including laying a gas pipeline in Bolivia and construction projects in the Middle East, I'd always contacted the giant conglomerate companies, thinking they would surely take care of me. I soon realized that not only did those big companies not need a small potato like me, but also, once they took all the necessary information, they would bypass finders and deal direct. Besides, with the big companies, there were so many steps to take until the final decision was made that it was not worth the time and the effort. Soon I learned how vulnerable the middle person's position was, and I realized that my only asset was to be connected with a company I could absolutely trust. Once I learned that cruel reality, I couldn't trust anyone. Everyone seemed to be a crook, out to take advantage of me.

In Seoul, I called Mr. Lee Hong Kyu, a businessman I'd met at one of the dinners I had attended when I first went to Korea with Anna Chennault a few years before. Mr. Lee was the president of a small export/import company called Cowman. Like many small companies in Seoul, his company lined up different factories for his clients, did the quality check before the shipment, and made sure orders were on time. Many foreigners new to business with Korea might assume it would be more economical to buy directly from the factory, but they soon discover that paying the middleman saves not only money but also headaches. This was especially true with companies like the French one, which wanted so many different items.

I hadn't seen Mr. Lee for over a year, but when I called, he was thrilled to hear from me. On the first night, he took all of us out to a fantastic full-course Chinese dinner. The next day he took the French representatives to all the factories and showed them samples. After three days of meetings, the French people left, and I stayed. Mr. Lee offered me a commission, but I told him I was already getting one from the French company, and commissions should be received from only one party. He insisted on giving his share. Finally I gave in and said I would accept only one percent from him. I might have been naive, but because I liked him so much and he didn't have a large company, I was more concerned about him making money than I was about my commission. We shook hands on it, and the deal was made.

When I came home, I had no way of knowing when the order would be shipped or how large it would be. But as soon as the first shipment was sent, Mr. Lee faxed me a listing of the items, the amount shipped, and the cost. That was the only way I knew what was happening. Even then, I had to keep calling Paris for my commissions, and I am not sure if I would ever have received all of them otherwise.

I felt fortunate to have known someone like Mr. Lee, one of the few men I've met who possessed true integrity and sincerity. After all these years, he still calls me now and then and asks how I am doing. In the Korean culture, honor is more important than an agreement. At the beginning, when I didn't know the system, businessmen usually backed off when I asked for a written agreement. Here in America, even if you have a written agreement, a person who can't pay, or simply doesn't want to pay, can declare bankruptcy and that's the end of it. In Korea, if the people who made the agreement can't pay the debt in full, they pay you a little at a time until they pay it off. As Master Park said, for me, there is nothing more important than one's character; I do what I say, and I keep my promises.

With my business, I knew I had to wait a long time before receiving commissions, and I had no idea how much I was going to get. I had to keep looking for new projects. I got to thinking that nowhere else in the world would I find every embassy on one street other than in Washington. I visited them to find out what services each country might need, and when I got the information, I flew to the respective countries. I began with the nearest countries: El Salvador, Guatemala, Jamaica, Venezuela, and Paraguay. I even went to Tunisia. I often slept at the airports to save on hotel bills and saved more by not eating dinners on my trips. I usually tried to stay only overnight because I was concerned about expenses, and because leaving Ed alone made me nervous. He was only nine, and I worried that Ron would find out.

One thing led to another, and things started to happen—though, as Master Park predicted, I also lost a lot of money, too.

I arranged meetings for Korean politicians when they came to Washington. On July 25, 1991, Y. S. Kim, the head of the opposition party in Korea, and his wife, Son Myung Soon, stopped in Washington after a visit to a research institution in Russia. I helped Chairman Kim set up meetings with various officials in town including Dr. Zbigniew Brzezinski, the formal national security adviser to the Carter administration who was working at the Center for Strategic and International Studies. As the chairman of the opposition party in a country that had been under a military regime for almost three decades, Chairman Kim never gave up fighting for the cause he believed in: a democratic country for the Korean people. He was held under house arrest for three years, and then he went on a hunger strike for a month and was released. He never gave in and was well respected by most Koreans, including me.

The week he was to arrive, one of the worst hurricanes in a hundred years hit Bethesda, with trees falling onto houses and electric lines. He arrived on a Monday, and I had arranged a dinner party on Friday for him before he left. I had invited around twenty people: the consuls from the Korean Embassy, all the State Department reporters, and Mr. David Gergen, who was the editor at US News and World Report and had worked in the White House under presidents Nixon, Ford, Reagan, and later Clinton. I thought it would be a great idea to conduct an unofficial briefing about Chairman Kim's visit to Russia and his political philosophy and agenda for the coming election in Korea the following year.

I prayed every day that the hurricane would end. It was summer, and we had no electricity, no air-conditioning, and no stove. The rain never stopped, and the electricity never came back on. The day of the dinner party, I cooked food at my mother's apartment—*bul-gogi*—on an outside grill while holding an umbrella. I lit candles everywhere and had to hold a candle to see who was there. Mr. Gergen, who was tied up with a deadline for the magazine, called several times to inform me that he was coming and would I please not let Chairman Kim leave before he could arrive. When the initial group of reporters left, Chairman Kim prepared to leave for his next function, but I kept telling him that he could not go until Mr. Gergen came. I can't remember everything they talked about, but what sticks in my mind is that the head of the Russian institution predicted that Chairman Kim would become the president of Korea, just as other leaders, like the German chancellor and the presidents of other nations, had been elected to their posts after visiting the institution. The following year, Chairman Kim became the first civilian president in three decades. Later, when I met his wife, she told me that because his birth sign is the dragon, every time he had an event, it rained.

Although I didn't expect anything from him, what I did for him in Washington was the best thing I had done. Whenever I went to Korea for business and gave him a call, he always told me to come to his residence on Sundays, as he was too busy to see me on the weekdays. Even if I arrived at seven in the morning, people were already sitting in the living room waiting to see him and ask personal favors. This went on until ten thirty, the time for him to go to church. I was always ushered into his small *ondol* room with a small low table. Then he would ask me what he could do for me and instructed his assistant to take care of my needs. His favorite restaurant was a Chinese restaurant in the Shilla Hotel, and he often invited me there. Once, I took along a well-known newspaper editor, Lee Uck Soon, and that particular evening we were ushered into a small private room that had a kitchen where the cook from the restaurant prepared our meal.

Of course, his assistants accompanied him everywhere, and people waited to catch glimpse of him and bow. Although he was in the news almost daily, it never occurred to me how important he was, as had often been the case with President Ford. Chairman Kim didn't have to help me, but he was a man of integrity who didn't forget what I had done for him in the States, no matter how small.

I loved his wife, too. She always had a big smile, was well educated, and did beautiful calligraphy. One evening, Madam Son took me and one of her closest friends out to dinner. We ate at the same Chinese restaurant where her husband took me often, but in the public dining area, not the private room. In the middle of the dinner, she laughed at something I said and turned to her friend and said, "You see? I told you how easy and funny she is."

My "business adventure" was like an old Korean saying, "*A mouse that was caught by the tiger's paw,*" which means that I didn't know what I was doing but had brought results. I tried to hold on to any straw for my survival. They say, "*Shoot for the moon. Even if you miss, you will land among the stars.*" Yes, I shot for the moon and found stars. One door had closed and another one had opened, a bigger one. Ron did me a favor by giving me only the child support, because it gave me the strength that I didn't know I had.

Edward, one month old

Ed with 100 day *Doryung* outfit

One year old, on Cherry Blossom Day

Mijee, my niece, and Ed at the
door of Air Force One

Ed is on Air Force #1, listening
to a secret message on earphone

Air Force One pass

Air Force One pass

Ed at 6 years old, proud to wear his Navy outfit

Tongkun's graduation with Ed

Dancing with Ed on Christmas Day

Ed's graduation at BU

Edward's wedding reception at the Hilton Hotel, January, 2008

Singing at Ed's wedding reception.

Dancing with Ed

My family picture. Front from left. my sister-in-law, Myung Ja,
me, Ed, his wife Erin, my other sister-in-law, Min, my youngest
brother KC. In the back, my niece Mijee and her husband.

My Japanese garden that I designed

Ed, me, Pastor Shirlen and his wife Linda

Ed and President Reagan, his sister, Caron, is in the back

1977
With mother in the Blue Room at the White House.
Mother and I were invited when the President YS Kim was
honored by Clinton.

With Hilary Clinton at the White House reception for
President YS Kim

With President of Korea Young Sam Kim
(1981, Hilton Hotel in Washington)

With President Kim at his residence (2007)

With President Roe Tae Woo

美「뮤지컬」서 主役맡아

뛰어난 춤과 노래솜씨로 人氣모아
"男便이 도와줘 잘해낼수 있었다"

前 白堊館대변인 「네션」부인 「심 宋」씨

국내에서 활약하던 무렵의
「신디·宋」여사.

총出演者 17명중 유일한 東洋人
첫번째 출연교섭엔 두려워 주저
말리던 아들도 「쇼」본후 態度바뀌

1977
Korean paper reporting my performance of
Drum Song at a dinner theater

I feel like I could fly up like a bird

Happiest time of my life

Me—Bamboo Heart

Woman's Home Is Her Castle

So be my roof beams short or long,
my pillars slanting or crook.
Do not mock my hut because it is so tiny.
For the moon and the mountain vines,
do they not all belong to me?

—Sin Hum (1566-1628)

He who hesitates is a damned fool.

—Mae West (1892-1980)

One of the hardest but most satisfying experiences I had after separating from Ron was the renovation. After I gave the party for Chairman Kim, I realized I had to make some changes to my outdated house or move. But I didn't want to move far from Bethesda, and the kind of place I was looking for would not only be expensive, but the moving cost would be huge. So considering how conveniently my house was located, I decided it was best to stay put. After we bought the house, Ron was away constantly, and when Ron was working for the White House, we were hardly at home, which meant we hadn't done anything to the house since we bought it in 1969. Not only too old and too small to begin with, it was now falling apart, and I realized that if I were going to entertain officials, and hold fund-raisers for politicians and events for future business, I had to do something. When President Ford had come, Ron was the somebody they came to see. Now I had to show that I was not just a mere single woman who didn't know what was happening in the world.

The house is right on the border of DC and Bethesda, a most prestigious area, and I could get anywhere in ten or fifteen minutes, especially to Kennedy Center, which is my "second home." I put my business on hold and started in. The plan Ron's architect friend had drawn up ten years before was a pretty dumb one. He wanted to move the kitchen outside, which would have cost a fortune, and planned to make two bedrooms out of three. I know that was one of the main reason Ron was hesitant about renovation. They say everything happens for a good reason, and it sure was good that we never followed that plan. I needed a big living room to entertain and a larger master suite built in a second-floor addition. I was introduced to a young architect and told him to design without limits—the old part of the house, the addition, the landscaping.

I had no idea how much it would cost, but I was not willing to compromise. The house symbolized for me a strong, new beginning. Compromising on the house meant a compromise in my strong, new life. Since I couldn't afford the bids from three builders, I became my own general contractor to save money and have more control over the process. At first it scared me when I read and heard about all the horror stories about picking subcontractors. *Well*, I thought, *if I survived my divorce, I should be able to survive anything.* I knew a woman who built mansions in Potomac, so I got names from her. I drove around the city, stopping at houses that were being renovated and talking to the workers. I picked a rough framer, an electrician, a drywall man, a plumber, a furnace man, a roofer, a siding-installer, a hardwood layer, a Dryvit (similar in appearance to a stucco wall) man, and a Latino stone layer. I compared the prices of all the materials, tons of plywood, Tyvek, hardwood, thousands of nails, gravel, and so on from the wholesale stores and ordered them all.

So it began. Every morning, the huge flatbed truck arrived with materials. I hired a man who operated heavy equipment, and it took three days for him to dig up the roots from the hundred-year-old sycamore that I had cut down on the patio where Ron and I had entertained our visitors every summer. It was so deeply rooted that the man's front end loader broke.

Most additions were built on the back of the house, but mine was to the side, completely altering the appearance of the house. I built a large sunken living room with eight-foot glass doors opening onto a big deck overlooking the park and swimming pool. To my new master bedroom, I added a walk-in closet as big as a bedroom so that I could put my dresses for all four seasons in one place instead of bringing them up and down from the basement. I added a steam unit and a Japanese sunken Jacuzzi bath, like the ones I'd loved in Asia. I knocked down the wall of the old dining room so that I could walk out to the new flagstone patio planted with azaleas and a camellia tree. A new fence was built all around. Then, of course, I had to have a completely new custom-made kitchen with glass-door cabinets, a built-in refrigerator, and black granite counter tops. My architect was an admirer of Frank Lloyd Wright, and he wanted everything to be a long straight shape, including the roof. I told him, "No, no . . . I wanted it to reflect me, the Asian." He seemed stuck. "Cindy, I don't know what I should do if you don't want a flat roof." I drew a picture of an Asian-style roof. And that is what I got.

From morning to night, people stomped in and out as if there was a war going on. Sometimes I thought I would go crazy trying to direct four or five workers at the same time: "Where does this fireplace go?" "No, I want the opening here." "No, the windows haven't arrived yet." "What size is the vanity and where are the faucets going to be?" I felt like an untrained symphony conductor or a traffic policeman in the middle of an intersection, blowing a whistle and directing the cars with his arm pointing this way and that. But I threw myself into the project with verve. I painted, caulked, stained, broke down the old brick walls, hauled dry wall, and threw all the trash into a high dumpster myself. I felt vigorous, and it's as though I was carving out all that was rotten inside of me. I started at seven in the morning, before the men came, and I usually didn't stop till midnight.

The owners before us had added a two-car garage with a lower roof. My architect thought it was easier to build a fake roof on top of the existing one. But my rough framer, who had built many mansions in Potomac, thought differently. He said we should remove the garage roof and build a new one straight to the main roof. The forecast was calling for rain in a couple of days. He thought that if I hired some laborers to help take the roof down, he could have the new roof built before the rain. I was nervous, but I decided to go for it. I hired five or six Latin American laborers. They climbed up the roof like ants and tore off all the shingles. Because of the threat of rain, they worked as fast as they could. At the end of the day, the room beneath, which was my office, was open like a stage set. While the men were tearing the old roof down, the carpenter was rushing to build the new one. But he couldn't finish before the clouds moved in and told me to get rolls of plastic from the roof store. I bought tons of blue plastic, and he covered as much as he could.

That evening, it started to rain. Water dripped everywhere. I ran around placing every container in the house beneath leaks that went all the way to the basement. The desk in my office was soaked, and that night, I called the carpenter and told him to listen while I held the phone close to water dripping in a bucket. Laughing, he said, "Cindy, what is going on there? It sounds as if some strange concert is playing, *ding dong, ding dong.*"

What else he could do? The next day, the new roof went up, covered with beautiful gray shingles that supposedly will last forty years, and complete with a gutter cap so that I never would have to go up and clean the gutter as I used to. The work stopped when the addition was finished and money was short, then started back up again when I got more funds. When the rough frame was done, I worked with one man who does the inside. I crawled into the ceiling and installed the rolls and rolls of insulation. I took bucket after bucket filled with stones and trash and dumped into a tall dumpster all day long. Addition and the renovation took more than two years to complete.

After the work was done, we had the coldest winter in a decade. Everybody had problems with water pipes freezing and bursting. One Saturday afternoon in February, I walked into my house and found the whole place flooded. I screamed. Water was pouring out from every recess in the living room. Turns out the plumber hadn't bothered to insulate the pipes in the attic when he'd installed the steam unit in the master bathroom. It looked as if I would have to navigate through my living room and my bedroom in a boat, and I even had to wear long rubber boots. Everything was ruined: my new Oriental rugs, the thick wall-to-wall carpet in my bedroom, all the dresses and handbags in my walk-in closet. I thought the whole house would collapse. In the past, I would have died from panic, but now I told myself to stay cool and follow an old Korean saying: *"Even if you are caught by a tiger, keep a clear head, and you will survive."* Now that I was my own person, there was nothing left to fear.

I called the county inspector, but before he arrived, I tried to move the huge Oriental rug, which was soaked and must have weighed a ton. I called a man who was renting the basement to help me, but as soon as I lifted that rug, my back gave way. I couldn't move and fell flat on the floor. I asked my tenant, Brian, to put a note on the front door and to get me a wireless phone and my Rolodex. I was still on the cold floor when the inspector came in. The poor man stood in the entrance, four steps above the living room floor, and looked down at me. I explained what happened to me and told him to go up and see my bedroom, which was still underwater, along with everything else. After he left, I called Mr. Rhee, the acupuncturist who had cured my sciatica years before, and he helped me into my son's room on the ground floor. My dog, Casey, never left my side, and for the first time I understood why my mother had been constantly fearful of being alone.

Of course, I survived, dried out the house, repaired it, and replaced the ruined items. I love my home. It is contemporary and Asian. In the summer, lying on my big bed, I can look at a tall oak tree from the sliding door and watch the squirrels running up and down building nests. In spring, the red cardinals and bluebirds come and sing. In the winter, when it snows, the park turns into a wonderland, every tree wearing a white bridal gown. If this is not heaven, what is?

I bought contemporary and Oriental-style furniture and an entertainment center with four-foot-tall speakers, as tall as my father's German-made radio. I also bought a CD player and a karaoke unit. I installed speakers in every room, as music is my breath, and I can't live without it. Last but not the least, I bought a baby grand Steinway piano. All my life I wished I could play piano. When I was twelve and thirteen years old, coming back from my grandmother's house in the evening after the sun went down, I would pass by one particular house. I always heard the girl who lived there practicing the piano. I stopped in front of her house and stood listening to Beethoven's "*Moonlight Sonata*" or "*Für Elise.*" I walked home with my heart heavy, as if I were carrying a rock. But I never uttered a word to my mother. What was the use? We could hardly afford the things that were essential to our survival. I knew that I didn't have the basic training to able to play as I wished, but as my father said, "The dream should never end as a mere dream." I took lessons and now I can play those pieces, and how I love it.

The cathedral ceiling in the foyer is paneled with cedar, which I painstakingly stained standing while on a scaffold for two whole days. Instead of a chandelier, as someone suggested, I hung a big round Japanese paper lantern. A big bookcase in my office is lined up with all the books I love to read. I had a landscape company dig up all the grass in front of my house, and I designed and landscaped a Japanese rock garden with Japanese maple trees, Asian pines, and stepping-stones leading to the street, just like my father saw at Mr. Ishihara's house when he was a young boy. A stone Buddha sits watching over me, with a spotlight on him at night. I even ordered two beautiful Japanese wooden lanterns from California. Later, I called my electrician to install outdoor spotlights and accent lights for the different trees. In spring, I plant beautiful flowers from one end to the other. Whenever I work out there, people stop to tell me how beautiful my garden is.

Renovating the house was one of the hardest things, both physically and mentally, that I have ever done in my life, but it was most rewarding. Every time I see the stars and the moon through the big skylight in my bedroom, it reminds me of the time when I looked up at the *Chusuck* moon, the harvest moon, through the hole in the roof after the fire in Yangsan.

Funeral

The hill is an old hill, but the river is not old,
How can it be old river, when it runs forever the man is like old
river, when he is gone he never returns.

—Hwang Jin

One who longs for death is miserable, but more miserable
is he who fears it.

—Wilhelm Zincgref (1591-1635)

Between back surgery and brain surgery, Mother had been in and out of the hospital for years. The Emergency Room at the Suburban Hospital in Bethesda became her second home. As soon as she was wheeled in, the nurses would say, "Are you here again, Mrs. Song?" When she was admitted, I went there every day, morning and night, to feed her and to be with her. All the doctors used to say I was the best daughter they ever knew.

By 2000, Mother had been in a nursing home for a year and a half. She was petrified to be alone, and although I'd hired a nurse to be with her night and day for six days a week, I also went there every day to feed her, and I even had to change her diaper and shower her when I couldn't find the nurse, which was usually the case. After all, when I was a little girl, didn't I promise to be like Shim Chung, who was so devoted to her father?

One evening a nurse called me and said she couldn't wake my mother. I rushed to the nursing home and went with her to Suburban Hospital by ambulance. Ed drove down the next day from New York, where he lived, and we stood next to her, still comatose. "Mother," I said, "Edward is here." I spoke to her in Korean. "*Halmony*," Ed said in Korean. "I am here." She made a strange moaning sound as if she wanted to talk. About 7:00 PM, a male nurse took her down for tests, and I went home, leaving Ed to have time with her. Around thirty minutes later, he called sobbing. "Mom, Grandmother stopped breathing."

The next morning, Ed and I went to Reagan National Airport to pick up my brother Young Chang, who was in a military academy in Newport , his wife, and his two teenage children. My brother went to the hospital to see Mother, but the hospital staff wouldn't let him. Then we went to Pumphrey Funeral Home in Bethesda and arranged for the funeral and cremation. Mother had one small Samsonite travel bag where she told me she kept the clothes to be worn when she passed away. In it was a blue *hanbok*, a pair of underwear, her rubber boat-shaped shoes, and white cotton socks. That evening, beside the open casket, Ed, me, cousin Sue, Young Chang, and Young Chang's wife and his children were there with her for the last time.

That night, Ed insisted that he call my other sister-in-law, Young Ja, to let her know about Mother's funeral. How long had it been since I saw her and her family last? My brother Tong-Ho had died about twenty-five years previous, and about ten years after that, my sister-in-law and Tong-Ho's oldest son cut themselves off from the rest of the Song family. But on the morning of the funeral, for the first time in several decades, all of our family was together. As someone said, Death is great reconciliation. Ron was there. I had not seen him for more than fifteen years. When Ed told me that Ron would like to come to the funeral, I didn't know what to say. But then I thought, after all, Ron was the reason we were all here, including my mother. When I was so much in pain during the divorce, a friend told me, "You know what? It'll take roughly two years to feel nothing when you see your ex." But for me, it took many, many years. Seeing Ron again, I felt as if I was seeing my favorite uncle.

Young Ja hugged the casket and couldn't stop crying. A Korean pastor performed the ceremony in English. Ed, in tears, said how he would miss his grandmother, who had practically raised him. Then Young Chang spoke:

"I am very heartened to see you on this occasion of my mother's passage. Thank you for attending this farewell ceremony. I also deeply thank my sister, Cindy. She has done so much in taking care of my mother in old age for the past several years.

"My mother, Choi Soon-Ok, was born in Busan, Korea, in 1917. She married early at sixteen. Through her long years of life, she achieved much, raising her five children. She was a proud grandmother of eight grandchildren.

"She had a good sense of humor. She was well liked. She was a good singer. She was a one-time champion of a Korean singing contest in Washington, DC.

"In 1970, our family came to the States, starting a new life in America. She coped with the new environment very well, learning English and working for a better life in America. I was most impressed with her efforts to pass the U.S. citizenship test in her old age. The American political system, the many citizenship concepts—she had to learn a lot of things to pass the exam. I remember her trying to memorize words like *judiciary* and *legislative.*

"With us today is my ex-brother-in-law, Mr. Ron Nessen. I truly thank him for bringing our family to the States despite many obstacles at the time. There were eight of our family members under his sponsorship, and that is a lot of people to nurture and care for. Everyone in the family was in school and at work. Thank you, sir. We owe you very much.

"We are very proud of her. Though her passage from this life is a big loss for the family, her challenging spirit will remain with us forever. Mother, we miss you very much. Please don't worry about us and rest in peace."

He could hardly contain himself from crying, since as the youngest, he was closest to her. I looked down at my mother's face and thought that after all these years, my responsibility to her was finally ended, my role as Shim Chung ended. That weight had been lifted from me, but it had left a space never to be filled again.

My mother's death had brought the whole family together again, and then adversity brought about more healing. In 2003, I discovered I had stomach cancer. I couldn't drive, I couldn't talk, I couldn't sleep. I became depressed, and Ron and my son came to my aid. Since Edward was in New York, busy with his job as a cameraman for movies such as *The Devil Wears Prada, The Bourne Ultimatum,* and *The Brave One,* Ron hired nurses who were with me twelve hours a day, a social worker to drive me to doctors and the hospital, and a psychotherapist to see me twice a week. I would be in bed for two years, and at the time I thought I'd rather be dead than go on living.

After my operation, Ron took me to my doctor's office. While I was trying to put on the gown, I looked at the long ugly scar all the way down my stomach. Crying, I said, "Ron, look at my stomach. No one will like me." He said, "Oh, Cindy, do you want to see mine?" He undid his tie, opened up his shirt, and showed a long scar on his chest. About five months before my operation, he'd had a quintuple bypass. Sitting in the doctor's office, two old people comparing our scars, suddenly seemed so comical that I laughed out loud. As usual, Ron gave me a peculiar look, as if to say, "What is so funny?"

I knew then that life wasn't over.

They say that time heals. Yes, it surely does—love, hate, making up, all of it seems as if it happened in another world. Through all the turbulence, pain, fear, and storms, I grew stronger as each new sprout grew out of each joint of the bamboo tree. Everything I wanted in my life was difficult, and therefore, the result was more special. Edward is the most important thing that happened to my life, and I am proud how I, a single mother, brought up a such wonderful young man. If I die tomorrow, I have no regret for having lived life to the fullest.

Acknowledgment

One day, in 1973, soon after Ron became press secretary, I was invited to a lunch at one of those posh restaurants in Georgetown. I didn't know any of the women except Mary Lynn Kots, the writer who had invited me, and I didn't know much about her, except that her husband, Nick Kots, was a writer and a Pulitzer Prize winner that Ron knew. In the middle of lunch, Mary Lynn told me that she'd studied in Japan and spoke a few words of Japanese. I told her that my father had been accused of being a spy and jailed by the Japanese. Suddenly her eyes lit up and she said, "Oh, you should write about it." She planted a seed in my head, although it was a far-fetched suggestion at the time.

But after my divorce, I had a strange urge to write my story. Not thinking seriously, I mentioned this to my brother, Tong Kung, who is a professor at one of the most prestigious universities in Korea. He said that if I was serious, I should write the story of the little Korean girl whose fate was manipulated by the history of Korea. The idea was great, but I had no idea how to go about it. Yet as Walt Disney said, "If you can dream it, you can do it."

First and foremost, what words can I use to thank my beloved son, Edward? He believed in me, encouraged me to write, and also recruited his father, Ron, to help me. English is my second language, and I thought that if I wrote down everything I remembered, along with what my mother had told me, I could find someone who could put it together. But finding a professional collaborator who could edit my outpouring of experiences into a publishable and readable volume was as impossible as my attempt to write a book on my own. Friends, acquaintances, and strangers were enlisted. Editors, co-authors, and ghost writers came and went, often charging me unconscionable fees for unsatisfactory work or no work at all. Ron enlisted a couple who didn't work out either. But he kept pushing me not to give up. I just didn't know my story would take almost 20 years to write.

Then, in 2003, I found out that I had stomach cancer. Ron and Edward did everything to help me survive. Ed was in New York working as a photographer and drove down every chance he had. Ron hired nurses for 12-hour shifts every day; found a psychiatrist whom I could see twice a week, and a social worker to drive me to the doctors. Every month, my brother Tong-Kun air-mailed me liquid packets of red ginseng in an aluminum container that cost over $500 and weighed over 20 pounds. I couldn't talk, I couldn't eat, I couldn't walk and I couldn't sleep.

Then, after I had cancer, chemo and radiation made me feel again like I'd rather die. I threw out everything I had—clothing, shoes, versions of my manuscript and tons of my family albums, including personally signed photos of Emperor Hirohito, President Ford and President Johnson. I didn't want to burden Edward with years and years of accumulation. (But I was lucky to find a few old pictures that I could use for this book) Then miraculously, I got better. Who says that only cats have nine lives?

My health started to improve at the end of 2005, and I picked up where I had left it off. Again, I didn't know where to go and what to do with my unfinished of manuscript. In desperation, in the summer of 2008, I went to The Writer's Center in Bethesda, MD, and registered to take a workshop taught by Barbara Esstman. When I laid eyes on her, I knew she would be the one to edit my story, and I was right. The rest is history.

Last but not the least, I want to thank Jim Cassatt, a long-time friend who gave me an old Samsung computer that his son threw away when I told him I needed one to write my story. I didn't know a thing about computers, and every time some strange thing occurred, I sent an SOS to Jim who would come over and show me how to operate it. (Of course, over the months of being banged on every night and every day, it finally broke down.) Also, sweet Barbara Cassatt, Jim's wife, who helped me with sentences when I got stuck. Without their unconditional support, I know I could never have even started.

Why was I so determined? I have nothing to leave to my beloved son after I am gone except the story of his mother, where she came from, and who she was. Now I can close my eyes with a smile on my face when I am ready to go. Also, without Edward's determination to make his mother better, I know I wouldn't still be here.

Finally, I am grateful to Rev. Jim Shirlen and his wife Linda who opened my eyes to see the greater source of God's love. They took me to the hospitals and doctors when I had no one else to take me after I moved to my Rockville condo from my big house in Bethesda with the pool I couldn't take care of any more. And I was delighted when he bought me a book, "*Write It When I'm Gone*," by Thomas M. DeFrank, after he read about me dancing with President Ford.

I have one more person I should not forget. In 1980, after my separation, I cried so much, night and day for months and years, that I had developed excruciating sciatica. It was as if someone was electrifying my leg. I could not walk, sit, or lie down. The American doctor only gave me painkillers. I thought my life had surely ended. Out of desperation I sought an acupuncturist. One day, after I sent Edward off to summer camp, I was introduced to Dr. Rhee, who resides in Great Falls. I went to him daily for half a year or more. I'd drag my leg when I got there, but felt as if I could fly by the time I left, even though my back and stomach were black from radiation burns. Again, he helped me, as he did recently after an aneurysm operation caused me excruciating back pain. Dr. Rhee is my life-saver, and as long as I live, I will continually seek him out.

I must also mention my dearest friend, Jocelyn Cheou, who helped me to electronically transfer hundreds of pictures to my publisher since I have no idea how to do it. Despite her busy schedule, working full-time and looking after her two teenagers, she was never too busy to help.

I want to say thank you to everyone who's touched my life, good and bad, because they are the sources of my being and who I am.

And finally, I must note that the names of some have been changed to protect their privacy.

Get Published, Inc!
Thorofare, NJ 08086
22 September 2009
BA2009265